South Asia in World History

The
New
Oxford
World
History

South Asia in World History

Marc Jason Gilbert

OXFORD
UNIVERSITY PRESS

OXFORD
UNIVERSITY PRESS

Oxford University Press is a department of the University of Oxford. It furthers
the University's objective of excellence in research, scholarship, and education
by publishing worldwide. Oxford is a registered trade mark of Oxford University
Press in the UK and certain other countries.

Published in the United States of America by Oxford University Press
198 Madison Avenue, New York, NY 10016, United States of America.

CIP data is on file at the Library of Congress
ISBN 978–0–19–976034–3 (pbk)
ISBN 978–0–19–517653–7 (hbk)

1 3 5 7 9 8 6 4 2

Paperback printed by WebCom, Inc., Canada
Hardback printed by Bridgeport National Bindery, Inc., United States of America

*Frontispiece: Mughal Emperor Akbar is shown in the midst of a theological
discussion with Jesuit missionaries.* © The Trustees of the
Chester Beatty Library, Dublin

Contents

Editors' Preface

This book is part of the New Oxford World History, an innovative series that offers readers an informed, lively, and up-to-date history of the world and its people that represents a significant change from the "old" world history. Only a few years ago, world history generally amounted to a history of the West—Europe and the United States—with small amounts of information from the rest of the world. Some versions of the "old" world history drew attention to every part of the world *except* Europe and the United States. Readers of that kind of world history could get the impression that somehow the rest of the world was made up of exotic people who had strange customs and spoke difficult languages. Still another kind of "old" world history presented the story of areas or peoples of the world by focusing primarily on the achievements of great civilizations. One learned of great buildings, influential world religions, and mighty rulers but little of ordinary people or more general economic and social patterns. Interactions among the world's peoples were often told from only one perspective.

This series tells world history differently. First, it is comprehensive, covering all countries and regions of the world and investigating the total human experience—even those of so-called peoples without histories living far from the great civilizations. "New" world historians thus share in common an interest in all of human history, even going back millions of years before there were written human records. A few "new" world histories even extend their focus to the entire universe, a "big history" perspective that dramatically shifts the beginning of the story back to the big bang. Some see the "new" global framework of world history today as viewing the world from the vantage point of the Moon, as one scholar put it. We agree. But we also want to take a close-up view, analyzing and reconstructing the significant experiences of all of humanity.

This is not to say that everything that has happened everywhere and in all time periods can be recovered or is worth knowing, but that there is much to be gained by considering both the separate and interrelated stories of different societies and cultures. Making these connections is still another crucial ingredient of the "new" world history. It emphasizes connectedness and interactions of all kinds—cultural, economic, political, religious, and social—involving peoples, places, and processes. It makes comparisons and finds similarities. Emphasizing both the comparisons and interactions is critical to developing a global framework that can deepen and broaden historical understanding, whether the focus is on a specific country or region or on the whole world.

The rise of the new world history as a discipline comes at an opportune time. The interest in world history in schools and among the general public is vast. We travel to one another's nations, converse and work with people around the world, and are changed by global events. War and peace affect populations worldwide, as do economic conditions and the state of our environment, communications, and health and medicine. The New Oxford World History presents local histories in a global context and gives an overview of world events seen through the eyes of ordinary people. This combination of the local and the global further defines the new world history. Understanding the workings of global and local conditions in the past gives us tools for examining our own world and for envisioning the interconnected future that is in the making.

Bonnie G. Smith
Anand Yang

Preface

Over a century ago, F. Max Müller, a pioneering scholar of world history, a field he knew as "universal history," gave a series of lectures arguing that whatever sphere of interest the human mind might select for special study, whether it be customs or languages, South Asia had to be considered because "the most valuable and most instructive materials in the history of man are treasured up there and only there."[1] The Nobel Prize–winning French essayist Romain Rolland regarded South Asia, in *Prophets of the New India*, as "the one place on earth where all the dreams of living men have found a home."[2] While both claims stretch the truth, the region holds a place in world history that is second to none, not only because of its unique status as home to arguably the world's oldest functioning civilization, but also because the region's largest modern nation, India, is currently vying with China for leadership of the world's economy by 2050.

South Asia's role as a touchstone for world history has much to do with its great size and population. South Asia is a triangular geographic region the size of Europe, more than 1,500 miles wide at its widest point from east to west and almost 2,000 miles long from north to south. It is the home of seven modern nations: the Federal Democratic Republic of Nepal, the Islamic Republic of Pakistan, the Kingdom of Bhutan, the People's Republic of Bangladesh, the Republic of India, the Republic of the Maldives, and the Republic of the Union of Myanmar (some would include the Islamic Republic of Afghanistan and exclude Myanmar). To world historians, South Asia is a subcontinent of Eurasia, set apart from the rest of the world by surrounding seas and great mountain ranges. Like North America, it is divided internally by mountain chains, river systems, a great desert (the Thar), and a dry, high plateau, the Deccan. These geographic obstacles have been surmounted by its human population, which has turned South Asia into one of the more densely populated places on earth. It is currently home to about one-fifth of the world's population, more than 1.7 billion of the world's 7 billion people.

Along with Egypt, Mesopotamia, and northern China, South Asia was one of the earliest of the "cradles" of civilization. It was physically larger than its contemporaries in Mesopotamia and Egypt. Its cities

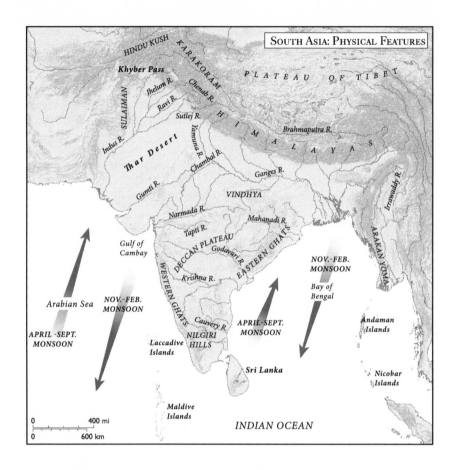

SOUTH ASIA: PHYSICAL FEATURES

HINDU KUSH

Khyber Pass

KARAKORAM

PLATEAU OF TIBET

Jhelum R.

Ravi R.

Chenab R.

SULAIMAN

Indus R.

Sutlej R.

Yamuna R.

HIMALAYAS

Brahmaputra R.

Gumti R.

Thar Desert

Chambal R.

Ganges R.

Irrawaddy R.

Narmada R.

VINDHYA

Mahanadi R.

Gulf of
Cambay

Tapti R.

DECCAN PLATEAU

Godavari R.

EASTERN GHATS

ARAKAN YOMA

NOV.-FEB.
MONSOON

WESTERN GHATS

Krishna R.

Bay of
Bengal

Arabian Sea

NOV.-FEB.
MONSOON

APRIL-SEPT.
MONSOON

Cauvery R.

APRIL-SEPT.
MONSOON

Andaman
Islands

APRIL-SEPT.
MONSOON

Laccadive
Islands

NILGIRI
HILLS

Sri Lanka

Nicobar
Islands

Maldive
Islands

INDIAN OCEAN

0   400 mi

0   600 km

benefited from innovations such as grid-patterned street plans, sewer lines, and flushable indoor plumbing. In classical times, its philosophical and theological schools figured in debates from Korea to the Greek city-state of Athens. The Roman economy was influenced by trade across the Indian Ocean to and from the bustling ports on South Asia's southern shores. Indigenized versions of its major classical religious traditions, Buddhism and Hinduism, took root elsewhere in Asia, while the region's monks, priests, and travelers spread literacy along with its epic literature and puppetry traditions, which together still influence Southeast Asia's performing arts.

During the period that in the West is commonly called the Middle Ages, South Asian merchants plied Asia's richest trade routes, selling across Afro-Eurasia much-in-demand cotton and silk to use in the manufacture of fine clothing. One of the early modern period's greatest writers, William Shakespeare, referred in two of his plays, *Henry*

IV, Part I and *The Merchant of Venice*, to the importance of Europe's trade with the region, including gemstones from its "bountiful mines."[3] Some scholars suggest that Britain's leading and sustaining role in the Industrial Revolution was made possible by its control of South Asia's vast material and human resources.

From 1757 to 1947, the British people sought to justify or excuse the exploitation of South Asia's land and people by claiming that they were backward, in need of civilizing, and had nothing to teach Europeans. However, even as the British began to assert their authority over South Asia, the region's classical language, Sanskrit, was found to have a common origin with the languages of Europe. This discovery was followed by further encounters with South Asia's philosophical, literary, and scientific heritage that led to the reshaping of intellectual traditions in Europe and the world over, as exemplified in literature in the work of the German writer Goethe, the American transcendentalist poets Ralph Waldo Emerson and Walt Whitman, and British writers such as William Wordsworth, Samuel Taylor Coleridge, and E. M. Forster. Physicist Albert Einstein is reputed to have said that by developing what today are called Arabic numerals, including the place-holder zero, the region taught the rest of the world how to count, without which no major scientific discovery could have been made. Einstein's colleague Erwin Schrödinger saw in the Upanishads justification for their scientific theories regarding the underlying unity of all things, which convinced Schrödinger that individual consciousness was only the manifestation of a unitary consciousness pervading the universe.

By the early twentieth century, many in the West, grown weary of the rationalism and materialism of the modern world, came to so admire what they called the "more spiritual" life of South Asia that they saw it as humanity's best hope for the future. However, when taken to such an extreme, this construction of South Asia's cultural heritage was far off the mark. While Americans and Europeans were right to admire one or another of the region's so-called otherworldly philosophies, many of these philosophies, and most of the region's peoples, were and remain no less materialistic than those found elsewhere. Since throwing off their British colonial yoke in 1947–1949, the nations of South Asia have resumed their place as sources of both philosophical light and material influence in world affairs.

South Asia's art and musical traditions also have had a global reach, but its cultural encounters with other societies have often been reciprocal. Western movie soundtracks today routinely employ the staccato beat of the tabla (small drums with tight drum skins) to heighten drama or suspense, while the Indian film industry in Mumbai (formerly called Bombay) is called "Bollywood," referencing the famous US film city. Its writers, including Rabindranath Tagore, V. S. Naipaul, Salman Rushdie, and Jhumpa Lahiri, have won the world's most respected awards in literature.

South Asian political systems all loom large in world history. The region's early dynasties, such as those of the Mauryans, Kushans, Guptans, and Cholas, figure prominently in the comparative study of the empires of the ancient world. The Sultanate of Delhi (1198–1526) is one of the earliest examples of this basic form of Islamic government. The Mughal Empire (1526–1858) is numbered alongside the Ottomans, Safavids, and Qing (Manchus) as an example of "gunpowder empires," a term commonly used to describe regimes melding effective bureaucratic management systems with the use of modern cannon and musketry.

South Asia is also known as the model for many modern colonial resistance and nationalist movements. The strategies of nonviolent social and political change through disobedience pursued by Mohandas Karamchand Gandhi helped hasten the end of the British Empire in India and, as interpreted by Dr. Martin Luther King, ended the legal trappings of racism in the United States. Aung San Suu Kyi of Myanmar successfully employed them to weaken the authoritarian regime in her country. The once-violent revolutionary Nelson Mandela and his pacifist compatriot Bishop Desmond Tutu employed Ghandi's methods in their fight to end apartheid in South Africa.

South Asia has experienced a variety of other global historical processes, such as major human migrations (including Indo-Europeans, Huns, Arabs, and Turks) and modern colonialism (Dutch, French, and Portuguese, as well as British). It is now a testing ground for solutions to the problems of poverty and social discrimination and also for addressing cultural and economic globalization through policies that yield economic development while preserving a sense of community cohesion and cultural tradition. Students of gender relations find South Asia of particular interest due to its complexity. Most of its societies are intensely patriarchal, and there are few regions where females are less valued. Yet there are no places on earth where more women have served as prime minister or president. Some of these include Sri Lanka's Sirimavo Bandaranaike, Pakistan's Benazir Bhutto, Nepal's Bidhya Devi Bhandari, India's Indira Gandhi, and Sheik Hasina and Khaleda Zia of Bangladesh.

Indira Gandhi's father and the first prime minister of India, Jawaharlal Nehru, wrote in *The Discovery of India* that the entire subcontinent contained millions of "separate individual men and women, each differing from the other, each living in a private universe of thought and feeling . . . Yet something has bound them together and binds them still."[4] It is true that, while South Asia's internal geographic and political divisions have led to a wide degree of regional linguistic and ethnic variations, its peoples have much in common in terms of patterns of dress, cuisine, social organization, and religious practice, if not always religious identity. Respect for gurus and pirs (great religious teachers) and religious pilgrimages are nearly universal among South Asians of all faiths. This "unity in diversity" has both supported episodes of imperial grandeur and also sustained its people in the absence of a subcontinental centralized state.

The forces of globalization, from interregional trade to European colonialism and the rise of "free-market" economics, have spurred South Asians of all stripes to go abroad in such numbers that they comprise one of the world's largest diasporas. Many countries have large minority populations of South Asian descent, ranging from Britain, with 8 percent, to Fiji, with between 46 and 49 percent South Asians.

South Asia holds a particularly strong attraction for those who wish to examine the role of very large-scale developments in human history, often called "Big History," such as the emergence of agriculture and global environmental history. South Asia's place in the history of agriculture can be gauged by the global use of the term "Asian," which is probably rooted in the Sri Lankan term for rice (arisi) employed by the Portuguese as they forged the first direct commercial sea links between Europe and Asia. The devastating droughts and famines that occurred in South Asia during the late nineteenth century were closely connected to a global ocean-warming phenomenon called El Niño. Along with global warming, these natural events illustrate the importance of environmental factors in South Asian as well as world history and remain major environmental concerns in the region. Some scholars see the progress of the Industrial Revolution in Britain as linked to its defeat of its European rivals in South Asia, which provided it access to the region's valuable material resources and markets. Today's booming South Asian high-technology industry reflects economic globalization through its role in the increasing shift of such jobs from the West to the East.

There may be no better way to approach the Big History of the world than through the examples provided by South Asia's connection with geological and weather factors whose influence is far greater than even El Niño. Scientists hold that approximately two hundred million years ago the continuous welling up of molten material from the earth's core forced one triangular piece of land to dive beneath its Eurasian counterpart. This process continues to this day, producing a massive upward thrust of earth that is now the world's youngest, greatest, and still-growing chain of mountains, the 1,600-mile-long Himalayas (Abode of Snow), and several associated ranges to its east and west.

The Himalayas and its neighboring mountain ranges influence South Asia's climate and related patterns of rainfall, temperature, and human activity by holding off arctic winds from the north, ensuring that most of the subcontinent enjoys a semitropical or tropical environment. They also play a role in generating the winds that drive the heavy rains of April–September and October–November. These monsoons offer relief from months of little or no rain and summer heat that can reach well over 100 degrees Fahrenheit. The wind generated by the monsoons secured South Asia's place as a fulcrum of early world trade: in the age of sail, ships traveling to and from South Asia, Southeast Asia, China, Africa, the Middle East, and Europe moved back and forth in keeping with the rhythm of monsoon winds.

The monsoons of South Asia are not, however, constant. Periodic shifts in the surrounding ocean's temperature and shifts in the wind currents in Central Asia can result in the failure of one or both of the monsoons, resulting in prolonged drought and often famine. Conversely, monsoon-related river flooding coinciding with high tides, oceanic cyclones, and tectonic plate movements have inflicted great damage to the subcontinent's human population. All over the world, changes in weather and tectonic plate movements have menaced entire cities and led to changes in the courses of rivers and coastlines. Together, these developments destroyed South Asia's earliest cities and today threaten its modern cities, as they have menaced and may soon destroy other urban areas across the globe.

Much of South Asia's place in world history may be less visible than weather and geological events, less visceral than colonial conquest and resistance, and less tangible than shifts in the global division of labor. It may rest in the region's ability to pursue innovative ideas generated from within, to absorb or adapt to new ideas imported from other regions, and to transmit or re-transmit these ideas into the wider world, a process exemplified by Gandhi's effort to help liberate South Asia from European colonial domination. Gandhi drew on indigenous conceptions of nonviolence (ahimsa) and a host of international influences, including the biblical Sermon on the Mount and the American philosopher Henry David Thoreau's pioneering ideas about civil disobedience, to create a method of sociopolitical action that would appeal to people not only in South Asia but also across the world. Gandhian methods loom so large in world history that one can easily lose sight of regional variations or adaptations of violent global resistance movements. These include movements and parties practicing "people's war," such as the Naxalites in India and Maoists in Nepal. South Asia has long been a site of global Islamist struggle waged there and elsewhere by the Taliban and Al Qaida.

South Asia's capacity for synthesis and adaptation is a recurring theme in efforts to gauge the region's place in world history. Yet this capacity is not unlimited. The respect given by many South Asians to diversity does not mean that all believe in equality. Moreover, the region's ability to draw inspiration from its traditional patterns of life to innovate in the face of rapid change has been severely tested over the centuries by forces as varied as religious fundamentalism, colonialism, nationalism, and laissez-faire or neoliberal economics. As these are global processes, both old and new, it is clear that the history of South Asia has much to tell us about the complex and increasingly interrelated world in which we live.

Chapter 1

South Asia and the World to 1500 BCE

Nearly four thousand years ago, one of the greatest port cities of the ancient world flourished east of where the Indus River meets the Indian Ocean at a site now called Lothal. Ships left from Lothal's seven-hundred-foot brick-lined wharf for places as distant as the Mesopotamian port of Ur, more than one thousand miles to the west. When these ships arrived at Ur and elsewhere in what is now called the Persian Gulf, the local inhabitants would have rushed to examine their valuable cargoes. These included the world's original cotton fabrics, wood, finely crafted gemstone beads, and key foodstuffs such as barley, rice, and wheat. These goods were the products of South Asia's first urban society, called Harappa after the name of the modern village closest to the site of one of the oldest and largest of its cities. Harappan cities and towns sprawled across the landscape of much of what is today Pakistan and northwestern India. Such was the size of the population of these settlements (some as large as fifty thousand) and their number (perhaps more than two thousand) that Lothal is only one of several ports of an urban complex that rivals those of Egypt and Mesopotamia. As the trade between Mesopotamian and Harappan cities was among the first direct and sustained contacts between the earliest urban societies, Lothal lies very near the roots of South Asian history and world trade.

It also lies close to the very beginnings of human history. The presence of stone tools dating to before 70,000 BCE leaves little doubt that human populations have long dwelt on the subcontinent. Subsequent patterns of development indicate a diversity of human communities and activities that remains a hallmark of the region. Its temperate climate and rich soils may have first attracted human groups to enter the subcontinent from the west and north, but they also subsequently drew Austronesian peoples from Southeast Asia to its eastern, central, and southern regions. In time, the subcontinent was home to foraging bands, pastoral nomads, and sedentary farmers, who varied greatly in their lifestyles. Some were organized along patriarchal lines, others were matriarchal societies.

After 4000 BCE, a new mix of human technologies and agricultural methods gradually added to the existing South Asian ways of life. Sedentary farming generated food surpluses that supported increasing job specialization, urban life, and long-distance trade. These surpluses also fostered literacy and large-scale building projects. This new pattern of human society is commonly called civilization, after the Latin word *civis*, or "city dweller," though today that term is used carefully so as not to suggest that non-urban dwellers are any less sophisticated or "civilized." After all, a song by a nomadic cattle herder can be as rich or poor in its expression of the human experience as that sung by a diva in an opera house or by a popular singer in a football stadium. When compared with other ways of living, such as hunting and gathering or pastoral nomadism (people moving with their herds of cattle), city dwelling offers the possibility of a richer diet and a higher standard of living. Yet civilization, with its bureaucratic administration and capacity to wage mass warfare, is often no less stressful than other forms of human society.

The emergence in South Asia of this new pattern of life, called the Neolithic or New Stone Age, can be linked to the Himalayas. When the subcontinent was formed, a vast watery gulf separated the northernmost section of peninsular South Asia, called the Deccan, from the foothills of the Himalayas. Monsoon rains make no headway in wearing down the Himalayas because the earth is pushing them up at the same rate that rain and snow act to erode them. Yet the process of erosion has been so relentless that the gap between the Deccan and the great mountains to the north and west was ultimately filled with mineral-rich runoff from the Himalayas. When this soil was spread upon the land by its flood-prone river systems, as in the valley of the Indus River in the northwest or across the vast region traversed by the Ganges and Brahmaputra rivers and parallel watercourses in the north (called the Gangetic Plain), the first peoples of northern South Asia enjoyed topsoil that still ranks among the world's most productive. This alluvial soil was not only rich in nutrients, but easily worked.

By about 3300 BCE, some South Asians in the valley of the Indus River witnessed the development of agriculture, the growing of food in amounts capable of generating food surpluses. This was made possible by the domestication of plants, such as wheat and barley, and the domestication of animals, such as the humped bull and water buffalo, which provided the means of sustaining all of the world's early civilizations. By 2600 BCE, many urban complexes had risen to maturity in the valley of the Indus River and beyond, reaching north to Shortughai, situated on the Amu Darya in northern Afghanistan, south toward today's Mumbai, eastward toward the head of the Gangetic Plain, and west to the border between Persia (modern Iran) and Pakistan.

The city now known as Harappa in the north of modern Pakistan is the site of one of the earliest and largest of these urban complexes and is the most common name given for the entire civilization. In the larger Harappan cities, such as Mohenjo-daro four hundred miles farther south, people traveled along streets laid out in a square grid pattern, the first of their kind. This city also shows evidence of the first town planning of any kind, with each city-center block of uniform length. Brick walls ten feet thick surrounded the elevated heart of these complexes. These massive walls seem built to protect against flood, rather than attack. Their gateways appear better designed to check incoming and outgoing merchant carts for sales receipts and tax payments on trade goods than for defense and lacked typical elements of ancient defensive fortifications, such as angled entrances to thwart a sudden rush or exposing an attacker to assault from above. Also, few weapons have as yet been found, and these are of such poor quality as to suggest a lack of need for them.

Harappan urbanites worked and lived in structures made of both mud brick and "burnt" or baked brick. The most impressive homes were those clustered on raised platforms, often as much as nine feet above the floodplain. These had their own baths and toilets connected by pipes to one of the most elaborate drainage and sewer systems in world history. This drainage system, when taken together with the system of locks controlling water levels and flow in harbors like Lothal, has led some investigators to conclude that Harappans were master hydraulic engineers. Shops and the dwellings of merchants and craftsmen located in the lower level of Harappan cities were concentrated along their north–south axis, while exclusively residential housing was located along streets running east to west. Industrial areas and factory buildings have also been identified, including a flour mill with circular brick work platforms and built-in mortars used to grind grain. Simple living quarters for workers were attached to the mill.

Daily material life was dominated by highly profitable farming and the most diverse manufacturing activity in the ancient world. Both were made possible by the region's fertile and mineral-rich alluvial soil, but Harappan society may still not have flourished had it not been for its

This artist's reconstruction shows a gateway into the city of Harappa. Uniform proportions of bricks and a lack of defensive works indicate a well-ordered and relatively stable society. Archaeologists found intact the arched bricked drain opening and other structures that were over four thousand years old. Painted by Chris Sloan, courtesy Harappa Archaeological Research Project

capacity to export its farming, metallurgical, and manufacturing surpluses. Tons of Harappan barley, cotton, rice, and wheat, as well as untold amounts of turquoise and agate, left annually from port cities such as those found near the modern villages of Lothal and Dholavira. These goods traveled to the cities of Dilmun (Bahrain) and Magan (possibly Oman) and further on to Mesopotamia, whose inhabitants knew the lands of the Indus Valley as Meluhha. Indus Valley pottery has already been found in Oman, where a recently discovered cuneiform inscription offers services to those who need a translator of the language of Meluhha. This suggests that ports in ancient Bahrain and Oman may have served to facilitate trade between the two civilizations. Phoenician middlemen may have carried that trade as far as Egypt.

Similar cargoes were dispatched northward from the city of Harappa overland to the Bactrian–Margiana civilization that thrived along the banks of the Oxus River in modern Uzbekistan. In exchange, South Asians received silver and gemstones, including lapis lazuli from Afghanistan and jade from China, which Harappans manufactured into valuable goods for internal consumption or export. Harappan cities produced precious jewelry, in part by drilling and shaping imported as well as local gemstones, including carnelian, a supremely hard stone. This they did with a skill so fine that carnelian beads made by them were the most treasured possessions of Mesopotamian kings and queens. Around 2500 BCE, the Mesopotamian queen Puabi was buried with Harappan-made items of copper, wood, and shells, as well as a gold necklace with carnelian beads and lapis lazuli. An ivory workshop found at Lothal suggests that elephants may have been domesticated to ensure that a supply of ivory was available to meet both foreign and domestic orders.[1]

This trade-fueled prosperity may have helped spur increased opportunities for work other than farming and, consequently, may have permitted a degree of job specialization unprecedented in the ancient world. As in other early civilizations, job specialization led to elaborate social differentiation and hierarchy in which the perceived value of an occupation determined social and political rank. Signs of such ranking by occupation have been found throughout Harappan society, ranging from bangles (gold for the higher ranks, gold-plated copper or tin for the middle ranks, and clay or seashells for common folk) to hairstyles and housing. On the other hand, Harappans seem to have seen death as a great equalizer. The cemeteries thus far excavated are unique among early urban civilizations in that their graves contain no personal wealth, such as jewelry, and offer no sign of the rank or power of the deceased. The disposition of their dead would indicate, at least in terms

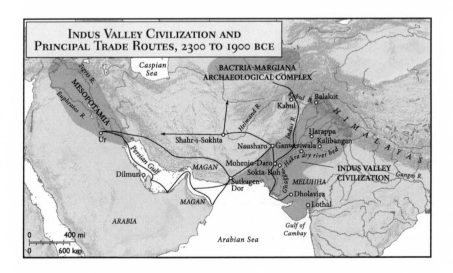

INDUS VALLEY CIVILIZATION AND
PRINCIPAL TRADE ROUTES, 2300 TO 1900 BCE

of cultural expression, that Harappan social divisions may have been less dramatic than elsewhere.

When initially explored by professional archaeologists in 1921–1924, the ancient rubble of Harappan cities seemed to yield few spectacular finds, suggesting that Harappa was a poor copy of Sumerian or other societies in Iraq, whose knowledge had somehow diffused eastward to form an "Indo-Sumerian civilization." However, further excavations revealed that the grid design of Harappan cities and their sanitation systems were without parallel in the ancient world. Moreover, their writing bore no relation to Sumerian cuneiform (script cut into wetted clay tablets). Harappans had also developed their own systems of weights and measures, including a decimal system. Their baked bricks of every size were manufactured at a fixed ratio of 1:2:4. Street corners were set at crisp right angles, a major feat of engineering. Harappan figurines have been described as masterpieces.[2]

Such discoveries were exciting, but paled in comparison to other finds, which collectively determined that the size of Harappan civilization in terms of territory was greater than Egypt and Mesopotamia combined, with settlements reaching into Central Asia. The discovery of dozens of Harappan-age sites along the dry bed of the Ghaggar-Hakra River further expanded the known range of Harappan culture. The riverbed runs parallel to the Indus River approximately one hundred miles to the east, crossing the border between present-day Pakistan and India. Immediately after the discovery of Harappan cities on the Indian side of the border, some nationalist-minded Indians began to speculate that the Ghaggar-Hakra riverbed may have more sites than neighboring Pakistan's Indus Valley. They have also argued that the now dry bed was the "lost" Sarasvati River mentioned in ancient Hindu texts, and that the name of Harappan civilization should therefore be changed to Sarasvati civilization. Such claims may prove to be valid, but modern nationalist arguments complicate the task of South Asian archaeologists who must deal with the poor condition of Harappan sites. The high water table means the oldest sites are under water or waterlogged and difficult to access. Many cities have been plundered by later peoples for their bricks. Most of all, archaeologists must work without the aid of written records due to their continuing inability to read the Harappan script.

The absence of a single grand fortress or palace on the citadel or highest mound at Harappa argues against a single authority and suggests that its people were not ruled by divinely connected rulers living in a central palace, as was the case in Mesopotamia, Egypt, and China.

The large number of substantial structures found there would be in keeping with a constant maneuvering for political power among a variety of interests in a less centralized, but complex, political system. Each city may have had its own leadership that functioned within a web of trade and production managed by shifting alliances between commercial or agricultural elites at the city's center.

Artifacts found at Dholavira, a sister port city of Lothal to its northwest, indicate that its citizens produced not only copies of wares made in the Harappan heartland but also goods stylistically linked to neighboring peoples. Other artifacts suggest that non-Harappan craftspeople migrating into such cities brought with them their own traditional arts, which led to a blending of cultures and artistic production. The evidence suggests that the people of Dholavira were able to reconcile different ideas and practices, a process known to world historians as syncretism.

In the absence of hard evidence, speculation is rife over the nature of Harappan religion. Scholars have attempted to reconstruct the Harappan religious outlook from the pictographs on Harappan seals, which are small, thin clay or soapstone tiles that may have been used as labels on merchandise. These seals often feature pictures of animals or human-like figures next to brief texts in the (undeciphered) Harappan script. Some of these seals are suggestive of religious beliefs, at least to those who believe that many South Asian religious traditions have Harappan roots. Fueling such speculation are seals of a possibly masked figure before whom offerings seem to be made. The figure sits with ankles over opposite thighs, phallus erect, and often orbited by elephants and rhinoceroses. Most South Asians today would recognize this figure as an early form of Shiva, a manifestation of the divine power governing all creation, including all animal life (*pasupati*). In this seated pose, now called the "lotus" or *padmasana* position (*padma*, "lotus"; asana, "seated"), Shiva demonstrates that meditation, when used to control the sexual drive, generates energy in tune with the internal spiritual, and hence cosmic, order.

Any attempt to project Shiva's current characteristics backward in time or to draw too fine a parallel with an ancient artifact (howsoever similar in appearance) is fraught with peril. However, this so-called Shiva prototype draws attention to other evidence supporting the view that Harappan peoples were greatly concerned with maintaining order, cosmic and otherwise. The standard proportions of bricks of all sizes produced throughout the society, the careful maintenance of the pattern of major streets and structures, the lack of visible signs of mass

A clay seal featuring a horned figure surrounded by animals and labeled with Indus Valley script dating from 2500 to 2400 BCE. *Some scholars suspect that the image is a religious one, depicting a Harappan forerunner of the Hindu deity, the Lord Shiva.* National Museum of India, New Delhi, India/Bridgeman Images SCP57227

conflict, together with the absence of palaces and temples, could all be taken to suggest that a sense of order was internalized in the hearts of Harappans, not imposed from above by priestly or monarchial decree. Without some sense of civic duty or cohesion, it is hard to imagine, for example, how a government could have cleared the wooden filters found in miles of Harappan drains. Such tasks may have been accomplished, as they were in Egypt, by instilling people with a deep devotion to a pharaoh-like authority, but the legitimization of such authority in Egypt was reflected in the construction of broad avenues leading to massive public buildings expressing and exalting the divine ruler's power to regulate society, features thus far absent at Harappan sites. The grid pattern of Harappan streets and standardization of building materials are more likely evidence of powerful guilds and municipal boards and serve a practical purpose, though they might also be fulfilling a collective view of an orderly cosmos.

The apparent absence of kings, brutal slave quarters, prisons, warfare, powerful weapons, or morally driven complex social hierarchies, together with orderly cityscapes, may seem like these cities together constituted an egalitarian, peaceable, utopian realm. Such a view does not take into consideration the hours of backbreaking labor supplied by factory and millworkers who no doubt lived in the poorer parts of town. Further, the discovery of a grave at Mohenjo-daro that holds the skeletons of a couple buried side by side could be taken to mean that the much later Hindu practice of a widow joining her husband in death (called sati) had Harappan origins. Yet the mere presence of husbands and wives buried next to each other is insufficient to support such a claim, and even so, it would only mean that early "civilized" South Asia was no more a paradise for women than it was in most other parts of the ancient world, where male dominance or patriarchy was common.

Harappan civilization reached its peak from about 2700 to 2000 BCE. Such was its influence on the world beyond its frontiers that the royal scribes of the great Mesopotamian king Sargon boasted that his great power was proved by the large number of ships with goods, such as wood from Meluhha, tied up by the quay at Agade,[3] his capital city on the Euphrates. Long after Sargon passed from the scene, rich cargoes from Meluhha still arrived in Mesopotamia, but by 1900 BCE Harappan ports, such as Dholavira and Lothal, and their Mesopotamian counterparts had disappeared or were in serious decline.

Harappan and Mesopotamian civilizations of that time seem to have fallen victim to common environmental forces. Harappan and Mesopotamian soils betrayed both societies. Each had long exploited great flood plains, where water overflowing the banks of their river systems could be captured by dams and distributed by levies to farms. The water-sodden land was then planted with crops that matured before the trapped flood waters fully evaporated. In South Asia, the possibility of two monsoon-driven rainy seasons greatly extended the crop-growing season. However, intensive plant growth, waterlogged land, and hot, dry summer climates cause rapid surface evaporation, drawing salts in the earth closer to the surface, where they slowly poison plant life through a process called salinization. Moreover, salt-permeated topsoil is easily blown away by passing winds, causing desertification. These conditions are further exacerbated where a hard substratum of bedrock impervious to water lies not far beneath the surface, as is the case in the valley of the Indus. Such soil formations mean water tends even more to stay close to the surface (a high water table), where the process of evaporation is greatest. Salinization is particularly deadly in regions experiencing a period of decreasing local rainfall, as the drier the air, the faster the evaporation, and hence the quicker the rise in salts to the surface. A further shift eastward of the monsoons may have been responsible for this decreasing moisture, encouraging a drying trend that became well established in Mesopotamia, in Canaan (Palestine), and on the western Indian subcontinent before 1800 BCE.

Throughout history, the combination of intense farming of flooded, waterlogged land in a dry climate with a high water table and decreasing local rainfall has proven deadly to human society. This same phenomenon brought an end to Peru's various Viru Valley cultures (dating from 1050 BCE) and that of the Sonoran Desert's Hohokam Indians (300 to 1450 CE) in the basin of the aptly named Salt River in Arizona. It seems that between 1900 and 1500 BCE, both the northeastern plains of South India and the land between the Tigris and Euphrates (Mesopotamia) experienced the ill effects of salinization. Crop failures in Mesopotamia may have led to poverty, which may in turn have reduced its trade with Harappa. The loss of a chief trade partner would have made it harder for Harappans to overcome the loss of their own agricultural surpluses.

Ironically, both civilizations' management of their natural resources may have figured in this mutual decline. Much of the Harappan–Mesopotamian bulk trade was in Harappan wood. Harappan woodsmen may have stripped much of the Indus Valley of its local forests for this trade and to provide fuel for the kilns that dried the bricks used widely in Harappan construction. Mesopotamians had already deforested the lands between the Tigris and the Euphrates, hence their need for outside suppliers of wood mentioned in Sumerian records. The removal of forest cover, for any reason, increases flooding, because trees hold water in the soil. The making of burnt bricks and the trade in wood, combined with drought, was a prescription for disaster.

Dramatic earth movements have often altered the course of human history: earthquake-related tsunamis alone have eradicated cities from ancient Mycenae (Crete) to Port Royal (Jamaica) in the early modern period. The fate of Harappans was probably sealed by a series of earthquakes and other tectonic-movement-related events between 1900 and 1500 BCE that uplifted land and shifted river beds so as to create even greater pooling of water in a time of flood, further increasing salinization. Increasingly unproductive land and declining Mesopotamian trade would have made it harder to fix the damage done by floods and earthquakes. Cities show signs of a slow dissolution of civic cohesion, including the rise of slums, the failure to maintain the grid pattern of streets, and a decline in the quality of crafts.

In South Asia, Harapan cities along the Indus and Ghaggar-Hakra rivers may have been the first to perish, as their life-giving waters shifted or largely dried up by 1900 BCE. Others cities, such as the port at Lothal, may have survived for perhaps two centuries longer until river courses either shifted away from or flooded over them. In an effort to avoid annihilation, Harappans may have moved farther east and south in search of fertile land and reliable rainfall. Such a migration might explain the ancient Harappan-like dam structures and cultural fragments found along rivers in the Deccan.

Language offers further evidence of Harappan migration. In an isolated valley above the Indus River, the earliest form of language found (called Brahui) may be related to the earliest form of the Dravidian language group, which is widely spoken in the southern regions of the subcontinent but has few clear connections to other language groups. If the Brahui-speaking inhabitants of lands once within the Harappan orbit are the descendants of speakers of the ancient Harappan language, so also are speakers of Dravidian. The idea of such an ancient lineage is very popular among Dravidian speakers. It is challenged by many other linguists, however, who argue that Brahui speakers migrated to their present location from their original home in the Dravidian-speaking south. Like the idea of "Sarasvati Civilization," this controversy indicates the complexities faced by students of the transition between Harappan society and its successors, but it is also a lesson on how the needs and desires of the present may impinge on an understanding of the past.

Of greater significance for South Asia's place in world history is that Harappan culture, from its outset, was connected to the wider world. South Asia continued those connections throughout its early history. King Solomon of ancient Israel imported peacocks from South Asia to enrich the atmosphere of his court. Caches of South Asian pepper and relics of South Asian teakwood boats have been found in Egypt dating from the time of Queen Cleopatra in the first century BCE. The earliest alphabets used in the Philippines and neighboring islands were based on South Asian models. Yet early South Asia's significance in terms of world history is far broader than direct connections between cultures: its first urban society offers a sobering example of the ways in which human action and environmental factors can combine to influence the course of a civilization.

Chapter 2

The Vedic Age, 1500–500 BCE

As the cities of the Indus Valley and Ghaggar-Hakra River systems declined, a society producing a poorer quality pottery than found in Harappan cities at their height began to proliferate across the northwestern reaches of the subcontinent. The makers of this so-called black ware were an initially illiterate, nomadic people who called themselves "noble ones" or, in their language, Aryans. Though their pottery was poor, their oral tradition was, as with most nomadic peoples, enormously rich, recalling days "when men roamed far" and "the conquering gods smote demons" and called for "the earth [to] vouchsafe to us good fortune and glory!"[1] This exhortation comes from the Vedas, originally an oral tradition whose songs of praise and sacrifice form the basis of what is known about Aryan society. This group was increasingly well established in the Indus River Valley and the Gangetic Plain after 1500 BCE, marking a new era in South Asian history called the Vedic Age.

The Vedas suggest that the Aryan people did not require the resources necessary to support urban settlements, such as agricultural irrigation. Its people were herders of cattle, which required only pastures for grazing. These herds provided meat for food and leather for shoes and clothing, as well as served as items for trade. As in many nomadic societies, the animals were venerated as a heavenly gift. Aryans followed a burial practice typical of nomadic peoples: they burned rather than buried their dead. As in many nomadic societies, Aryan women were honored not only as wives and bearers of children but also as warriors and moral philosophers. Such was their status that an early proverb held, "Where women are honored, there the gods rejoice, but where they not honored, there rituals are without fruit."[2]

And rituals mattered a great deal. According to the Vedas, Aryan successes or failures depended on the support of their gods, and the gods depended on them. Only through the sacrificial offerings humans made to them were the gods able to serve mankind. These ritual offerings included a sacred drink made of soma, a now extinct plant with hallucinogenic properties. Typically, priests poured these offerings into a fire that freed their powerful inner essence to be gathered up by the messenger god Agni, who carried it up to his heavenly cohorts dwelling above the clouds on the top of a sacred mountain called Mount Meru. The warrior god Indra, strengthened by soma offerings, was able to destroy the demonic enemies of his servant-people. His tasks included freeing the divine cow, Vac, from the hands of a serpent-demon god of chaos, Vitra, who would deny Vac's milk to humankind. Vitra also halted the rivers that sustained Aryan pastures and the soma plant that linked man and god—that is, until a thunderbolt launched by a soma-powered Indra split Vitra "like a tree-trunk split asunder with an axe" and "let go the seven streams to flow."[3]

Aryan ceremonies were presided over by priests called Brahmins, whose name signifies that they were the keepers of the divine principle known as Brahman (literally, "the sacred breath"). Brahman was invested in all things, material as well as spiritual, but was accessible only through ritual sacrifice, just as Indra was accessible through the offering of soma. The Aryans believed that the first man, Purusha, sacrificed himself to create the four varnas, or social orders of men and women: the Brahmins arose from his severed head, Kshatriyas (warriors) from his arms, Vaishyas (herders and merchants) from his trunk, and Shudras (slaves; later, most farmers) from his thighs. Vedic priests chanted a prayer calling out to Brahman "who propagates knowledge of the Vedas . . . for a Kshatriya prince for the safety of kingdom; a Vaishya for rearing the cattle; a Shudra for hard labor and service."[4] Only the first three of these varnas could wear a sacred thread worn like a sash across the upper torso from shoulder to the opposite hip, invested on males only and marking them "twice born" (by birth and spirit), who could alone fully partake of Aryan religion and society. The Shudras existed to serve the twice born, who in turn served the gods through ritual sacrifices. Brahmins claimed superiority over all others, so much so that even if others "none a Brahman, espoused a dame, and then a Brahman took her hand, he is her husband and only he."[5]

With their compact social structure, and divinities and ritual practices as portable as a simple fire altar for sacrifices, the Aryans were well suited to survive the increasingly arid environment of the northern tier of the subcontinent. In search of pasture and other resources, they spread east until the dense woods of the Gangetic Plain stopped them. Their progress resumed after 800 BCE, when their use of iron axe blades enabled them to clear a path through these forests. By then, the Vedas had coalesced into a fourfold collection of sacred hymns: the *Rig Veda*, the *Sama Veda*, the *Yajur Veda*, and the *Arthava Veda*. The contents of each complements the others: the *Rig Veda* is chiefly devoted to divine knowledge, the *Sama Veda* sets that knowledge to melodies sung at religious rituals, the *Yajur Veda* guides priests in the conduct of those sacred rites, and the *Arthava Veda* is a record of spells and incantations. These works, perhaps the oldest of the world's surviving sacred texts, were written in an early form of Sanskrit. Sanskrit is a member of a family of languages spoken by an ethnically diverse group of societies, which is thought to have spread from Central Asia into Europe and northern Iraq and Iran as early as 3000 BCE. Horses together with soma and other plants mentioned in the Vedas strongly suggest that Aryans were migrants originally from Central Asia where these flora and fauna were known to have flourished.

Today, this linguistic family is called Indo-European after the range of its influence. The speakers of Indo-European languages, including Iranians, Scandinavians, and Dorian Greeks (who succeeded earlier Mycenaean culture in the eastern Mediterranean), used nearly identical terms for key words such as "mother" and "father" and also worshipped similar atmospheric deities—gods of thunder, dawn, and so on. The gods of the Indo-European speaking Aryans dwelt on Mount Meru, while the gods of the Indo-European speaking Greeks lived on Mount Olympus. The Greek carrier of prayers offered to the gods via a sacrificial fire was called Hermes. The Aryan deity corresponding to Hermes was Agni, which in Sanskrit means "he who is born of fire."

Hymns in the *Rig Veda* describe the Aryan sky god Indra as not only "the slayer of Vitra," but one "who stormed the castles of the foe."[6] When placed alongside early, and now discredited, physical evidence, this description lent credence to a theory that invading Aryans destroyed the cities of the Indus Valley. However, its great walled cities show no damage from an attacker, and in any event, Aryans did not arrive in the Indus Valley until after the cities' abandonment.[7] The transition between Harappan and Aryan societies may or may not have been accompanied by violence, possibly including the subjugation of some Harappan people, but is best viewed as a gradual process. The most persuasive evidence for a slow process and cultural integration is that Harappan sites near the head of the Gangetic Plain show no sign of a "dark age" taking place after the decline of Harappan civilization, and there is some evidence of the Aryan adoption of Harappan hydraulic engineering, exemplified by the large heated pool found at Mohenjo-daro.

Early Aryans were not builders of dams or reservoirs, but thereafter no Aryan municipality or religious complex was without a tank or pool for cleansing. Some blending of Aryan with Harappan ways may have been inevitable given the impact of the Aryans' expansion into the Gangetic Plain, where they experienced a slow but dramatic shift from nomadic life to settled agriculture—a lifestyle familiar to Harappans, but which challenged the Aryans' deepest moral and philosophical beliefs.

Vedic South Asia offers world historians a rare opportunity to explore several global themes; foremost among these is the shift from nomadic to settled life. The transition to agriculture, and the ensuing need to control land and water to raise crops, became the source of competition among previously allied Aryan clans. Warfare among them became endemic and more deadly due to the development of iron weapons during what has been called the "Iron Age" (1300 BCE–700 CE). Iron tools meant more efficient means of clearing land for growing food; they also freed more men and resources for battle. As result, after 800 BCE, the Gangetic Plain became dotted by large cities protected by two parallel high wooden palisades or walls with the space between them filled with pounded earth. Aryan hymns that once sang of Aryan battles against their common foes, of the glories of power over others, and of the joys of material wealth, came to speak of the sorrow of war that pitted brother against brother, of the burdens of kingship, and of material wealth turned to ashes. The impact of these developments is reflected in the two great Aryan epic poems, whose earliest origins lie in that time: the *Mahabharata* and the *Ramayana*.

The *Mahabharata* is attributed to the legendary sage Vyasa. It has its origins in oral traditions coalescing after 800–700 BCE, when Aryan society began to address the ethical dilemmas and material conflicts that even the most righteous Aryans had to negotiate when making their way in this war-torn world. The core of this epic concerns a legendary battle at Kurukshetra, located on a plateau separating the Indus and the Ganges River Valleys—a location so strategic that the fate of South Asia was often settled there. At Kurukshetra, the forces of the five sons of Pandu (the Pandavas) faced off against their cousins, the Kuravas, with whom the Pandavas had been raised and educated as children after the deaths of their own father and mother. Pandu was the eldest child of Bharat, the ancestor of all Aryans (Bharat is the short form of the name of today's Republic of India in its own languages). His sons therefore had an absolute traditional claim to rule that kingdom. Out of the lust for power common to all men, the Kuravas attempted by various foul means to prevent the Pandavas from assuming their political inheritance. When these methods failed, the eldest of the Kuravas, Duroyodhana (meaning "unyielding fighter"), was unrepentant: "Should we not pursue selfish ways when we have power or are rich?"[8] He then forced the Pandavas into battle to decide the fate of the kingdom. The Pandava army was led by Arjuna, the Pandava brother who possessed all the qualities and abilities of the ideal Aryan warrior, especially his skill with a bow. On the field at Kurukshetra, the *Mahabharata* tells us, "Arjuna displayed his full prowess, as heroes [of the opposing forces], hoping to win glory . . . came before Arjun as he let loose his shafts. They fell by the thousands. Arjun carved a path through the Kuravas."[9] The Pandavas emerge as victors, but the unprecedented event of kindred Aryan families slaughtering each other raised moral questions only to be resolved in the *Mahabharata* after centuries of spiritual contemplation.

The *Ramayana*, attributed to the poet Valmiki, illuminates the difficulties that the divine King Rama confronts as he attempts to quell rivalries within the newly emerging Aryan states and absorb non-Aryan peoples of vastly differing lifestyles. The poem emerged slightly after the *Mahabharata*, about 750–500 BCE, but has been much rewritten by poets thereafter. Prince Rama, his wife, Sita, and his brother Lakshmana find themselves in temporary exile in a dense forest due to a succession dispute. Sita is kidnapped by a demon, Ravana, a denizen of Sri Lanka, who might have served to express Aryan fears of contact with non-Aryan peoples to their south. Rama rescues Sita with the help of a monkey-general, Hanuman, perhaps representing non-Aryan allies brought into the Aryan fold.

After a truly epic battle, King Rama returns with Sita to his capital but must convince the doubting populace that Sita has not been defiled by Ravana while in captivity. They may have seen self-interest and dishonor in Sita's righteous appeal for leniency for the defeated foe. "A superior being does not render evil for evil . . . A noble soul will ever exercise compassion [as] who is without fault?"[10] Rama finds himself unable to quell the gossip of his scandal-obsessed subjects that begins to disorder his kingdom. Full of shame over that failure, Rama asks Sita to undergo a public test of fire. She agrees, but not before calling out to the king's assembly that she has never been unfaithful to Rama in act, thought, or speech. She then prays for protection to Agni, the Lord of Sacrificial Fires, and rushes headlong into the fire. Many variations of this story were composed over the centuries, but in the most popular, Agni hears Sita's call and raises her from the fire, unharmed, to sit beside a chastened King Rama on his throne, where they rule as examples of true justice. In other versions, the lesson is harder. Despairing of justice, Sita calls upon the Earth, her divine mother, to take her back into her arms:

> If I have been true and virtuous, performed every duty,
> If I have been honorable and good, Mother Earth, hear my plea.
> Have mercy on your gentle child; take me back in your arms.[11]

The ground then opens and she disappears into it, never to return. Sita's defense of wifely purity would become conflated with the much later custom of sati (meaning a good woman or true wife), in which a widow joins her husband's corpse on his funeral pyre. In any case, Rama thereafter becomes the model of an ideal king and his rule the embodiment of good government.

A ceremony called the Ashvamedha (horse sacrifice) provides further insight into this era of transition from a nomadic to a settled society. The Ashvamedha began with a highly ritualized ceremony during which the Brahmins (priests) offered prayers to a great steed, which was then released to wander for a year followed by a king's courtiers, who were to subjugate all the people and land that the horse traversed. Upon its return, the horse was sacrificed, during which women of the royal household, including the queen, participated in rituals meant to associate the virility of the horse with that of the king. After this, the Brahmans chanted, "May this Steed bring us all-sustaining riches, wealth in good kine [cows], good horses, manly offspring. Freedom from sin may Aditi (mother of the gods) vouchsafe us: (may the sacrificed) Steed with our oblations gain us lordship!"[12]

This ceremony, set against the larger canvas of Vedic society, suggests the growing importance of settlement or territoriality, but also the existence of some equality of influence among the king, or raja (ruler), his warriors (also of the Kshatriya class), and the Brahmins, who conducted the Ashvamedha, thus reflecting the emergence of a true ruling class, rather than either a pure theocracy or mere military dictatorship. Such relative egalitarianism has led some scholars to idealize the evolving Aryan or Vedic state as a democratic republic rather than a consultative monarchy. It was more likely the latter, perhaps necessarily so. Most ancient societies required a mechanism for balancing the roles of warriors, priests, and other contending parties. The Vedic ruler may have used his powers to act as that balancer. The balancing nature of Vedic kingship may have played a role in the origins of the region's complex social hierarchy, dubbed the "caste system" by Portuguese visitors in the sixteenth century after their own word for social classes (castas).

The roots of caste may be in Harappan precedent or in varna, the four major Vedic social divisions. Yet the king's grant of patronage to clan lineages that served him, or his demotion of groups that offended him or his Brahmin advisors, may also have played a role. The Vedic ruler's powers were great, but he may have required the compliance of warriors and priests to bring order to an increasingly complex world.

These relatively small early Vedic courts ultimately proved unequal to the growing competition within their communities and the increasing number of other peoples encountered as Vedic society expanded to the east and south. Sons of kings vied to succeed their fathers, and once-united Vedic clans vied for control over new lands. Royal Brahmin advisors may have sought to blame the unrighteousness of Kshatriyas for these divisions, while Kshatriyas may have blamed Brahmins for lost military campaigns which the Brahmins had blessed.

To defend their tenuous authority, Brahmans and Kshatriyas restricted admission to the ruling class at the expense of Vaishyas and Shudras. There were also groups of *mleccha* (outcastes), people who could not be easily assimilated into Aryan society even as slaves, such as the aboriginal peoples called *adavasi* living in rainforest areas or in the more remote sections of the Deccan plateau. Eventually Aryans refused to marry or eat with anyone of perceived lower social status. The task of advising the king about which non-Aryan peoples (or even Aryan clans) should be afforded what degree of status could pit the twice born against each other. Brahmins might consider some low-ranking Aryan chiefs contemptible, while Kshatriyas might regard the same group as indispensable military allies worthy of higher rank. Moreover, Brahmins or any group who did not function as exemplars of ideal Aryan social roles (for example, Brahmins living as farmers, not priests) could be assigned lower social rank.

Sometime between 800 and 500 BCE, pressures within Vedic society reached the point where some Kshatriya men and women began abandoning their role in the ruling class and retreated to forest clearings, where they sat down and critically discussed the growing dilemmas and divisions facing their people. Martial duty and death with honor were central to Kshatriya existence, but those of this class who had retired to the woods had to wonder: since victory in battle did little to change the competitive and violent nature of the world, of what use was battle, or even human existence? The record of the poetic forest dialogues produced by those Kshatriyas and others who raised these challenging questions came to be known as the Upanishads (meaning "the texts produced by those who are seated in discourse near others, or before a teacher"). Most of the more than two hundred known contributors to this text concluded that their existing knowledge of Brahman (the divine), dharma (the correct moral path, order, or law), and ritual sacrifice was not wrong but was too literal an interpretation of reality. Brahman was seen as the source not only of the sacred but also the profane or material world. All was Brahman, a divine power or consciousness that, unlike human existence, was eternal and at peace within itself, two characteristics human life clearly lacked. Since all was Brahman, the world seen by men and women was merely maya (illusion) arising from the desire for self-advancement and the pursuit of material gain.

Upanishadic thinkers believed that, though blinded to the true reality of Brahman by selfish desire, men and women remained connected to it through their atman (souls). They proclaimed that the soul was indivisible from Brahman. They recognized that karma—a lifetime's desire for the things of this world—might bind the soul, preventing its entry into the realm of Brahman at the time of death. Having no spiritual outlet, the soul was later presumed to migrate into another being of desire entering this world of illusion. The Upanishads acknowledged that living things could not help but be attached to the material world around them and offered a way to achieve moksha or *mukti* (liberation) from samsara (the cycle of rebirth) by reducing that attachment through an austere life of fasting and meditation. Fasting unto death was considered the ultimate act on this path to salvation, but was not strictly necessary, as the small amount of karma remaining at the death of one who had renounced the material world could be burned away by the purifying flames of the funeral pyre. The significance of the Aryan fire sacrifice was thus reduced, but remained potent. Liberation from samsara was an act of sacrifice, not by the burning of a material substance like soma, but by the internal burning away of *tapas* (desire) born of attachment to this world.

Spirited chela (students) joining the gurus (master teachers) in their ashram (forest retreats) did not hesitate to challenge the logic behind these principles, which were tested before assemblies that included princes and at least one learned woman, named Gargi. The most pointed of the questions they raised was, if everything was Brahman, "why was it that Brahman could not be seen, while all else was visible?" This question so puzzled an Aryan king (King Janaka) that he promised to give "a thousand cows and a bull as big as an elephant for the answer."[13] The *Chandogya Upanishad* offers the clearest expression of that answer through a dialogue between the sage Uddalaka Aruni and his young son Svetaketu. When Svetaketu is asked by his father to dissolve salt in a cup of water, he does so. When then asked to take it out, the son confesses that he cannot even see the salt. His father asks him to taste the water, which Svetaketu finds salty. His father then leads his son to the logical conclusion: just as the salt cannot be seen but can be tasted, Brahman is everywhere, though unseen.[14] The writers of the Upanishads affirm that

> this whole world is Brahman ... whose body is imbued with life-principle, whose form is light, whose conception is truth, whose *atman* (Self) is space containing all works ... all desires ... this Self, my Soul within my heart, is greater than the earth, this sky ... This Soul, this Self of mine is that Brahman.[15]

Once the unity of the human soul and Brahman was ascertained through the development of *jana* (spiritual knowledge) and self-denial, a soul could attain liberation from samsara. Since the Upanishads advocated the practice of self-denial to a degree beyond the capacity of even most Kshatriyas and made no direct attack on the authority of the Brahmins, they were not a call for radical religious or social change. However, they ultimately altered the spiritual and social structure of South Asia.

The concept of karma ultimately provided a rationale for bringing order to an expanding and complex Aryan society in ways acceptable to Brahmin and Kshatriya alike. Higher or lower status would come to be legitimized by reference to a divine process, which would often be associated with the perceived spiritual purity of social categories as distinct as specialized occupations. For example, those born into powerful Brahmin lineages were deemed to have earned their *jati* (privileged birth positions) as priests because of merit acquired in a previous life. At the other end of the social spectrum, peasants and slaves could be deemed to have earned their lower *jati* status by their past selfish acts. Only acceptance of one's status at birth could ensure a higher status upon rebirth. Performance of another's social place in the dharma (moral order) would guarantee a lower status in the next life. Thus each *jati* needed to avoid contact with those beneath them. Of course, priests and rulers could make these assignments to suit their mutual needs. When a turn in political fortune raised a clan described in the *Arthava Veda* as "despised" to that of powerful kings, Brahmins had no difficulty assigning them to a *jati* of suitably higher status.

The stresses of the Iron Age sparked a global emergence of new philosophical traditions. The Upanishads opened a door of philosophical perception that was to influence not only South Asian society but also ancient Greek contemporaries. Athens had its share of South Asian philosophers in residence, and Athenians witnessed a funeral held according to Vedic rites. Both Socrates and Plato believed in reincarnation, the immortality of the soul, and in a division between the absolute (divine) and relative (human or material). In his "allegory of the cave," Plato offers a theory of maya (illusion) similar to that found in the Upanishads.

The writers of the Upanishads may or may not have anticipated or approved of the eventual social uses of the law of karma. Several of them were closely associated with low-status Aryan or non-Aryan rulers to whom Brahmins gave scant respect. Other Kshatriyas who took refuge in the forest rejected outright not only the notion of *jati* but also much of Aryan society. Two of those Kshatriyas who took to the forest were former princes who developed their own pathways to liberation from the snares and evil fruits of worldly desire.

Sometime between 599 and 527 BCE, Prince Vardhamana of the eastern Gangetic kingdom of Vaishali concluded on his own that knowledge such as that now associated with the Upanishads was useful, but not nearly sufficient to achieve moksha (spiritual liberation), let alone justify a reordering of society. This prince, commonly known as Mahavira (Great Hero), shared the Upanishadic view that attachment to existence meant continued rebirth into this world, but he also believed that the true difficulty of that attachment lay in how casual selfish human acts, especially the ill treatment of animals and the exploitation of the natural world, caused *himsa* (harm), were a source of karma, and led to rebirth. He enjoined all those seeking liberation to be harmless (ahimsa, "acting without harm"), saying, "All breathing, existing, living, sentient creatures should not be slain, nor treated with violence, nor abused, nor tormented, nor driven away."[16] Only when the discipline of ahimsa was internalized could humanity's karmic burden be properly identified, lessened, or avoided. It was true that sitting in the forest half-naked while fasting and meditating would generate less karma than, for example, coveting the material possession of others. But to Mahavira, the making of the commonest clothing and even small physical movements, such as breathing, could be fatal to tiny life forms and thus doom the unwary soul to rebirth.

Mahavira's advocacy of self-denial through nonviolence and not doing harm to living beings, together with his establishment of clear modes of conduct (chastity, resisting the temptation to amass possessions, abstaining from lying, and not stealing from others), attracted a small but devoted following who came to consider him the most recent in a line of twenty-four Tirthankaras (spiritual guides) whose merit had triumphed over the cycle of rebirth. This *jaya* (victory), achieved without priestly rituals or social distinction earned in a prior life, led to the formation of a new dharma known as Jainism, perhaps the first faith to make ecology a form of religious practice.[17] While the number of adherents to Jainism was and remains small, Jain philosophy has made an impact on the subcontinent far greater than its numbers would suggest. Mohandas Karamchand Gandhi was raised in a region rich in the Jain tradition of ahimsa, and it was the centerpiece of his social and political philosophy which helped to liberate South Asia from colonial rule.

Mahavira was not the only Kshatriya concerned with the karmic results of thoughtless living and the spiritual value of ahimsa. Siddhartha Gautama (563–483 BCE), a prince of the Shakya clan's state to the north of Vaishali, also advocated these principles. Like Mahavira, he addressed the same spiritual issues as the philosophers of the forest and spent time as one of them. Also like Mahavira, he found unacceptable the idea that the social order of the living should be based on the presumed spiritual merit acquired in a past life. He eventually developed a vehicle of salvation along a middle path between the worldly rituals of the Brahmins and the extreme rejection of the material world advocated in the Upanishads and by Mahavira. The teachings of Siddhartha, who later was known as a *bodhi* (possessor of wisdom) or Buddha (Enlightened One), came to form the basis of Buddhism, a religion destined to influence many cultures within and beyond Asia.

At the age of twenty-nine, Prince Siddhartha saw stark examples of the common fate of all humanity: old age, sickness, and death. What struck Siddhartha most about these encounters was how, despite the universality of these experiences, no human being was ever prepared for them. He then realized that all human grief, confusion, frustration, and pain were born of ignorance that everything in the material world was in constant flux and decay. In the midst of these thoughts, he encountered a wandering ascetic who may have been a follower of Upanishadic or Jain thought and whose calm demeanor suggested a way out through self-denial.

Shortly thereafter, Siddhartha abandoned his royal life and joined an ashram. He quickly excelled in the practice of self-denial to the point of being able to fast unto death without pain. However, this achievement brought him no peace, as it offered no insight into the operation of the spiritual world. He ended his fasting and began mediating until he achieved nirvana, a state of consciousness beyond any form of attachment to the self, where he gained the understanding he sought. He then began preaching a dharma that could bring the wheel of rebirth to a halt in as little as one life.

The Buddha's followers codified his teachings, often expressed as the Four Noble Truths. Three of the Noble Truths are conditions or states of knowledge born of Siddhartha's earliest spiritual encounters. All emotional connections and material things deemed worth possessing, such as loved ones, health, and wealth, are in a constant state of *anicca* (transition or decay); this uncertain hold over what seems to matter most in life produces frustration that grows inexorably into *dhukka* (a condition of suffering), and only through *vidya* (insight, from the root "to see") into the truly transient nature of all things can *avidya* (blindness, or ignorance of the true nature of existence) be dispelled. Once aware that the world of desire offers nothing permanent and thus nothing worth possessing, the conscious mind awakens to nirvana—not a place, as all thoughts of places arise from a desire for permanence, but a state of consciousness wherein all desire for the self has ceased to exist. The fourth Noble Truth is the name given to the Buddha's offering of an Eightfold Path by which a seeker of nirvana practices non-attachment through mental focus, proper action, expressing one's purpose, relations with other individuals, relations with the larger community, daily life, examining one's actions, and contemplating one's existence. Buddhists hold that a follower of the Eightfold Path resembles a lotus flower, rooted in the mud of a pond (the world of *dhukka*) while its petals reach up to the sun to receive its light (nirvana), hence the mantra, or spiritually directed phrase, "Om mani padme Om" (Divine awareness is found in the lotus).

Buddhists, like Jains, condemn lying, stealing, and violence, but Buddhists see these acts as merely the choices of people blinded by pain and self-delusion. When faced with any loss at the hands of another, a Buddhist's typical response is to pray that the perpetrator may someday free herself or himself from the anger that is poisoning their life. As for losses beyond anyone's control, Buddhists typically remark that "all things are impermanent."[18]

So great was the Buddha's ability to make such abstract truths accessible that he also came to be called Shakyamuni (the Sage of the Shakyas). His followers agreed on what came to be regarded as "The Three Jewels": that men and women (the Buddha preached to both) could take refuge from the transitory world by following the practices he pursued during his exemplary life, by studying his lessons about the true dharma, and by participating in the sangha (Buddhist monastic orders) he organized to provide a self-reinforcing community for those attempting to walk the Eightfold Path.

BUDDHA
ABOUT 1ST CENT. FROM TAKHT-I-BAHI.
Given by C.E. Pitma.c, Esq. 1989.

A standing Buddha, first or second century BCE, whose lost hands are in abhaya-mudra, *a gesture of reassurance designed to dispel fear and accord divine protection. The statue's natural pose suggests a realism not found in the Greek art of this period, which idealized the human body.* © The Trustees of the British Museum, 01613029260

Like Jainism, Buddhism became a doctrine distinct from the ritual practices of the Brahmins and the philosophers of the Upanishads. Unlike the Brahmins, the Buddha held that the Vedas were products of unenlightened human discourse or mere legends. He also rejected not only the concept of a social order based on karma (the fruits of one's desire) in an earlier life but also any royal or Brahmanic authority deployed to enforce it. He did not reject either the law of karma or samsara but sought to demonstrate logically that karma merely determined the material or social circumstances into which one was born, with no further effect on that individual's progress toward liberation. A child born of a Brahmin was fortunate in wealth and education, but even a Brahmin's path in life was what the Brahmin made of it. Advantages of birth were thus no guarantee of righteousness; birth rank or inherited wealth often proved an impediment. The Buddha also advocated the doctrine of *anatman* (no soul), by which he meant not that the self or individual life or spirit was empty of value, but that its value existed only in how it engaged others. Comfort given freely to sick friends is of value to them and is of no cost in karmic terms. The expectation that such comfort will be returned has no value; usually ends in frustration; and is a sure path to selfish thought, selfish action, and hence rebirth. The Buddha reasoned that the identity of each atman or personal soul was thus relational; it did not exist in and of itself, but was constructed out of one's encounters with others, an idea that, centuries later, would be addressed by the European Enlightenment philosopher John Locke.

The Buddha lived at the end of the age in which people had begun to use iron for implements. Historians speculate that heavier weapons and tools favored male strength and so eroded the status of women. Whatever its cause, women's status declined as agriculture advanced due to iron technology (which spurred the manufacture of better axes, better plows, and better weapons). Whereas women had participated in the discussions that produced the Upanishads, not long afterward they were prohibited from reciting them, and a view emerged that women could attain salvation only after being reborn as males. The Buddha's response was to admit women to monasteries as nuns alongside male monks.

Since the Buddha described nirvana as the product of an internal spiritual awakening, not the negation of the material world, he rejected both the Vedic passion for immersion in the world, and also the Upanishadic and Jain view that liberation from samsara required extreme self-mortification (such as starvation). He told his followers that these were "the two extremes that he who has given up the world

This first- or second-century BCE carving depicts a group of Jain monks. Jainism, an ascetic or self-denying religion that developed contemporaneously with Buddhism, was pursued by monks, here identified by their nudity, which symbolized their renunciation of all materialistic pursuits. Brooklyn Museum, Gift of Georgia and Michael de Havenon, 87.188.5.

ought to avoid. A life given to pleasure and lust—this is degrading, sensual, vulgar, ignoble, and profitless; and a life given to mortifications, this is painful, ignoble, and profitless," He explained to seekers that it was "by avoiding these extremes that [he] found the Middle Path that leads to insight" and hence to nirvana.[19]

True living was a life in balance, wherein one fulfilled the needs of the body, mind, and spirit, while living in harmony with nature and other people, abhorring violence, and remaining open and adaptable to changing circumstances. Hence modern Buddhists, like their Jain counterparts, seek to peacefully protect the environment, knowing that in doing so, they are simultaneously protecting their bodies and advancing their spiritual liberation.

In the first centuries after the Buddha's death, most adherents to the "Middle Way" believed it was best pursued along the lines of the Buddha's own life, which was spent in discourse with seekers of arhat (individual enlightenment). Accordingly, these Buddhists called their path the Way of the Elders, or Theravada. They advocated living as monks and nuns supporting each other in pursuit of nirvana. However, there were others who developed another means of pursuing the Middle Way. If a person's attainment of nirvana were an end in itself, some Buddhists reasoned, the Buddha would not have devoted his life to spreading the knowledge he acquired: that he did so was an expression of selfless compassion. Thus, it was better to become increasingly enlightened, like the Buddha himself, and gradually gain salvation through learning and preaching among others suffering from the pains arising from ignorance in the form of a bodhisattva (a "Buddha in becoming") than as an arhat, who sought only personal salvation. They dubbed themselves Mahayanists (followers of a Maha, or Greater, Way)

Mahayanists who claimed that Buddhism required a greater involvement in the world than monastic living came to call the Theravadin way the Hinayana (the "lesser" or "narrower" way), but the two doctrines in time came to share much in common. Theravadins accepted the centrality of compassion to Buddhist thought and action, while Mahayanists embraced the concept of the monastic life to a considerable degree. Each sect enriched the Buddhist world with its own evolving variations of the Buddha's teachings. Theravadins added to the human store of knowledge through their rational philosophical discourse. The Mahayanist tendency to see the world itself as a great laboratory for spiritual learning ultimately led to its pioneering of an observational form of practice called Chen in Buddhist China and Vietnam and Zen when it spread to Japan. Zen practitioners draw lessons from human frustration. Moments such as having to stop at a red light when one is already late for work are perceived as opportunities for connecting to others or for healing reflection instead of outbursts of road rage. Thus, Buddhism's spread throughout South Asia to Central and Southeast Asia, China, and Japan came to enrich other Asian societies and, ultimately, became a part of the world's philosophical heritage.

CHAPTER 3

South Asia's Classical Age, 321 BCE–711 CE

By 600 BCE, much of the forests that were home to the Kshatriya and other writers of the Upanishads, as well as the Aryan chieftains from whom Mahavira and the Buddha were descended, fell within the larger orbit of a loose-knit state called Magadha, located south of the Ganges River. Around the late fourth century BCE, about a century after the sages of Jainism and Buddhism had died, the Nanda clan had usurped the power of Magadha's existing rulers and quickly developed Magadha's rich mineral deposits to support a large standing army. The Nandas soon used their armies to expand their frontiers to the limits of both the Indus River and the Ganges River plains. Nanda aggression roused the enmity of other Aryan clans, leading local Brahmins to call the Nanda dynasty the "killers of Kshatriyas," a phrase intended to suggest the Nandas were beneath Kshatriya rank and thus not entitled to be rulers. Aiding the Nandas in their wars of expansion was a force far more powerful than mere propaganda: a small group of foreign mercenaries called Yavanas (the Sanskrit word for the Greeks) who deployed a deadly combination of arms and a fighting formation called hoplite, in which soldiers fought in ranks or phalanxes rather than in individual combat, as had been the norm among Aryans for centuries.

The presence of Greek warriors on the Indo-Gangetic plain was a result of great change in Greece itself. With the collapse of Athens and the decline of Sparta following the Peloponnesian Wars (431–404 BCE), Greece had descended into chaos. Disgruntled ruling elites had left many Greek warriors unemployed or even banished from their home city-states. Some warriors found service in the imperial court of Greece's most hated enemy, Persia. Other Greeks passed through the Persian Empire into South Asia via Afghanistan and the northernmost city-states of the Indus River Valley. Under the Persian king, Cyrus the

Great, the Persian Empire claimed the Indus River Valley as its own in the mid-sixth century BCE, but what little political authority they had there was generally exercised through autonomous Aryan princes. In 330 BCE, King Philip of Macedonia (a land to the north of Athens) united and reinvigorated the city-states of Greece. After his death, his son Alexander asserted his authority over all the territories of Greece's traditional enemy, Persia, as far as the Indus Valley. But his goal there was not merely to assume control over the easternmost lands that Persia claimed as its own. Alexander was set on earning the status of a divine hero by passing down the Ganges River to reach the legendary East Sea (the Bay of Bengal in the eastern Indian Ocean), as had, in Greek legend, the hero-turned-god, Dionysus.

Neither the autonomous Aryan states of the Indus Valley nor the Nanda rulers to their south were aware of Alexander's aspirations to divinity, but Alexander's almost two-year-long pacification campaign in Afghanistan left no doubt about his imperial intentions. Aryan warriors engaged Alexander to the north of the Khyber and continued to oppose Alexander's forces as he marched to the Indus River, where he barely defeated a local ruler known to the Greeks as King Porus. Porus, in return for being allowed to retain his throne, provided Alexander with logistical support and local levies. However, even with such aid, the resistance of other Aryans was skilled and fierce enough to give Alexander's mixed Macedonian and Greek forces pause.

After receiving reports suggesting the great size and military might of the Nanda state that lay between Alexander and his ultimate goal, Alexander's warriors grew concerned over his desire to advance down the Ganges to the Indian Ocean. Exhausted by years of continuous campaigning and bloodied by even the small states on the northern banks of the river they called Indos (hence its name, the Indus, and India), Alexander's men begged him to bring their adventure to a halt. With his men in a state of virtual mutiny, Alexander declared that his forces would return to Persia by sea and land in July 326 BCE. This decision proved almost as deadly as the military debacle his soldiers had anticipated. His army had to fight its way down to the mouth of the Indus River, where some boarded ships for their journey home. Most of those ordered to march home along the desert coastal strip between the Indus and Persia perished from lack of food and water. Worse, most of the Greek-led colonies Alexander had established during his sojourn in India were almost immediately overrun by local Aryan rulers, though Greek settlements persisted in Bactria (in northern Afghanistan and neighboring Central Asia).

Not long after Alexander was forced to abandon his plan for further conquest, a young Aryan named Chandragupta Maurya visited Alexander's Greek-style reconstruction of the ancient city of Taxila, just east of the Indus. He may have been a fugitive or an exile from the Nanda domains. He may or may not have met Alexander, but Greek historians believed that he told Alexander's men that even he "lacked but little of making himself master of those countries since its king was so hated and despised on account of his baseness and low birth."[1] In 322 BCE, Chandragupta acted on his perception of Nanda weakness. He overthrew the Nanda dynasty by exploiting their unpopularity, by avoiding open battle with its numerically superior army, and by acquiring Greek mercenaries to use against them. This waging of guerrilla or asymmetrical warfare was part of a brilliant campaign plan devised by Chandragupta's Brahmin strategist, Chanakya. In less than two decades, Chandragupta employed Chanakya's strategies and Magadha's resources to conquer most of the subcontinent and establish South Asia's first imperial state, known as the Mauryan Empire (322–185 BCE).

The conquests of Alexander the Great in the name of Hellas (the Greeks' word for their homeland) encouraged the spread of Persian and Greek concepts of government and the arts throughout the eastern Mediterranean and much of Asia. The imperial idea, the control of many peoples and/or territories under one rule, may have been one of them. Certainly, empire was a realistic solution to late Vedic wars and social divisions. Under Chandragupta and his successors, the imperial idea took the form of a unified centralized bureaucracy featuring many departments and a civil service under the authority not of a mere king but of a *chakravartin* (he whose wheel runs everywhere without obstruction).

Alexander's successors, who maintained ambassadors at Patiliputra in Magadha, recorded in glowing terms the city's emergence as the capital of South Asia's first true and perhaps greatest imperial state. One of these Greek ambassadors, Megasthenes, described the city as "wealthy and beautiful," with "lavish palaces" and protected "by a wooden wall nine miles long and a mile and a half wide . . . with 570 towers and a moat that was 900 feet wide." He also noted that the empire drew upon the cultivation of "reeds which produced honey without bees" [sugarcane] and "trees which grew wool" [cotton] and that its roads, well maintained by a public works department, supported a trade network that extended from Greece to Southeast Asia. Megasthenes was perhaps

The Buddhist artistic encounter with Greek-influenced Central Asia is illuminated by this second- or third-century CE *example of the Greek hero Hercules holding a club usually wielded by the bodhisattva Vajrapani to keep the Buddha from harm.*
© The Trustees of the British Museum, 00276040001

most impressed by the empire's moral and political economy, even in times of war.

> [T]There are usages observed by the Indians which contribute to pre-
> vent the occurrence of famine among them; for whereas among other
> nations it is usual, in the contests of war, to ravage the soil, and thus to
> reduce it to an uncultivated waste, among the Indians, on the contrary,
> by whom husbandmen [farmers] are regarded as a class that is sacred
> and inviolable . . . even when battle is raging in their neighborhood
> [they] are undisturbed by any sense of danger, for the combatants on
> either side in waging the conflict make carnage of each other, but allow
> those engaged in husbandry to remain quite unmolested. Besides, they
> neither ravage an enemy's land with fire, nor cut down its trees.[2]

The design of the administration of the empire owed much to Chandragupta's advisor, Chanakya (also known as Kautilya), who provided a rational basis for imperial rule. He argued that logically, as well as historically speaking, "big fish swallow the little fish," a principle of imperial state formation that endures to this day. He also developed the more complex, but equally enduring, mandala or "circle" theory of diplomacy. According to this theory, a state's closest neighbors usually posed the greatest threat to its security because the closer the neighbor, the more likely it was to compete for local resources and have similar geopolitical goals, while more distant states, being neighbors of the near neighbor, were natural allies against them. Chanakya's principles form the central core of the Arthashastra, a classic text on government that came to constitute a manual for the application of South Asian laws and the punishment of the law's violators (*danda-niti*, meaning literally, "rule by the rod"). This text also considered the economy as coequal to concerns of diplomacy and military strategy, which suggests that Chanakya may have been the true father of political economy as well as modern political theory.

Chanakya probably had a hand in the process by which Chandragupta dealt with a second Greek invasion, led by Seleucus Nicator in 305 BCE. It is said that Chandragupta defeated the Seleucid army by deploying an army of sixty thousand men and nine thousand war elephants against them, but for Chandragupta and Chanakya, the making of a lasting peace was more important than military victory. Chanakya may have negotiated the subsequent treaty, which included Seleucus's own daughter (or another ranking princess-bride) being given in marriage to Chandragupta in exchange for the Macedonian general's surrender of any claims to most of Afghanistan, all of Baluchistan, and the Indus Valley. In return, Chandragupta gave Seleucus five hundred battle elephants, a paltry concession on the part of Chandragupta that proved vital in Seleucus Nicator's defeat of Greek rivals to his claim as heir to Alexander's empire in what is now Iran and Iraq.

Like Chanakya, Chandragupta was a philosopher as well as a master soldier and diplomat. Late in life, he transferred power to his son Bindusara and became a Jain monk. Bindusara remained in contact with the Hellenistic world, once reportedly asking Seleucus Nicator's heir, Antiochus I Soter, for samples of items for which his empire was well-known: "sweet wine, figs and a sophist (a philosopher who engaged in debates among philosophical schools)." The first two were sent, but the philosopher was not because, as Antiochus seems to suggest, he did not control the principle source of sophists, which was the city of Athens.[3] As for Bindusara's request, given the conflicts of the age over the nature and purpose of existence and the nature of the state, he may have thought he could not have too many philosophical schools represented at court.

Chandragupta's son Bindusara completed the conquest of the Deccan begun by his father, leaving to his son Ashoka, who ruled from 273 to 232 BCE, the task of consolidating Mauryan rule there and asserting control over Kalinga (modern Orissa), a state on the southeastern coast. The conquest and pacification of Kalinga proved costly: possibly over one hundred thousand lives were lost, including ten thousand of Ashoka's own men. According to Buddhist sources, the carnage of this campaign so awakened the Buddha nature within Ashoka that thereafter he swore to practice ahimsa and rule through Buddhist *dhamma* ("dharma" in the language of Buddhist texts). Though his interest was likely an evolving one, rather than a sudden conversion (he was a lay Buddhist before Kalinga), his regret over the price of that conquest and the growth of his personal faith is clear from one of his edicts:

> After the Kalingas had been conquered, the beloved of the gods [Ashoka] came to feel a strong inclination towards the dhamma, a love for the dhamma and for instruction in dhamma . . . Indeed, the beloved of the gods is deeply pained by the killing, dying and deportation that take place when an unconquered country is conquered. Even those who are not affected by all this suffer when they see friends, acquaintances, companions and relatives affected. These misfortunes befall all as a result of war, and this pains the beloved of the gods.[4]

Ashoka's decision to embrace Buddhism did not mean a withdrawal from public life, as his grandfather had done at the time of his conversion to Jainism. Rather, Ashoka came to regard Buddhism as a means of legitimizing his new regime.

After Kalinga, Ashoka consolidated his empire by enabling the centralized bureaucracy begun by his father to reach down through ministerial departments to provincial governors and further down to the headmen managing village affairs. He also expanded his father's road and revenue systems, then perhaps the most efficient communications and fiscal systems in the world. He replaced the "rule of the rod" with Buddhist moral precepts that he believed offered greater stability than mere force could ever secure. The political costs of imposing Buddhist values such as ahimsa (for example, by prohibiting animal sacrifice) were great, but Ashoka believed those costs would lessen as the people perceived the benefits of a less violent society.

Ashoka was seeking to justify a new manner of government—an empire—through a set of moral teachings that had not been the dominant religious philosophy of the people. Ashoka dealt with this problem in part by sponsoring what is now known as the Second Buddhist Council, at which Buddhist scholars, then mostly Theravadins, sought to suppress heresy and otherwise create a more authoritative doctrinal base. Ashoka was an active participant in its deliberations in a way that perhaps showed his commitment to Buddhism both on a personal level and as a means of justifying the unprecedented power and sweep of Mauryan rule.

Ashoka's propagation of evolving Buddhist doctrine as state policy was accomplished by edicts inscribed on prominent rock faces and on stone pillars he had erected across the length and breadth of the subcontinent. These inscriptions warned officials to respect the people and the people to respect the authority of the ruler in his unceasing vigilance to advance the public good:

> I have given this order, that at any time, whether I am eating, in the women's quarters, the bed chamber, the chariot, the palanquin, in the park or wherever, reporters are to be posted with instructions to report to me the affairs of the people so that I might attend to these affairs wherever I am. There is no better work than promoting the welfare of all the people and whatever efforts I am making is to repay the debt I owe to all beings to assure their happiness in this life, and attain heaven in the next.[5]

Though the rock and pillar edicts praised the value of the unity arising from adherence to a single religious pathway and announced laws based on Buddhist precepts, they proclaimed that "security from persecution" was as important as Buddhist practice. It is well they did so, as local records indicate that the edicts were not always received with enthusiasm. The edicts do make clear that Ashoka's goal was not to promote a religion, but to advance the secular value of moral practices which increased "the mercy and charity, the truth and purity, the kindness and honesty of the world."[6]

As this "globalist" phraseology suggests, Ashoka also sought to extend the benefits of Buddhist values beyond the boundaries of even his vast empire. According to tradition, he sent his son Mahendra to Sri Lanka, then an allied state, to advance the teaching of Buddhism there. Other Ashokan missions spread Buddhism westward to the Mediterranean, north toward Tibet (and hence to China), and eastward to the kingdoms of Southeast Asia, including Burma, Java, Sumatra, and Thailand, whose rulers grasped the value of the political legitimization that could accompany the adoption of Buddhist values. For centuries to come, in lands as distant as Korea, Buddhist rulers with imperial ambitions of their own would claim the status of *chakravartin* that Buddhist scripture accorded Ashoka, though he himself never took that title. Though other Asian rulers interpreted this South Asian model within their own cultural context, one Ashokan element persisted: a Thai king, when asked to explain how his Buddhist state tolerated other faiths, is said to have replied that Buddhist kings are masters of men's bodies, not their souls.

Ironically, only the last Mauryan emperor, Brihadratha Maurya, contemplated declaring himself a universal ruler, but he was assassinated by one of his generals shortly thereafter, in about 185 BCE. Mauryan rule ended with a whimper, rather than a bang, due to a flaw inherent in all dynastic regimes: the need for one clan or family line to generate able leaders over several generations. In its last fifty years, the empire was led by no fewer than six weak rulers. Yet neither political chaos, economic collapse, nor cultural transformation followed the fall of the Mauryans. Power passed relatively smoothly to other successor states in the north and to large kingdoms in the south. The unity and efficiency of the Mauryan revenue and road systems sustained the health and stability of the region, permitting the dynasty's successors to prosper and benefit from South Asia's contacts with the wider world.

In both their rise and their decline, the Mauryan achievement had a wide influence on the ancient world. They gave shape to South Asia's "Classical Age," the epoch when its dominant traditional pattern of politics, literature, religion, and arts emerged. During this time, South Asian religious ideas were expressed through new schools of religious philosophy and practice. Manuals defining political and social behavior were developed, while Sanskrit epic literature was refined and spread throughout South Asia and beyond due to the growth of transregional trade. As the exchange between Seleucus Nicator and Chandragupta can only begin to suggest, these developments paralleled and influenced the nearly simultaneous reformulation of the traditions of the ancient world, in China as well as in the Mediterranean, which marked what came to be called the classical ages of all three societies.

Greek philosophers from Plato to Aristotle seeking a prime mover or an unseen ideal world behind the veil of material existence discussed these issues with South Asian philosophers in Athens, hence Greek accounts of the funeral pyre of a Brahmin in Athens. Buddhists and Brahmins came to live in Alexandria, Egypt, when that city succeeded Athens as a center of the philosophical world. Clement of Alexandria, who lived in the second and third centuries BCE, knew these Brahmins well, once remarking, "They drunk no wine nor eat any animal food."[7] While Clement sought to meld Greek philosophy and early Christian thought, he remained ambivalent about the teachings of Brahmins, perhaps because early Christian philosophy ran on parallel lines, making Christian thought less unique. Clement favored gnosis (knowledge of a pathway by which a human soul can return to God), while Upanishadic philosophers sought to link atman with Brahman.

Alexandria was also home to the Greek ship captain who authored the *Periplus of the Erythraean Sea* (Manual for Going Around the Red Sea), a guide for Greek captains who were the primary players in the Greco-Roman world's trade through the Red Sea to South Asia. This manual supplied information about each major South Asian port's facilities and commodities on offer there, thus greatly facilitating trade between South Asia and the Mediterranean. Greek merchants trading between Egypt and the South Asian port of Barygaza on the western coast of the subcontinent (near the present-day port city of Surat) were thus well informed as to the best use of the monsoon winds and of the great commercial opportunities there.

> There are imported into this market-town wine, Italian preferred . . . also copper, tin, and lead; coral and topaz . . . gold and silver coin, on which there is a profit when exchanged for the money of the country . . . There are exported from these places . . . Saussureacostus [a medicinal plant], bdellium [a myrrh-like gum resin], ivory, agate and carnelian, lycium [a medicinal herb], cotton cloth of all kinds, silk cloth, mallow cloth [canvas], yarn, long pepper and such other things as are brought here from the various [other] market-towns.[8]

This trade was further spurred by the Roman conquest of Egypt in 33–30 BCE, which put Romans in direct contact with South Asian merchants, who had established a community there. The Roman elite's demand for South Asian goods soon outstripped that of the Greeks.

Romans were major bulk importers of one of the commodities listed above—cotton—that was so famous for its quality that they called it by a Latinized version, *carbasina*, of its Sanskrit name, *karpasa*. Romans also purchased South Asian parrots and peacocks to adorn their homes, and tigers to pit against African lions (and sometimes men) in the Colosseum and other Roman venues. In 50 CE, over a hundred ships laden with goods purchased in South Asia rode the monsoon winds to Roman-controlled Arabia. These goods included fine furniture. A table leg carved in Taxila was found in the ruins of Pompeii, the city destroyed by the volcano Mount Vesuvius in 79 CE.

Since the Greco-Roman world produced little that was of value to South Asians, it had to pay for its purchases in gold and silver. A Tamil poem praises the thriving port city of Muziris, which benefited from the "beautiful vessels" of Westerners "arriving with gold and departing with pepper,"[9] but this boon to the city's merchants was of deep concern to Roman officials, who feared that the drain of their most precious metal would ultimately undermine the empire's financial stability. They even considered a ban on trade with the subcontinent. To cut costs by getting closer to producers, Greco-Roman merchants settled in India, where they could supervise the transit of goods, some of which traveled overland as well as by sea to the subcontinent's southeast coast and back to ports on the west coast and from there on to Roman Egypt. The trade across the Indian Ocean ultimately was rivaled by a network of land routes, the fabled "Silk Road," which stretched from Korea to its terminus in the eastern Mediterranean, passing through Bactria in the northernmost reaches of the subcontinent.

Bactria was once occupied by Greeks who had been banished from their homeland or otherwise had reason to join the Persian Empire during its wars with Greece. On his arrival in Bactria, Alexander the Great slaughtered most of these Greeks as traitors and began resettling the region with fresh colonists, who founded a line of kings ruling an independent Indo-Greek kingdom. One of these kings, Menander I (ruled about 165–155 BCE), converted to Buddhism and was greatly admired by Greek historians. Bactria served as a Silk Road hub and a major conduit of Greek knowledge and culture into South Asia, though its political identity was eclipsed by the rise of the Kushan Empire (30–375 CE).

The Kushans were a nomadic warrior people who lost their lands to the Chinese imperial expansion that followed the rise of the Han Dynasty in China. They found a new home in lands that stretched from Central Asia to the Indo-Gangetic Plain, where they ruled as a Mauryan successor state, a step facilitated by the conversion of their greatest king, Kanishka I (ruled about 144–172 CE), to Buddhism. Strangers in much of their new South Asian homeland, the Kushans embraced all of the cultures (including all of the deities) of the people they now ruled. This policy was made visible in their Greek-style coinage, which featured the symbols of virtually every religion known to these regions, from Buddhism to Zoroastrianism. Eager to expand their empire, and open to cultures other than their own, the Kushans sought trade relations with the Roman Empire when the Romans became their neighbors after defeating the Parthian Empire in northern Persia. This contact marked the true beginning of Silk Road exchanges between the Romans and the Chinese. Both Roman and Chinese sources noted that the Kushan kings not only made secure the trade between their two peoples, but provided products such as the cotton cloth, perfumes, pepper, ginger, and wool carpets that were as valued in China as in Rome.

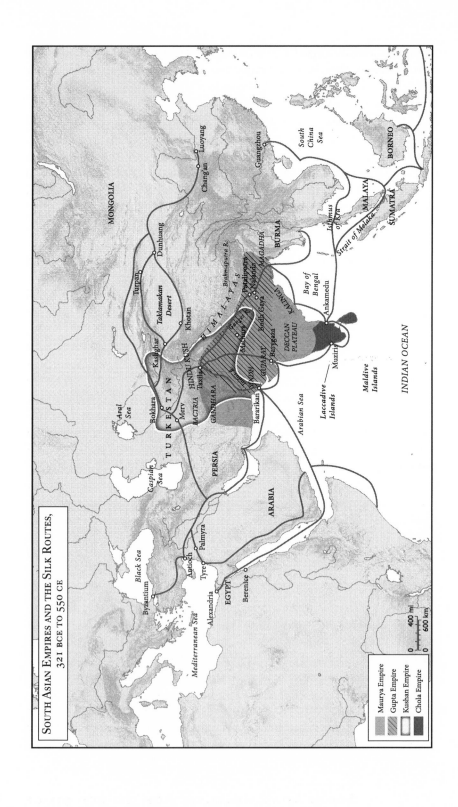

SOUTH ASIAN EMPIRES AND THE SILK ROUTES,
321 BCE TO 550 CE

Maurya Empire
Gupta Empire
Kushan Empire
Chola Empire

The Kushans, however, were more than middlemen. Under the rule of Kanishka I, the cities of Gandhara and, later, Mathura, flourished as points of contact between Greek craftsmen and Buddhist artisans. The latter were impressed with the blend of realism (true forms in nature) and idealism (an attempt to grasp the ideal essence of things— their spirit—thus without flaw) that was characteristic of late Greek and Hellenistic art. In Gandhara and Mathura, local artists drew upon Greek styles and stone-carving techniques to serve an emerging demand for devotional images of the Buddha, which may have been encouraged by contact between Greek and South Asian cultures. These devotional images heralded major changes in South Asia, which included the rise of a second great imperial unification of the region, under the Guptas. They also foreshadowed changes in South Asian art and religion that, when spread via the Silk Road, influenced both Asia and the wider world.

It is widely believed that the Buddha told his followers that he had merely tapped into the truth of the universe: he was not that truth itself and thus was unworthy of worship. Theravadin Buddhists clung to this ideal, but gradually began to use images associated with his life as a focus of meditation. These images initially included the pipal tree under which he attained enlightenment, his sandals, and the stupa (domed or mound-like structure) built to protect his human remains. In time, rock carvings or paintings appeared featuring stories about his previous lives (the Jatakas). These stories included his renunciation of his life as a prince, his near fasting unto death, his first teaching of the wheel of law, and his *parinirvana* or passing from this earth. Mahayanists embraced this practice. They believed that the Buddha's compassion was such that at his death he entered into a heavenly realm, where devotees could draw upon the accumulated merit of the Buddha's past lives to wash away their karma and thereby attain nirvana.

Mahayanists won many converts throughout Asia by arguing that local sages were bodhisattvas or, like Buddha, were celestial beings. Some Chinese and Japanese Buddhists believe that nirvana, or at least a place in the realm of these celestial Buddhas, could be achieved by merely uttering on their deathbed "Amitaba" or "Amida," the potent names of one of these heavenly Buddhas. They worship bodhisattvas such as Avalokiteshvara, once a disciple of the historical Siddhartha Gautama, who has postpones his own salvation until every last man and woman is released from samsara. The supreme embodiment of compassion, Avalokiteshvara is worshipped in Tibet as Chenrezig, who is said to be incarnated as the Dalai Lama. In East Asia, Avalokiteshvara is worshipped in female form as Guan Yin or Kannon, as compassion is most often regarded as a feminine quality. Theravadin missionaries also preached with great success that the Buddha drew on the same source as indigenous sages and deities.

The origins of the rise of devotional Buddhism is a matter of great debate. Some argue that it arose from exposure to Greek worship of hero-gods, who had conquered death and through whose intervention the Greeks sought to live on in spirit, if not in the flesh. However, the devotional forms of worship that came to characterize this aspect of Buddhist practice arose out of indigenous concerns and were ultimately expressed within evolving indigenous aesthetic traditions. Whereas the gods of Hellenistic mystery religions could withhold their blessings, Buddhist deities appeared in stone and in paint as compassionate beings who existed only to offer to all the means of escape from suffering.

At the very least, the efforts of Greek artists to render spiritual concerns in stone offered South Asian artists new techniques and forms to express their own ideas. Working alongside Greek artists first in Gandhara and later in Mathura (to the northwest and to the east of the Indus Valley respectively), South Asian sculptors produced devotional Buddhist images that initially reflected Hellenistic Greek stylistic conventions, most particularly the nimbus (light radiating from the head), a distant, patrician gaze, and heavily draped clothing. In time, South Asian artisans elongated these figures, turned their gazes inward in self-realization, and lent their clothing the translucence typical of the finest Indian cotton. The best-known example of the artistic synthesis today called Greco-Buddhist art is that of the "Fasting Buddha." The clothing on this seated figure is rendered transparent by the skill of the artist, as is the Buddha's remaining flesh, which clings to the exposed ribs of the cadaverous Siddhartha, portrayed perhaps at the moment of his realization that this extreme proof of his control over material desire, while powerful, was not the pathway to full enlightenment.

Greco-Buddhist art later appeared alongside figures displaying a Greco-Roman influence resulting from increasing trade contacts with Roman merchants at Amaravati and elsewhere in the south. All three styles—Gandhara, Mathura, and Amaravati—spread across the subcontinent and throughout Asia as a result of the commerce that Buddhism itself fostered. Buddhism's anti-caste sensibilities offered increased social and economic opportunities for the lowest order of the twice born, the Vaishya or merchants. Buddhist centers located along major trade routes, such as at the great rock-cut monastery at Ajanta in the Deccan, became places of pilgrimage where grateful merchants stopped their journeys and made offerings in support of these institutions.

The Mauryan imperial epoch heralded an era of dynamic political and religious change with a transregional reach largely due to the spread of Buddhism. Yet Buddhist influence would soon be equaled or surpassed by parallel developments in the Brahmin world that were to lead to the emergence of a second great South Asian empire, that of the Guptas in northern India. The Guptan Empire, from the installation of Chandragupta I in 320 CE to its decline at the hands of foreign invaders in about 550 CE, never approached the size and administrative cohesion of the Mauryan imperial achievement, but exceeded it in terms of global trade and influence. Its rise to prominence owed much to its encouragement of a revival of the authority of the Brahmins, whose traditional religious belief system had not been wholly eclipsed despite the Mauryan Empire's support of Buddhism. Guptan patronage of a Brahmin-led reformation of their traditions helped marginalize Buddhism in the land of its birth, while at the same time inspiring new social and cultural ideas that came to influence South Asian civilization.

The Guptan Empire has been called a "theater state," in that it established and maintained itself less by *danda-niti* (violent conquest and rule by force) than by the performance of religious rituals and other expressions of cultural power that legitimized its authority. That authority lay somewhat more lightly on the people of South Asia. The Guptas did not directly administer the three-quarters of the subcontinent they conquered by military force or threat of force, but sought instead to rule through alliances with local and regional rulers, some of whom paid them tribute. Their legitimacy was thus tied to their status as sponsors of new Brahmanical religious ideas.

The Guptan-supported religious revival and the political power associated with it were so potent that for more than two hundred years, Guptan art, literature, and science flourished, setting standards against which many South Asians still measure their achievement in many fields and profoundly influencing the politics and culture of neighboring Southeast Asia. Aiding in this era's global reach were the contributions of contemporary states in South India, such as the Pallava in the south and its successor states, the Pala Empire based in Bengal, and the Pandya, Chola, and Chera seaborne empires that formed along the subcontinent's southern coasts, which carried Guptan-style religious revival and economic influence throughout Asia.

Much as South Asian artists had responded to Greek artists and works, Chinese artists, working with South Asian migrant artists or from their models, initially sought to use South Asian themes and styles directly. However, they, too, quickly came to adapt them to serve their own sensibilities. For example, the elongated figures appearing in both stone and paint that adorn the rock-cut prayer halls of the Buddhist center at Ajanta clearly influenced the cave-temple art of the Wei Dynasty in China, but soon thereafter South Asian dress and body images of Buddhist figures gave way to familiar Chinese dress and appearance as the Chinese "indigenized" the Buddha image. Strong South Asian influences in architecture as well as sculpture can also be seen among the Khmer in Cambodia, the Cham in Vietnam, and at Borobudur and Prambanan in Java, all of which evolved to express indigenous culture.

Indigenization was also a characteristic feature of the South Asian political forms that passed to eastern Asia via trade as well as through missionary activity. South Asian merchants and adventurers were attended by scribes, as well as monks and priests. They brought with them literacy in the form of South Asian scripts, and intriguing literature in the form of the Jatakas (stories about the Buddha's exemplary earlier lives) and epic tales such as the *Mahabharata* and *Ramayana*. They also disseminated concepts of government which later helped give rise to Southeast Asian states and empires, such as that of Angkor, of the Thai and of the Champa on the Southeast Asian mainland, and at Borobudur and later Srivajaya on the island of Java. These indigenous rulers added to their existing legitimacy by claiming to be *devaraja*s (divine kings), and by holding indigenized court performances of the *Ramayana*, such as the Thai *Ramakien*. In each case, local deities, motifs, and ethical dilemmas were woven into South Asian plots and themes. This process also can be seen in Asia's puppetry traditions, most of which have their origins in South Asian puppetry and performance art.

The cultural flowering that occurred under the Guptas and was spread farther afield by its successors is astonishing in its content as well as its global reach. The Guptan-era master playwright Kalidasa produced works such as *Shakuntala* that, like the much later works of William Shakespeare, used everyday life to examine enduring truths and employed a plot point revolving around mistaken identity. Sanskrit texts, or sutras, also addressed universal human concerns, like sexuality and love, which were the focus of the *Kama Sutra*, attributed to Vatsyana. Buddhist monks visiting Japan in the mid-eighth century, writing in Sanskrit, not only spread knowledge of Buddhist doctrine, but, in the hands of a Japanese Sanskrit scholar named Kukai, may have influenced the formation of Kana orthography (a way of writing the Japanese language) as well. In the field of mathematics, the fifth-century CE scientist Aryabhata may have been the first to employ the concept of zero and made breakthroughs in astronomy, such as the theory that the Earth revolved on its own axis and also that it orbited around the sun. Other mathematicians developed a base-ten numerical system (the decimal system), along with identifiers that Europeans obtained though Arab hands and therefore called "Arabic" numerals.

Chinese Buddhists, on pilgrimages to the land of their religion's birth, portrayed daily life in the Guptan Empire in glowing terms. From their accounts, the more stringent aspects of Mauryan administration (registration of passports, severe punishments for theft) seem to have been abandoned or modified (fines instead of executions). Serious crime remained rare. The Chinese monk Faxian, who traveled across the Guptan domains in the early fifth century, noted that in the north "the people were well off and happy," while in the city of Anuradhapura in Sri Lanka, "the dwellings of the merchants are very grand; and the side streets and main thoroughfares are level and well-kept [and on holy days] a lofty dais is arranged where ecclesiastics and laymen come together from all quarters to hear the Law [Buddhist dharma] expounded."[10] Everywhere religious sects maintained houses of charity that offered support for weary travelers such as himself, and at no time was he molested or robbed.

Monks like Faxian and South Asian merchant travelers were instrumental in spreading a Guptan-era invention: granulated sugar. Cane sugar (*sakara*), which originated in Southeast Asia, was known to Megasthenes, the Greek ambassador to the Mauryan court. Cane sugar syrup, dried and crystallized in pans, came to be known as *kandha* (candy). In approximately 500 CE, Guptan artisans learned how to turn sugar cane juice into crystallized granules, making sugar easily transportable. Within three hundred years, knowledge of the production of granulated sugar appeared in China and the Middle East, where Christian Crusaders encountered it about 1200 CE. By 1500, Venice had established granulated sugar production in the eastern Mediterranean, making a sweet tooth affordable to Europeans. To satisfy it, Europeans globalized sugar production via a slave-based plantation system that ultimately brought misery to generations of laboring people from Africa to Hawaii and generated capital that spurred the Industrial Revolution.

Life under the Guptas was not always sweet. The Sanskrit texts produced during this era, largely written by Brahmins, extolled the moral virtues of a hierarchy of classes, in which Brahmins stood at the top. Those who violated their caste duty or who married below their assigned caste status were driven to the margins of society, while those occupations dubbed by Brahmins as ritually "unclean," usually jobs closely connected with the material aspects of life, such as sweepers (garbage collectors), were cast out of the system altogether. Brahmin writers mandated that mere contact with such "outcastes" was so spiritually polluting that they should wear noisemakers to warn others of their proximity, hence the later term, "untouchables." Including the *adavasi* (the ancient indigenous people of South Asia's forests) and other non-Aryan groups, the *mleccha* (those outside the system) amounted to as much as 20 percent of the region's population. These same texts prescribed the full subordination of women to their fathers and husbands. All women were to be chaste and obedient to men and strive to make themselves attractive to them. Kalidasa's play, *Shakuntala*, features a scene wherein a princess-bride is enjoined to be subservient and "never be angry with your husband, even if he is less faithful than a man should be . . . as to do otherwise is to bring shame upon your family."[11]

Some of these social burdens may have been lightened, at least in spiritual terms, by the increasingly devotional aspect of late Vedic and early classical worship. Some Vedic divinities came to be understood as manifestations of divine knowledge that were expressed in forms both male and female (as in Devi, the divine female principle). Perhaps under the influence of Buddhist thought, or springing from a common search for truth, these evolving Vedic divinities became vehicles, or manifestations, of compassion as well as of the knowledge that resides in Brahman. The Lord Shiva emerged, perhaps as a greater understanding of a virile Harappan figure posed in a lotus position or of the equally virile Vedic god Rudra. He appears on earth to teach moral lessons and combat evil. His cosmic dance of creation and destruction as Shiva Nataraj, "Lord of the dance" (*nata*, "dance"; raj, "ruler"), announces an ever reoccurring cycle of the death and rebirth of the universe, but reassures mankind that the righteous should not fear it. The Lord Vishnu, a deity once associated with the Vedic god of divine order, Varuna, emerged as an aspect of Brahman who has taken many avatars (forms) to defend the cause of righteousness on earth. These avatars came to include Rama of the *Ramayana*, as well as the Lord Krishna, who first appeared in the *Mahabharata* as a prince who drove the chariot of the hero Arjuna.

In a major section of the evolving *Mahabharata*, called the *Bhagavad Gita* (Song of the Blessed One), the great Pandava warrior Arjuna, commanding the Pandava armies, hesitates to open battle with the Kuravas and their allies, many of whom he had known all his life:

> The long-awaited time for war had arrived—a terrible fratricidal war . . . Suddenly seeing the horror of it before him, Arjun gazed at his relatives and friends arrayed across from him; men who were like fathers, brothers, sons, and grandsons, as well as teachers, uncles, friends.[12]

Images of Shiva as Lord of the Dance (nataraja) *are among the most powerful representations of Hindu devotional worship. The deity embodies the forces of creation, regeneration, destruction, preservation, and salvation.* ©Victoria and Albert Museum, London, 2006AK9833-01

Krishna then explains to the shattered Arjuna that he is wrong to hesitate: by defending his side in the great battle, he would do no wrong in killing his relations and teachers. He tells Arjuna that his cause is just and that it is the duty of Kshatriyas to defend justice at all costs, lest evil triumph and add to human suffering. Krishna goes on to explain that, at a deeper level, those he is facing in the battle could not be killed. He tells Arjuna:

> Our bodies are known to end, but the Self [atman] is enduring, inde-structible, immeasurable, constant and primordial. It is not killed when the body is killed. You have no cause to grieve for all these creatures, Arjuna! Look to your own duty, do not tremble before it.[13]

Arjuna then asks what will happen if he fails in his duty as a warrior. In reply, Krishna says that there are many pathways to divine knowledge other than being obedient to one's place in society and that each of these paths offers release from the wheel of samsara. These include the older ways of knowledge, such as the performance of rituals, meditation, and yoga (the discipline of linking mind and body). However, one path is open to all, even those who failed in pursuing any other: salvation through bhakti (devotion to God). When challenged by Arjuna as to how he knows this, Krishna demonstrates his divine identity (as Brahman) by offering him a vision of the universe, spiritual and material, embodied in Krishna for the purpose of this teaching. Krishna then tells a no longer doubting Arjuna, "He who turns to me shall never be reborn."[14] Thus reassured, Arjuna fights and wins his battle, and righteousness triumphs.

Parallel to the development of bhakti was the emergence of the concept of *varnashramadharma*: that a righteous life could be pursued by living according to the dharma (religiously ordained duties) of one's varna (social role) at an appropriate ashrama (place or stage of life). For example, a Brahmin should seek the knowledge of religion as a student, but then go on to serve as a priest or as a householder with a family, not as an ascetic. Upon seeing the birth of one's grandchildren, it was appropriate to withdraw with one's spouse to a forest retreat to practice detachment, and only thereafter does one live out one's life as an ascetic, alone with no worldly attachments. Most texts denied this last stage to women, but in practice, few men or women reached the final two stages, as *varnashramadharma*, like Buddhism, offered a middle way between abandoning the world and indulging too deeply in its pleasures. Moreover, bhakti in this context meant that failure at any stage of the life assigned to one at birth, or in any performance of religious duty, was potentially redeemable via divine grace. Through prayer came access to the love and the compassion within Brahman that could undo the fruits of one's own selfish desire.

This holistic approach to religion was sealed by the inclusion of Buddha as an avatar of Brahman through Vishnu, as were Krishna and

Rama. Of course, though the Buddha had accepted that one was born into a social role on earth that was prescribed by one's acts in an earlier life (karma), he had rejected the idea that one was locked into that role or suffered "bad" karma for leaving it behind. To him, each birth was a new chance to develop divine knowledge unfettered by the social position into which one was born. He also rejected the divine authority of the Vedas: they were mere stories. However, with Brahmins promoting the idea of divine grace in a way that offered the promise of social stability and salvation to all who accepted their lot in life, the obstacles to the absorption of Buddhism into late Vedic thought began to shrink, helping to forge a revised and still evolving religious mainstream or dharma that many today call Hinduism. The rise of Hindu kings such as the Guptas aided in the emergence of the revised dharma. Guptan rulers and their successors supported Buddhist institutions, but may have begun to assign people to their place in the evolving Brahmin-approved social hierarchy, within which a group's rank was often determined by the ritual purity of the *jati* (approximate to occupations) into which they were born.

Buddhism, without royal patronage to summon in defense of its rejection of caste, was vulnerable to decline. Moreover, Buddhist monasteries were chiefly along trade routes, which strengthened ties to merchants, but not to kings. At the same time they remote enough to isolate Buddhism's leadership from the common people. An increasing Buddhist focus on tantric studies (esoteric or highly wrought philosophical exercises and actions) also alienated the masses. As a result, Buddhism slowly lost its popular appeal and disappeared from the Gangetic Plain and the Deccan, though its tantric form took root in Tibet and its more orthodox forms flourished in Sri Lanka and Southeast Asia. Many Buddhist as well as Jain concepts, such as vegetarianism as a practice of showing respect for life, became near-universal practices.

Yet even as the spiritual dimensions of South Asian culture expanded, its political culture declined. By 500 CE, multiple ills beset the Guptan Empire. These included internal dynastic disputes over succession, foreign invasion, decline of trade or revenue, and the revolt of tribute-paying allied states. The Guptan Empire barely survived the initial assaults of a nomadic people from Central Asia known as the Hephthalites (Huna or White Huns). The Huna, who were pushed across the Eurasian land mass by an expanding China, menaced the Gupta domains, moved west to crush the Sassanid Dynasty in Persia (224–651 CE), and helped bring about the collapse of the Western Roman Empire in 527 CE. The Huna invasions also disrupted trade along the Silk Road, which was a key source of Guptan wealth. By 515 CE, Huna advances into the Gangetic Plain further cut into Guptan imperial revenues and undermined its authority.

By 550 CE, little remained of Guptan administration, though as is common in South Asia, imperial decline did not mean collapse, but led to the rise of large and powerful successor states. Of these the mightiest was the seventh-century empire built by Harsha Vardana. At this time, Chinese Buddhists were arguing over the finer points of the religion originally brought to China by monks such as Bodhidharma, around 400 CE. One of these Chinese monks, Xuanzang, left a record of his purpose for coming to Harsha's domains in about 633–637, as well as his observations of Harsha's empire. He wrote, "Though the Buddha was born in the West, his Dharma has spread to the East, in the course of translation, mistakes may have crept into the texts . . . When words are wrong, the meaning is lost, and when a phrase is mistaken, the doctrine becomes distorted." While Xuanzang found Buddhism in decline, Harsha Vardana himself appeared to be a strong patron of Buddhist culture and had strengthened the Buddhist center at Nalanda by donating the income of a hundred villages to its support. Nalanda then had an enrollment of ten thousand students, some from Mongolia, Korea, and Tibet, as well as China. Xuanzang recorded a conversation with Harsha Vardana which began with the emperor relating to him a story he had heard about the compassion of a Chinese ruler. A delighted Xuanzang replied that it was his own emperor who had "reduced taxes and mitigated Punishments," and that "as to his moral influence and his profound edification of his people, it is too exhausting to narrate in any detail!" "Excellent!" Harsha Vardhana, said. "The people of your land must have performed good deeds in order to have such a saintly lord."[15] More significant in terms of cultural exchange, after Xuanzang's visit Harsha sent a mission to China in 641 CE, which established the first diplomatic relations between China and the subcontinent. In response, two Chinese ambassadors were dispatched to Harsha's court, but on arrival they found that Harsha had died, his successors had not possessed his vigor, and Harsha's empire had passed to a Hindu prince.

Still, such was the continuing strength of classical political values, Sanskrit literature, and Hindu religious appeal that even the Huna invaders were soon absorbed as local ruling elites. Moreover, as the Guptan imperial state weakened, a new one emerged in Southeast Asia. According to legend, Theravada Buddhism had long since taken root in Burma (now Myanmar) due to the efforts of a son of Ashoka Maurya.

By 1100 CE, Buddhism and Burmese society had fashioned a "classical" culture out of a synthesis of indigenous and Guptan characteristics.

Like Burma, Sri Lanka was believed to have been brought into the Theravadin fold by missionary efforts launched by another of Ashoka's sons. The reign of the first female ruler in South Asia, Queen Anula (reigned 47–42 BCE), suggests the superior status enjoyed by women in Buddhist Sri Lanka. Sri Lankan kingdoms repelled no fewer than eight invasions by the Guptas and its southward-looking, seafaring successor states (the Cholas, Pandyas, Cheras, and Pallavas), which spread Hinduism across Southeast Asia as far as the island of Bali in what is today eastern Indonesia. Sri Lanka's kingdoms flourished until at least 1186 CE, due to the double bounties flowing from their location along the Silk Road's sea routes between China and the Mediterranean and Sri Lanka's place as the center of the world's cinnamon production.

Whereas during this same historical period classical Roman roads and baths fell into disuse and its people turned to a new religion, Christianity, South Asia's traditional pattern of life, religion, and government persisted. Vedic religion evolved into a rich, more complex form of dharma. At the same time, Sanskrit became the basis of most of South Asia's developing languages and literatures. Empire continued to be a common pursuit, if hard to maintain. Perhaps most important, trade links with the wider world by land were eventually reestablished and the region's seaborne trade and cultural influence across the southern seas flourished as never before, providing vehicles for continued economic renewal and growth. Even as Buddhism faded on the subcontinent, it was becoming a world religion via the Silk Road and its associated maritime South Asian trade routes.

Chapter 4

Islam in South Asia, 711–1556

Long before the coming of Islam, Arab merchants were active in Indian Ocean commerce alongside Guptan sailors and those from the Chola, Pallava, Pandya, and Chera seafaring empires based along the southern coasts of the subcontinent. Arabs eventually established settlements in the lower Indus Valley, which connected the trading zones of the Red Sea, the Persian Gulf, and the Indian Ocean to Central Asia, a major source of horses destined for Arabian markets. Arabs also settled on the southwestern coast of the subcontinent, known as Malabar, joining with Hindu merchants to create a virtual monopoly of the Indian Ocean trade. In the eighth century, this expanding Arab community called Al-Hind or Hindustan[1] was incorporated into a near-global empire of great material as well as spiritual strength. The engine of this transformation was the message of Allah (God) delivered through the Prophet Muhammad in Mecca and later Medina between 613 and 632. This revelation is known as Islam (submission to the will of God), and its followers are known as Muslims (those who submit to the will of God).

Muslims pursue a faith largely consistent with the spiritual teachings of Allah's earlier revelations, which, according to Islam, preceded, as well as included, what is commonly known as the Old and New Testaments: "The same religion has He established for you as that which He enjoined on Noah—which We have sent by inspiration to thee—and that which We enjoined on Abraham, Moses, and Jesus: Namely, that ye should remain steadfast in religion, and make no divisions therein."[2] Allah is thus believed to be the same supreme deity referred to by Jews as Elohim and as Jehovah by Christians, whose prophet Jesus (Issa, in Arabic) Muslims believe to be misconstrued as divine. He was human, as were Abraham, Moses, and the Prophet Muhammad. The revelations vouchsafed to the Prophet Muhammad expressed God's concern that his people were then, as at the time of Moses and Jesus, under moral stress and drifting away from faith in the one true God. This drift could be corrected by avoiding the behaviors that were beginning to draw humanity away from God, such as alcoholism and drug addiction, and also by developing a stronger sense of the oneness of God and the equality of all believers. To accomplish this, Muslims were enjoined to declare their faith in the oneness of God and in Muhammad as his Prophet; pray at set intervals five times a day; observe a month of daytime fasting during the ninth lunar month to encourage peace and reflection; give alms (charity) to the needy; and go to Mecca on pilgrimage at least once in one's lifetime. These and other precepts gleaned from the *qur'a* (recitations) of Allah were gathered together to form the Qur'an (collection of recitations). The Qur'an, supplemented with examples of righteous living drawn from the life of the Prophet Muhammad, became the common core of sharia (Islamic law) across the Islamic world.

This manner of belief, expressed in Arabic, was a matter of great pride to the Arab people and to all Muslims, who came to believe that it was the last revelation from Allah to be received before the Day of Judgment mentioned in earlier revelations. However, the tenets of Islam raised suspicions among Jews and Christians, who believed the revelations associated with Moses and Jesus were unique and each sufficient until God's final judgment upon mankind. The Qur'an enjoined peace among all people who had received God's word, but this was not to be. Conflict between the newly energized Arab Muslim community and the fading power of the neighboring Christian Byzantine (eastern Roman) and Zoroastrian Persian empires resulted in a Muslim-dominated Middle East. Muslims took this success as a mark of God's desire to see the new faith become a universal terrestrial, as well as spiritual, empire.

That terrestrial empire took the form of a caliphate, derived from *khalifa* (he who stands in the place of the Prophet), the title first held by early Muslim leaders elected by senior members of the community after the Prophet Muhammad's death in 632. Soon afterward, the caliphate became a hereditary monarchy and succession disputes erupted between various factions, who advocated claims to the title of caliph advanced by members of the Prophet's family or closely related Arab lineages. One such claimant, the Umayyad clan, ruled the Islamic world from Damascus in Syria (661–750) until being overthrown by the Abbasids, who ruled from Baghdad (762–1258). Both regimes claimed to defend the Sunna, the traditional form of worship pursued by the vast majority of Muslims, thus called Sunnis. However, a rival political and religious faction, the Shi'a, challenged both Sunni authority and the common interpretation of Islam. The Shi'a believed that the defeat and death of the Prophet Muhammad's cousin and son-in-law, Ali, in an early civil war between Muslim factions had prevented the emergence of righteous Muslim government and deprived the faithful of obtaining access to a true understanding of the Qur'an itself (Shi'a is an abbreviation for *Shi'at Ali*, "party of Ali"). The Shi'a, or Shi'ism, became a haven for all those who challenged the legitimacy of Umayyad and Abbasid rulers or found fault with Sunni practice.

All Muslim regimes and sects took an interest in South Asia as Islam spread eastward. The Arab Umayyad caliphs were the first to take serious note of the region, having received reports of pirate attacks launched from Sindh against Muslim Arabs in the Indian Ocean. According to Muslim historians, Sindh's Hindu and Buddhist leaders failed to respond to Umayyad demands for assistance against the pirate menace, prompting an Umayyad and later Abbasid-led occupation of much of the land along the western bank of the Indus. These operations did not, however, lead to a sudden clash of civilizations, because the Umayyads had initially been more interested in booty than conversion and they, and the early Abbasids, also recognized the need to access the knowledge and administrative skills of local Buddhist, Hindu Rajput, and Jat populations.

The Qur'an specified that protection should be given to followers of previous books of revelation given by Allah. The Qur'an held these previous texts to be older and thus inferior revelations of Allah, but their followers were deserving of protection and toleration on the condition of paying the *jizya*, a tax paid by military-age non-Muslims in lieu of military service (since in theory only Muslims should serve in defense of the Islamic state). Jews and Christians were already classified as *dhimmi*s (protected people). Since the purpose of the Islamic state was to preserve the community of Islam, living according to what they believed was the last of these revelations, Muslims expected non-Muslim peoples living among them, even those with books of revelation of their own, to acknowledge the supremacy of the Islamic state. However, at this juncture, few major steps were taken to restrict private non-Muslim religious practices or the operation of their houses of worship within the Islamic world.

This tolerant posture governed the policies followed by the Umayyad governor of Iraq, al-Hajjaj ibn Yusuf, who in 711 sent his battle-tested seventeen-year-old relative, Mir Muhammad Qasim, to conquer Sindh. Qasim accomplished this in two years of brutal fighting during which those who opposed him faced dire consequences, including the enslavement of women and children and the looting of towns.

But Qasim allowed those who submitted to his authority to retain their power, wealth, and families. Thereafter, in keeping with his own way of thinking and at al-Hajjaj's express orders, Qasim allowed Hindu and Buddhist houses of worship to remain and even new ones to be constructed, generally without interference. By what became known as the "Brahmanabad Settlement," no non-Muslim Sindhi was prohibited from following his religion. Moreover, Buddhists and Hindus were granted the same *dhimmi* status as Jews and Christians and were likewise required to pay the *jizya*. Over time, this tax came to be seen as a sign of second-class citizenship, but Qasim then won great favor by appointing Hindus to high administrative posts while leaving minor Hindu cities to rule themselves. At the same time, many Buddhists, outflanked by Muslim and Brahmin rulers, may then have converted to the religion of the new rulers, as lower-ranking Hindus may also have done, because Islam offered an egalitarian status among believers that the caste system did not.

Mir Muhammad Qasim's successors as governors of Sindh were not always as tolerant, but they learned to speak the Sindhi language and otherwise acculturated themselves to local ways. Into this rich, if fragile, atmosphere of cultural exchange Muslim Sufi missionaries arrived to play a major role in the conversion to Islam of many South Asians. Named for the simple common wool (*suf*) clothes they wore, Sufis often approached non-Muslims with open hearts and open minds. Sufis in Sindh were among the most liberal-minded of Sufi sects. They sought union with God through practices often shunned by orthodox Muslims, such as openness to the ideas of other faiths and the veneration of pirs (mystic Sufi saints). Sufis lived selflessly in pursuit of divine love and wisdom, a practice which appealed to Hindus, who venerated sages, and to Buddhists, who respected Sufis as pursing the way of bodhisattvas. By 800, Sufis were gaining converts to Islam in Sindh, many of whom became respected commentators on Islamic law in Abbasid Baghdad.

Sindhi Muslim merchants and bankers were soon found in major Syrian towns. Sindh's reputation for producing excellent doctors led to their treatment of several Abbasid caliphs, including the illustrious Harun al-Rashīd (ruled 786–809). More important in terms of world history, Sindhi mathematicians shared with the Arab world the knowledge of the Sanskrit-based South Asian numerical system, which became known as "Arabic" in the West, along with other advanced mathematics developed during South Asia's classical age.

Sufi missionaries were to spread new agricultural resources and techniques throughout South Asia. Like European orders of monks, Sufi religious orders were repositories of knowledge. During the Muslim conquest of eastern Roman lands and of Persia, they learned hydraulic techniques (including methods of water conservation) and how to raise a variety of agricultural plants of high commercial value, which are known collectively today as the "Islamic Tool Kit."[3] These methods and practices were well suited to difficult environments such as the drier areas of Sindh and the jungles or otherwise marginal lands, which, coincidentally, were areas of the subcontinent where Hinduism was not well established. This may help explain why conversion to Islam occurred so rapidly there: Sufis offered the inhabitants of these lands new and highly profitable forms of agriculture and an egalitarian religion appealing to those on the margins of, or less traditionally committed to, Hindu society. These developments have led some Muslims to boast that Islam brought "civilization" to Sindh, while some Hindus believe it was in fact the other way around, as Sindh helped educate and civilize the new Muslim Arab kingdoms, which in turn helped carry the knowledge of India to Europe. It seems fair to say that they are probably both right.

By 1000, Sindh was entirely integrated into the Islamic world, but its place in that world, and that world itself, changed radically in the ensuing decades. By then, the authority of the Abbasid Empire had gone into such steep decline that it began to splinter. Its provincial governors, backed by local Islamic jurists and political philosophers, began to wean themselves from the idea of a terrestrial caliphate (with all members of a Muslim community united under a single rightly guided polity) in favor of rule by a local ruler, a sultan, whose position was legitimized not through association with the family of the Prophet but by the *sultan* (power) he exercised in preserving the faith.

Over the next three hundred years, under the stress of Islamic expansion and Mongol invasions, philosophers such as Abu Hamed Muḥammad ibn Muḥammad al-Ghazali urged Muslims to support any ruler so long as he defended the faith and did not call on a believer to disobey the laws of God. To draw a bright line defining what those laws were, Taqi ad-Din Ahmad ibn Taymiyyah favored an interpretation of sharia that unified religion and state after the fashion they believed had been current during the era of the first four caliphs, or *salafiyya* (predecessors). Any later legal theories or compromises with non-Muslim religious traditions were to be abandoned until Muslim and non-Muslim life were distinct from each other. According to Salafist doctrine, practices such as veneration of saints, which was regarded as an adaptation of Christian ideas, were to be eradicated, as was any trace of idolatry.

Muslims had previously understood that the world was divided into realms ruled by hostile infidels, known as *dar-ul-harb* (the Abode of War), and realms under Muslim rule, known as *dar-ul-Islam* (the Abode of Peace or Abode of Islam). The former might, through jihad (struggle), become the latter. Under this emerging approach, even the Abode of Islam could be a place of struggle against pretenders to true belief. Any Muslim leader who departed from the Salafists' revised orthodox view, and even those Muslims who obeyed him, could be considered unbelievers, targets of jihad in the form of holy war, and could be sentenced to death, as had apostates in the early years of Islam.

Salafism eventually had a considerable effect upon the policies of newly formed Muslim sultanates created by the Turks in South Asia. Turks were a Central Asian people who had been earlier conquered, often enslaved, and had converted to and assimilated into Islam, sometimes as military men of high rank. One of these, Mahmud of Ghazni (ruled 997–1030), pursued periodic destructive raids into the north of India from Afghanistan. Unlike the Muslim Arab rulers of Sindh, he regarded Hindus as idol worshippers, but it was more likely the pursuit of the wealth of northwestern al-Hind, rather than theological concerns, that drove his expeditions. These included the looting of richly endowed Hindu temples. Such looting was not unknown among Hindu rulers, who plundered the royal temples of their rivals in wartime. However, Mahmud's attacks over thirty years were sufficiently bloody and broad in scope that his own brilliant court scientist and historian, Muhammad ibn Aḥmad Biruni, considered that his sultan's actions had created an "inveterate" prejudice among Hindus against Muslims.[4] There is no doubt that Mahmud's invasions came to fuel a Hindu memory of trauma at Muslim hands that influences Hindu-Muslim relations to this day.

In 1192, one of Mahmud's lieutenants and eventual successors, Muhammad of Ghur, defeated the chief opponent of the Muslim raiders, the Hindu Rajput Raja Prithvi Raj Chauhan, outside of his capital at Lolkat. By 1198, Turkic warriors had established their own capital there, which they named Delhi ("heart," hence "capital"), and used it as a base to conquer most of the Indus Valley (which they called Hindustan) and the Gangetic Plain. From 1198 to 1240, conflict between Turkic clans over control of the sultanate commanded much of their attention. This competition briefly featured a female ruler, Sultana Razia (ruled about 1236–1240), whose life, like many of the sultans, was cut short as part of deadly endemic rivalry among the Turkic nobility. The early sultans (and sultana) were so busily engaged in conquest and elite competition that they had little interest in seeking the conversion of Hindus to Islam, or in interfering with those apolitical and mystically oriented members of Islam's Sufi order who sought to build bridges with the local population. They did nothing to halt the spread of the "Islamic Tool Kit," as there was no better means of generating agricultural prosperity and profitable trade and thereby enhancing their tax revenues.

In 1258, a Mongol invasion of Islamic Persia severed the Delhi Sultanate from its Middle Eastern ties. Its sultans customarily offered prayers for the health of the Abbasid caliph in Baghdad. In an effort to preserve the illusion of the unity of the Islamic world, they continued to do so, even after it was known that the caliph had died at the hands of the Mongols without a successor. Another Turkic people, the Seljuks, stopped the Mongol conquest of the rest of the Middle East, but the Mongol destruction of Baghdad, the seat of Muslim arts, literature, science, and law, put an end to centuries of progress in those fields.

The Mongol invasion and its turbulent aftermath drove many Muslim intellectuals to seek refuge in the Delhi Sultanate, whose culture they enriched. Further Mongol invasions, including drives into the subcontinent itself (1221–1327), directed Muslim flight, both Sunni and Shi'a, to the western and central portions of the Deccan, where they established rich sultanates of their own. In succession, the regimes of the Bahmanids, Bijapur, Golkunda, Ahmadnagar, and Berar offered a home to Persian and other displaced or mobile Muslims, particularly architects. In 1367, a Spanish Muslim architect took the Grand Mosque at Córdoba in Muslim Spain as his model for the Bahmanids' Jama Masjid (mosque) at Gulbarga. Bidar's Mahmud Gawan madrasa (school), built in 1472, followed the style of that at Khargid, in Persia. The delicate Persian-influenced symmetry of the tomb and mosque of the Bijapur ruler Adil Shah II (ruled 1580–1627) may have influenced the design of the Taj Mahal. Yet conflicts among these Deccani sultanates helped sustain the great Hindu empire of Vijayanagar to their south.

Vijayanagar (City of Victory) was established by two brothers, Harihara and Bukka, of the Hindu Sangama family in 1336 to check the Muslim march south. Its rulers accomplished this task quite successfully for more than two hundred years by wisely employing their own version of Chanakya's "mandala theory": the more distant neighbor of your closer enemy is your friend. Vijayanagar made an alliance with the Bahmani sultans' own northern rivals, the Delhi-breakaway sultans of Gujarat and Malwa. This Hindu-Muslim alliance was reflected in the Muslim quarter in Vijayanagar's capital, which was as vibrant as the Hindu precincts of the city, home to perhaps half a million people.

The Qubt Minar (Tower of Victory) at the Quwwat'ul Islam (Power of Islam) Mosque was constructed in 1220 CE in Delhi from materials obtained from the destruction of more than twenty local Hindu and Jain temples. Photo by Nadezda Murmakova/Shutterstock 122062321

When the Portuguese visitor Domingos Paes visited the capital in 1521–1522, he called it "the best provided city in the world . . . as large as Rome and very beautiful to the sight."[5]

The burden of sustaining the Delhi Sultanate amid these increasingly challenging conditions was taken up by Ala-ud-din Khalji (ruled 1296–1316), who was one of a very few of the world's rulers to beat back a Mongol invasion. Building on that success, he experimented with price controls intended to lower the price of essential goods. He also introduced changes in land assessments meant to free the individual cultivator from the abuse of landlords and place Hindus on a par with Muslims in terms of tax payments. However, the new overall tax rates were too high and so far departed from prevailing orthodoxy (Muslim law mandated separate tax policies for Muslims and non-Muslims) that he was assassinated with the connivance of the ulama, the traditional Muslim learned elite or clergy. Nevertheless, these policies were so pragmatic in their aim that they were later pursued by Muhammad ibn Tughluq (ruled 1324 to 1351) in the first half of the fourteenth century.

In 1333, Abu Abdullah ibn Battuta, a learned Muslim from Tangier, on a quest for knowledge of the wider Islamic world, heard that

Muhammad ibn Tughluq, Sultan of Delhi, promised to shower wealth and high rank on all Muslims who came to enrich his court with their talents and skills. Ibn Battuta knew nothing of Delhi or of the sultan. Nonetheless, his spirit of adventure, and desire for gainful employment, led him to Delhi, where the sultan appointed him chief judge at a salary beyond his wildest dreams. Upon his arrival, he was overwhelmed by the city's magnificent walls, its central mosque, and its public amenities, which together comprised what he believed was "the greatest city of al-Hind, and even of all the Islamic lands in the East."[6]

However, Ibn Battuta was surprised to find that though Muslims had ruled at least a part of al-Hind for almost six hundred years and had come to dominate the northern tier of the subcontinent politically, they were still a small minority in the country. Most lived in islands of settlement among a Hindu population that frequently rebelled against Muslim rule in the north and whose rajas still controlled much of the south. Moreover, the diversity of Islamic belief and political practice shocked him. The enigmatic Muhammad bin Tughluq supported orthodox Islamic institutions and, through military conquest, was expanding their reach. But he was so bent on melding the new territories of his conquests into a sustainable whole that he not only employed Hindus in his administration, but also supported what some Muslims viewed as their idolatrous practices to such an extent that they claimed that al-Hind had fallen under Hindu rule. While working as a judge in the islands known as the Maldives, Ibn Battuta had been shocked that women before his court were barely clothed. On the other hand, he considered that the Muslim rulers of Malabar on the nearby southern coast of the subcontinent were contravening Muslim law against cruel punishments by impaling his Hindu subjects alive. Conditions in South Asia forced Ibn Battuta to ask what a good Muslim was to do in the face of such diversity, and how far Muslim law should be bent to accommodate it. He was neither the first nor the last observant Muslim in South Asia to find it hard to locate a middle ground between the requirements of maintaining an orthodox Muslim way of life and the necessity of adjusting to the multicultural realities of the South Asian cultural and political landscape.

Muhammad ibn Tughluq sought to strengthen his sultanate by a clever combination of emerging Salafist ideas regarding the closer identification of religion and the state and the belief that, in the current condition of the Islamic world, the sultan could rule by fiat if necessary so long as believers were not asked to violate God's laws. In effect, he sought to follow orthodoxy strictly in his role as defender of the faith, but would bend received Islamic law with regard to relations between Muslims and non-Muslims in order to strengthen the Islamic state in South Asia, whose vast non-Muslim majority made concepts such as the Abode of Islam and the Abode of War impractical.

An example of Muhammad ibn Tughluq's approach can be found in Ibn Battuta's account of how, like all Salafists, the sultan was ill-disposed toward Sufis, though less for their unorthodox practices than for their holding aloof from the state, as Sufis considered it impossible to maintain spiritual values while enmeshed in politics. The sultan did not appreciate the finer points of this argument and considered their position disloyal. Ibn Battuta noted how, when one Sufi—a friend of Ibn Battuta's—called the sultan a tyrant for demanding his appearance in court and refused to recant that charge, the sultan had him executed. The orthodox ulama cheered the sultan's action, but were not pleased when the sultan issued new taxes and ended the *jiyza* paid by Brahmins. The ulama held that neither the new revenue streams nor the exemption from the *jiyza* were sanctioned by the Qur'an. In response, the sultan deprived those ulama of their political authority due to their unwillingness to recognize that the new taxes enriched the state and that the end of the *jiyza* strengthened its political cohesion. The combined result was economic stability and security for Muslims, and thereby the sultan fulfilled his duties as a Muslim ruler.

When many of the sultan's Turk, Afghan, and Persian courtiers joined the ulama in their opposition to his policies, Muhammad bin Tughluq attacked their power base by seeking to end the *jagirdar* system, by which officials of merit were assigned a *jagir* (farmlands) whose revenues they exploited as a means of their own support. Ibn Battuta's own luxurious lifestyle was made possible by a stipend of five thousand silver dinars from the revenue of two and a half villages of Hindu families, whose average income may have been as low as five dinars a month. In the sultan's view, this system was not merely unjust and deprived the government of revenue, but threatened the state: *jagirs* were supposed to revert to the sultan after the death of their holders but had become hereditary, giving *jagirdars* resources they could use to overthrow any regime.

Believing that his new approach to Muslim politics could be the salvation of Islam, Muhammad bin Tughluq became an ardent imperialist. During his reign, he launched wars of conquest in every direction. He sent Ibn Battuta to China to serve as his ambassador, no doubt to explain his aggressive expansionist policies in Central Asia. The sultan's campaigns were not always successful, and Ibn Battuta's mission was thwarted by storms and other accidents of travel, but under Muhammad bin Tughluq, the sultanate's frontiers reached their greatest extent. To better administer the territories he had seized in the Deccan, the sultan moved his entire capital seven hundred miles south to Daulatabad. This action particularly outraged the largely foreign-born nobility at court, who vastly preferred the pleasures of Delhi to the hardships of the war-torn Deccan. The move south proved untenable in the long run, as the sultan had to return north to address the persistent threat of Mongol invasion.

However, the incorporation of these new territories and the selfish behavior of his courtiers served to strengthen Muhammad bin Tughluq's view that the sultanate's continued survival depended on drawing non-Muslims into the orbit of the Islamic state. When dealing with Hindu rebels and rajas, he meted out harsh punishments and offered them the choice of conversion or death, but, as his removal of the *jiyza* obligation from Brahmins suggests, he was prepared to be generous to those Hindus and Buddhists who supported his regime. He also built rest houses for monks, celebrated Hindu festivals, and permitted the construction of a temple for the veneration of the cow. These actions, along with the removal of the capital to Daulatabad, met with considerable opposition and even armed revolts from Muslims, but not from Hindus, who began to see him not as an alien ruler but as an indigenous one.

Muhammad bin Tughluq's policies did not survive his death. His cousin and successor, Sultan Firuz Tughluq, a pious and unassuming ruler from 1351 to 1388, guided the sultanate back to orthodoxy. In terms of religious affairs, Firuz Tughluq reestablished the influence of the ulama at court, while winning the support of Sufi mystics by promising to allow them freedom from being involved in politics. He engaged in traditional public works, such as building madrasas (religious schools) and hospitals. He also removed taxes on, and restored privileges of, both Muslims and non-Muslims that were sanctioned by the Qur'an. In practice, this meant that Hindus were still considered *dhimmi*s, their property and lives thus secure, and that existing non-Muslim houses of worship were therefore to be left unmolested, but it also meant reinstating the *jiyza* on all Hindus and the reimposition of strict rules prohibiting the building of new temples. As he noted in his memoirs, his piety demanded the severest punishment to be meted out to those non-Muslims who "erected new idol temples in the city and the environs in opposition to the Law of the Prophet, which declared that such temples are not to be tolerated. Under Divine guidance I destroyed these edifices, and killed those leaders of infidelity who seduced others into error, and the lower orders I subjected to stripes [whipping] and chastisement, until this abuse was entirely abolished." He continued in the same passage to relate how, upon learning of a long-tolerated open-air prayer meeting of thousands of Hindus and some Muslims, "I went there in person and ordered that the leaders of these people and the promoters of this abomination should be put to death."[7]

Moreover, to win back the support of the Turkic nobility, Sultan Firuz Tughluq stopped employing Hindus in the higher ranks of government and distributed a large part of his empire among Muslim civil and military officers via restoration of the *jagirdar* system with the inevitable results: loss of revenue and increased opportunities for nobles to build alternative centers of power. Firuz Tughluq's relatively quiet reign may have come as a relief from the turmoil of Muhammad ibn Tughluq's experimental redesign of the sultanate. However, the sultanate lacked both the stability and the resources to resist a new wave of Turkic-speaking invaders from Central Asia, led by Timur (known in Europe as Timur Ling or Tamerlane).

Timur was a conqueror of Eurasia much feared in Europe. He was born in 1336 near Samarkand, then at the center of a portion of Central Asia known to Persians as Mughulistan (Land of the Mongols) and known to Turks and Mongols themselves as the Khanate of Chatagai. Local ethnic groups freely mixed in this part of the world. Timur's clan was originally Mongol but had adopted the language and culture of the Turks. In time, Timur saw himself as heir to the great Mongol conqueror, Chinggis Khan (often spelled Genghis).

In 1398, as his forces prepared to attack Delhi, Timur was advised that the one hundred thousand prisoners of war already in his camp posed a security risk. He wrote in his autobiography that after giving the question much thought with regard to morality and practical policy, he concluded that it

> would be entirely opposed to the rules of war to set these idolaters and foes of Islam at liberty, so that no course remained but to make them all food for the sword . . . and [he ordered] that whoever neglected to do so, should himself be executed and his property given to the informer. When this order became known to the champions of Islam, they drew their swords and put their prisoners to death.[8]

Timur's forces easily took the city, after which it was sacked by his Turkish soldiers, though not on his order. After three days of looting and the killing of thousands of the city's inhabitants, Timur carried off hundreds of artisans and craftsman to build a new mosque at his capital at Samarkand. Timur appointed a vassal, Khizr Khan, to rule Delhi in his place.

After Timur died in 1405, Khizur Khan reestablished the Delhi Sultanate with himself as its ruler, but less than a decade later, the rule of Turks gave way to that of Afghans, who established the first non-Turkic sultanate at Delhi in more than 250 years. However, the new Afghan rulers, known as the Lodi Dynasty, soon fell victim to lack of political innovation, endemic infighting, Hindu discontent, and the breakaway of its provinces led by its own nobles, all factors that had previously weakened the Turkish sultanate. As a result, the last Sultan of Delhi, Ibrahim Lodi (ruled 1517–1526), a capable military leader, took every possible precaution to ensure his army was ready to face the challenge posed by the arrival of Timur's descendants in 1526.

Timur's passing had inaugurated a struggle for control over his domains among his relations, including his grandson, Zahir-ud-Din Muhammad Babur (Babur meaning "the Tiger"). Though Timur's descendants called themselves Chatagai, or Timurids, Europeans, following the Persian word for Mongol (Mughal), came to call them Mughals. Babur's dynastic line, under any name, was not destined to rule over Central Asia as Timur had done, but its impact on South Asia would be far greater and longer-lasting than Timur's had been. Between 1497 and 1502, Babur had seized and then lost control of Samarkand, the capital of Mughulistan, to family rivals and other empire builders. He then fled to Kabul, Afghanistan, from where he failed in many further attempts to recover his ancestral lands. He later gave thanks to God for this disappointment, for it ultimately focused his attention on Hindustan. His conquest of this lost legacy of Timur became a reality in part because of his political flexibility.

Though nominally a Sunni Muslim, Babur was so intent on building up his forces that he posed as a vassal of the Shi'a Safavid ruler of Persia, who hoped to use Babur to advance the Shi'a cause in Central Asia and against the Sunni Ottoman Turks in Anatolia. Babur then adroitly gave the Ottomans his promise not to attack them in return for their military aid, which he received in the form of the newest of battlefield inventions, the matchlock gun and cast cannons, as well as instructors to train his men to use them. With Safavid and Ottoman aid, the Mughals would soon join these two powers in a triumvirate of warrior-driven, expansionist, and both militarily and bureaucratically efficient early modern states, now often called "gunpowder empires" due to their common proficiency is using such weapons to conquer lands they sought to control, as Babur was about to do.[9]

THE DELHI SULTANATE, VIJAYANAGARA EMPIRE, AND THE MUGHAL EMPIRE

The Delhi Sultanate (1335)
Mughal Empire (1707)
Vijayanagara Empire (1520)

After fully establishing himself in Kabul, Babur learned from Afghans in that city that many of their countrymen were in rebellion against their own sultan, Ibrahim Lodi, and that the Afghans living in the Punjab, a rich, well-watered land that stood between Kabul and Delhi, would support him in an invasion of the country. At a field near the village of Panipat, close to the sites where Arjuna faced his kinsman-foes and the Turks secured Delhi for Islam in 1192, Ibrahim Lodi brought an army of one hundred thousand to confront Babur's force of about twenty thousand, unaware that the Mughals had new weapons and had learned to place them among and between carts drawn up into a defensive wall. The flanks of this wall were defended by world-conquering Mongol-style cavalry formations that stood ready to envelope any enemy weakened by attacking that wall. On April 21, 1556, the sultan's army advanced into and was shattered by a deadly firestorm of cannon and muskets. Mughal cavalry destroyed what was left.

After Babur's decisive victory at Panipat, the Mughal army, a mixed force of Uzbegs, Turks, and Afghans, marched down the Gangetic Plain

Babur's army, with its wheeled cannons, is shown in battle against the army of Rana Sanga in 1527. Babur's use of cannons allowed him to defeat armies much larger than his own. © The British Library Board, Or. 3714

to join Punjab in the west with Bengal in the east. They were poised to conquer much more when Babur died at the age of forty-seven. His son Humayun ascended his father's throne in 1530 under the false impression that his three younger brothers would be satisfied with ruling their large empire as junior partners. They proved capable not only of rebelling against him but also of rebelling again after being defeated and pardoned. These betrayals so weakened Humayun's position that he was forced to flee to Afghanistan in 1540. There, like his father, he looked to the Safavids in Iran, who, still seeking allies against the Ottomans, gave him the resources to reconquer Hindustan.

Had Humayun not been forced to flee and instead had the luxury of merely pursuing policies of the Lodi Sultanate, the reign of the Mughals might have differed little from its Turk and Afghan predecessors. However, in Humayun's absence, Sher Shah Sur, an Afghan, seized power in the Punjab and the Gangetic Plain, and set in motion a course of events that later Mughals exploited to acquire a much sounder footing in South Asia. Sher Shah Sur was a commander in Babur's army who used the opportunity provided by Humayun's conflict with his brothers to methodically conquer the rich eastern provinces of Bihar and Bengal, drive Humayun into exile, and establish a short-lived dynasty (1540–1555). In the fashion of Muhammad bin Tughluq, Sher Shah Sur worked to establish a state that was worthy of the support of all his subjects. He employed innovative revenue policies that protected peasants from abuse by the nobility, began the Grand Trunk Road which linked the northwest of the subcontinent with Bengal in the southeast, and minted a standardized silver coin, the *rupiya*, that was the precursor of the modern rupee, the currency of India, Pakistan, Sri Lanka, Nepal, Mauritius, and the Seychelles.

Like Muhammad bin Tughluq, Sher Shah Sur waged jihad against rival Hindu rulers, but pursued a policy of toleration toward his own Hindu subjects. However, unlike his Turkic predecessor, Sher Shah Sur's actions were now well in tune with developments at the grass-roots level of both Muslim and Hindu society.

South Asian belief systems were hard pressed to accommodate or absorb the Muslim cultural, political, and social influence, particularly when Muslim regimes sought legitimacy through the pursuit of orthodox interpretations of Islamic law that called for the marginalization of non-Muslim faiths and peoples. The coming of Islam thus represented both a challenge to Hindu traditions and serious test of its capacity for indigenizing foreign peoples and for synthesizing old and new ideas. At the same time, their experiences in South Asia forced Muslims to reexamine their fundamental patterns of politics and belief. This Hindu-Muslim encounter resulted in the deepening within both faiths of a desire for union with God over ritual observance and led to the emergence of a South Asian Islam that its followers carried to Southeast Asia and southern China, much as the region's past empire builders, traders, and travelers had earlier helped diffuse Buddhism and Hinduism outward from the subcontinent.

Since the time of Ibn Battuta, Sufi mystics had not been deterred by the hostility of the orthodox ulama from taking an ecumenical or inclusive approach to Hindus in their common pursuit of union with God. In the fourteenth century, Amir Khusrau (1253–1325), one of the greatest of South Asia's Chisti Sufi poets, wrote: "O, he who sneers at the Hindu's idolatry, learn also from him how worship is done," and that

> Though Hindus do not believe in the
> religion in which we do,
> In many matters they and we believe in
> the same thing.[10]

The Chisti order shared in the growth of the devotional aspect of worship that was sweeping religious thought across much of the subcontinent. By promoting the worship of Krishna through ecstatic song and dance in Bengal, Chaitanya Mahaprabhu, a Hindu ascetic and social reformer, elevated bhakti (Hindu devotionalism) to great heights in the early sixteenth century. In the early fifteenth to the mid-sixteenth century, a religious leader in the northwest of the subcontinent, Guru Nanak (1469–1539), received a revelation from God urging him to bring Hindus and Muslims together. His teachings and those of his immediate successors led to the emergence of an egalitarian faith called Sikhism.

These movements emphasized the sheer joy of union or connection with the divine essence of the universe, be it Allah or Brahman. Their common goal was illuminated by the poetry of a humble fifteenth-century weaver known as Kabir, claimed by both Muslims and Hindus as one of their own. His poems reflected concerns common to the Upanishads and Buddhist thought ("Take your seat on the thousand petals of the lotus, and there gaze on the infinite beauty") and the Sufi desire for union with God ("Bring the vision of the Beloved in your heart").[11] Kabir and his foremost disciple, Dadu, rejected religious formalism, both Hindu and Muslim, while embracing both faiths. As

Dadu wrote, "I am not a Hindu, nor a Muslim . . . I love the merciful God."[12]

Adherents of these devotionally oriented movements reinvigorated Hindu belief and pride in the face of Muslim conquests and missionary efforts, while Muslim emphasis on the oneness of God may have encouraged monotheistic trends within Hinduism. Islam and Sikhism remained clearly distinct faiths from Hinduism and from each other, but both took on aspects of Hindu culture and society, including shadings of caste.

The fullest measure of Hindu, Buddhist, and Muslim religious accommodation was achieved in Southeast Asia. Sufi converts from among long-distance traders in Sindh and neighboring Gujarat proved effective missionaries to the islands of Java and Sumatra, whose people were eager to form cultural bonds with their merchant partners, if on their own adaptive terms, as had been the case in their absorbing Hindu and Buddhist beliefs. After their conversion to Islam, they continued their laws allowing for the active role played by women in their societies, while theatrical versions of the *Mahabharata* and *Ramayana* were performed with an Islamic veneer, often with Muslim sultans in the roles of Hindu princes.

In keeping with these accommodationist times, Sher Shah Sur and the Afghan rulers of the Delhi Sultanate who succeeded him were more tolerant of religious diversity than perhaps any that preceded them. However, Afghan dynasties were neither sufficiently inclusive nor sufficiently orthodox to reinvigorate Islamic rule in the north. None proved able to rise above the traditional internal conflicts that had opened the door to Humayun's successful return in 1555. Yet, during the fifteen years of Humayun's absence, the inclusiveness pursued by Sufis and by Sher Shah Sur and his Afghan successors was just enough to enable a Hindu official, Hemu Chandra, to become their commander in chief. After Humayun's death in 1556, Hemu Chandra led the Afghans to a series of victories against the Mughals of such magnitude (including the seizure of Delhi) that he took the title of Samrat Vikramaditya (an emperor as brave as the sun), a royal title once held by powerful Hindu rulers. Yet Hemu Chandra retained the loyalty of his Afghan supporters due to the respect he afforded them and by his generous distribution of the spoils flowing from the occupation of Delhi. In the late fall of 1526, he marched toward Panipat, with a Hindu commanding one wing of his army and a Muslim Afghan commanding the other. They were eager to engage what remained of the Mughal army gathered there in the name of Humayun's thirteen-year-old son, Akbar. Once again that battlefield proved pivotal, determining whether the fragile course of Hindu-Muslim accommodation, if continued, would be directed by a Hindu or a Muslim. The outcome, settled by the flight of a single arrow, would facilitate the ascent of what became one of the greatest empires in world history.

Chapter 5

The Great Mughals, 1556–1757

On November 5, 1556, Samrat Hemu Chandra Vikramaditya, leading his army from atop one of his several hundred war elephants, was making good progress against rival Mughal forces, which his forces greatly outnumbered. With victory within his grasp, he fell victim to the oldest and most perfected weapon in the Mughal military arsenal: the bended bow. An arrow pierced his eye, its point emerging from the back of his head. His body fell from his mount, to the consternation of his troops, who soon fled the battlefield in the certain knowledge that dead rulers make poor paymasters. Bhairam Khan, an able Mughal general and regent to Jalal-ud-Din Muhammad Akbar, the thirteen-year-old son of the late Mughal emperor Humayun, had Hemu's body brought to the victorious Mughal camp. He directed Humayun's heir to cut off the fallen Hindu leader's head, so that Akbar could claim the title of Ghazi, or "warrior of God." Akbar declined, telling his guardian that had Hemu been alive, he might do so, but no credit could be acquired by dismembering a dead man. Bhairam Khan then ordered Akbar to slash Hemu's body with his sword, after which he himself cut off Hemu's head.

Over the next four years, relations soured between Akbar and Bhairam Khan, and even members of Akbar's family attempted to assassinate him to order to replace him with their own favorite as Babur's heir. Bhairam Khan eventually launched a failed revolt against Akbar's authority and was banished on the traditional, if thin, excuse that he was leaving on a pilgrimage to Mecca. In an effort to simultaneously break away from court politics and keep any disloyal elements within his army occupied, Akbar, now established as the *padishah*, or emperor, embarked on an eight-year war to reconquer the provinces lost to Hemu and the Afghans and thereby expand the Mughals' revenue base so as to provide his empire with greater stability. These goals were achieved through battles in which Akbar displayed utter fearlessness, brilliant generalship, and a capacity to win the respect of ally and foe alike, through diplomacy or violence, as the situation required. He did not hesitate to wage a jihad against those Hindu Rajputs who defied his authority, but he also won them over as allies by including them in his administration, and bonded with them by taking as his first and favored wife a Rajput princess.

Despite his relative youth, Akbar had considerable life experience to guide the governance of his empire. He had been born in Sindh while his father was fleeing Hindustan because of the acts of Akbar's uncles, the first example of the intra-family warfare he came to loathe. His father's ensuing alliance with the Persians exposed him to the grandeur of Persian culture and engendered in Akbar a respect for Islamic Persia's Shi'a thought, which helped to broaden his own philosophical and spiritual horizons beyond the Sunni orthodoxy found in most Muslim courts. He also had before him Sher Shah Sur's experiments in efficient, innovative administration. Most important of all, the multiethnic origins of the Mughal line and the inclusiveness of Mughal policy in Central Asia predisposed him toward political and cultural accommodation when engaging the enormous diversity of South Asia's population.

Whatever the strength of these possible formative influences, from the mid-1560s onward, Akbar sought not merely to win his diverse subjects' acquiescence to Mughal rule, but to bring them to identify their interests with it. Akbar tried to unify his subjects in ways that are more typical of modern states, with a level of success that many modern states have since failed to achieve.

Akbar's effort to create an inclusive state worthy of broad-based support began with his reformation of the bureaucracy and army. As much as possible, officials in both the Mughal military and administrative service were awarded the equivalent of a salary out of the general land revenue, rather than being directly assigned peasants' lands to fund their activities, as had been the case in the time of Ibn Battuta. Akbar directed that each administrator and high military officer be assigned a *mansab* (rank) whose value would amount to the normal cost of supporting a certain number of troops for state service, from five hundred men (a local commander) to five thousand men (a provincial governor). This *mansabdari* system included a separation of nawab (executive/military) functions and diwan (financial) responsibilities at the provincial level. By dividing these functions between these two offices, he sought to prevent the corruption that would be sure to follow otherwise. This idea, a separation of powers used to create checks and balances, was not to be employed in the West for two hundred years. It was central to Akbar's parallel efforts to prevent officials from unjustly enriching themselves by overtaxing peasants and to stop them from building a local revenue base to fuel a breakaway from imperial authority.

To further address this problem, Akbar ensured that officials could be transferred from one post to another across the empire at any time, and he banned the common practice of allowing the transfer of their accumulated wealth to their offspring. The latter step had an unintended but positive result. Local centers of administration became great nodes of craft and artistic production because, since Mughal officials could not bequeath to heirs or take their wealth with them to their next post, they spent their funds on artists and craftsmen who built and decorated their local courts to the highest artistic standards.

Perhaps the most noteworthy of Akbar's attempts to prevent the financial oppression of the peasantry and thus further assure internal political stability was carried out by his Hindu finance minister, Todar Mal, who improved upon Sher Shah Sur's sliding-scale land revenue system based on seasonal crop estimates, so that, in the event of drought or other calamity causing a drop in crop yield, tax rates or collections could be reduced.

Akbar's most significant administrative innovations were directed at indigenizing his state. Hindus like Todar Mal occupied key official posts, which usually included the commander in chief of the army. Akbar also favored the appointment of South Asian–born Muslims over the foreign born and sought to place as much provincial administration as possible in the hands of local Hindu rulers, who pledged their loyalty to the Mughal state. Akbar allowed these rulers to retain their traditional authority by assigning them to high *mansab* rank, and by subtler forms of attachment: armed Hindus guarded Akbar's throne, a powerful gesture of trust that served to indicate that all who appeared before the emperor could expect to receive justice.

Akbar encouraged a literal melding of Mughal and indigenous elites by encouraging intermarriage. His youthful experience among Afghan and other Central Asian troops had taught him that these warriors had been assets in creating the empire, but they were accustomed to being kingmakers and thus their loyalties were inherently fragile. An indigenized ruling elite would pose much less of a danger to both the emperor and the empire. Akbar led by example, not merely marrying into the powerful Rajput house of Amber in 1563, but also ensuring that his heir would have a Hindu mother. His son Jahangir followed suit, making such alliances a tool through which indigenous elites entered the court.

All of Akbar's reforms were meant to serve as a means to draw people into the orbit of the Mughal state in general and to the emperor as its head. All grants and awards, including *mansabdari* assignments, were gifts of the emperor, bestowed to create an intimate personal bond between the emperor and his officials that, if broken by either party without just cause, would lead to a serious loss of honor. These investitures at once centralized authority in the emperor, but were deliberately seen to be reciprocal: the empire's legitimacy was dependent on his just rule.

A further aspect of Akbar's indigenization policy was the giving of grants to Hindu and Muslim cultural and religious institutions, as well

Akbar's beloved Hindu wife, Jodha Bai, gives birth to their son, the future Emperor Jahangir. After this event, Akbar gave her the name of Maryam-uz-Zamani (Mary of the Age). She practiced her religion at court and was an excellent businesswoman, trading internationally in spices and silk, a living expression of early Mughal multiculturalism and the freedom granted to women of the royal court. Photograph © 2017 Museum of Fine Arts, Boston, 14.657

as to individual poets and artists, including Mian Tansen, now considered the font of modern Hindu music. He also supported the work of artists, architects, and stonemasons, who developed a syncretic style (today called *mughlai*) that blended Hindu and Muslim cultural forms. This style was most apparent in architecture, which mated the Persian dome with the elongated pillars of the Hindu *nata mandapa*, or temple dance hall, to form *chatri* (umbrella-like pavilions) that graced the sides and corners of Mughal palaces and fortress towers. During the sultanate, royal tombs were squat structures well suited to the Central Asian climate of high winds and brutal winters. The Mughals built their tombs on raised plinths pierced by arches, lending a lightness also found in their palace architecture, which featured balconies and chatri-topped towers, that captured the cooling breezes passing above the plains of semitropical South Asia.

Akbar also sought to make his empire popular by advancing general living conditions through public works, improvements in living quarters for the urban poor, and the regulation of alcohol. Moral laws such as the latter were typical of Muslim rulers keeping to shari'a, which mandated them, but to these regulations Akbar added prohibitions against the needless slaughter of animals, and restricted his own eating of meat to specific days of the week, which appealed to Hindus and Jains opposed to violence. Moreover, drawing on the active role women played in Mongol society, the emperor was not afraid to challenge the patriarchy of both South Asian Muslims and Hindus by seeking to improve the condition of women. He discouraged child marriages among all his subjects and permitted the remarriage of widows, which was against Hindu custom. He also sought to end the practice of sati among Hindus by requiring permission to be given by local police, who were expected to discourage the act. To keep women safe from molestation, Akbar encouraged merchants to establish separate market days for women.

Akbar intended all of his social reforms to support his larger object of not merely religious neutrality, but what was called *sulh-i-kul*, or universal harmony. He was convinced that most Hindus and Muslims would prefer such a policy to the periodic fracturing of society and state over social and religious issues. It would also reduce the impression that the Mughal regime was an alien one. To achieve these ends, he abolished most levies paid by non-Muslims, including the *jizya* (1564), and introduced an edict of religious toleration (1593).

Akbar's emphasis on religious tolerance, while politic, may have been rooted in personal convictions arising from his Chisti Sufi orientation. He had been drawn to the teachings of Moinuddin Chishti of Ajmer, who earned the title of Benefactor of the Poor during the Delhi Sultanate. At Fatehpur Sikri, some miles from Agra, which, along with Lahore, was the preferred capital of the early Mughals, Akbar directly received the teachings of another Sufi master of the same school, Shaikh Salim Chisti. Shaikh Salim returned this act of piety by assuring Akbar that God would grant him the male heir for which Akbar devoutly prayed. Soon thereafter, Prince Selim, the future Emperor Jahangir, was born of Akbar's Hindu wife. This event fulfilled Akbar's prayers for a son and also his personal desire for the House of Timur to have roots in Hindustan. To mark this event, Akbar built a beautiful white marble shrine for the shaikh and a magnificent new capital at Fatehpur Sikri. A traveling Englishman, Ralph Fitch, visiting Agra and Fatehpur Sikri in 1584, found both cities "considerably larger than London and more populous." He observed:

> Fathepur towne is greater than Agra, though it had the same compliment of 1,000 elephants, thirtie thousand horses, 1,400 tame Deere, 800 concubines, such store of Ounces [a big cat similar to a snow leopard], Tigers, Buffles [water buffaloes], Cocks & Haukes, that is very strange to see.[1]

Contemporary Mughal historians described the new city as having become by 1596 "a rendezvous of merchants from all the known quarters of the globe."[2]

Akbar also built a hall of worship (Ibadat Khana) at Fatephur Sikri where he hosted debates on religious topics, chiefly among learned Muslims, but these proved deeply disappointing. Akbar was sickened to find that most of these divines sought to belittle their opponents. Two of the most honored Muslim theologians at court engaged each other in bitter personal attacks as well as doctrinal differences. Both were great hypocrites. Each would later prove to be bent on preventing the other from amassing a personal fortune or allowing others to use his own office to so. To Akbar, who had been drawn to Chisti Sufism because of its denial of the self as well as for its eclectic mysticism, orthodox Islam increasingly seemed desolate of true spirituality.

The poor performance of Muslim clerics at the Ibadat Khana encouraged Akbar to open it to Hindus, Jains, and others so that he might explore other avenues of religious knowledge more closely. This caused much distress to one of the most orthodox of Akbar's court historians, Abdul Qadir Badauni. Badauni noted that Akbar spent his life exploring the "most diverse phases and through all sorts of religious

A section of the main courtyard of the royal city at Fatehpur Sikri, built at the orders of the Mughal emperor Akbar in 1570. The platform in the center of the photograph was the site of musical and dance performances. Note the chatri, *or umbrella-like towers, at top left that are characteristic of Mughal borrowings from Hindu architecture.* Photo by Nickolay Stanev/Shutterstock 84457321

practices and sectarian beliefs, and collected everything which people can find in books, with a talent of selection peculiar to him and a spirit of inquiry," all of which were "opposed to every Islamic principle."

> The result of all the influences which were brought to bear upon him, [there] grew as gradually as [moss] upon on a stone the conviction in his heart that there were sensible men in all religions . . . among all nations.[3]

Akbar was aware of Badauni's criticism, and bristled at Badauni's illiberal ideas, but believed that there was no point in having historians if they were not free to record what their intellect dictated.

In pursuit of his quest for religious knowledge, Akbar began what was to be a long Mughal association with Jesuits, a Catholic order that had become famous in Mongol circles for its devotion to scholarship as well as missionary work. Arriving in the Portuguese settlement of Goa in 1541, the Jesuits hoped to convert local princes and other political elites, who would then lead their subjects to convert. A lack of results forced them to realized that the Muslims were impervious to their call and that Hindu elites feared loss of social status as a result of close contact with foreigners (who were considered *mleccha*, or among the lowest of the low). Moreover, high-caste Hindus refused to worship side by side with those from inferior castes, as Christians did. Thereafter, the Jesuits largely rested content with making converts from the lower orders, with limited but better success. They never quite abandoned their dream of converting a Mughal prince, though from the first, Akbar informed them that the quest for religious truth was not a contest, as is reflected in his request of the Catholic King Philip II of Spain to send Jesuits to reside at his court. Akbar wrote:

> Most men are so fettered by the bonds of tradition that they never investigate . . . the religion in which he was born, excluding [themselves] from the possibility of ascertaining the truth which is the noblest aim of the human intellect. Therefore, we associate . . . with learned men of all religions, and thus derive profit from their exquisite discourses and exalted aspirations.[4]

Unfortunately, many of the Christians who participated in Akbar's discussions were not only as petty and argumentative as the Muslim scholars at his court, but also stooped to insult the religion of Islam. This collective rancor may have helped propel Akbar to create the Din-i-Ilahi.

The Din-i-Ilahi, or divine discipleship, has often been interpreted as an attempt by Akbar to create a universal religion suitable for his multicultural state. Initially, that may have been on his mind when he announced his wish to create a community of seekers devoted to exploration of religious truth with Akbar himself at its head. However, some of his most devoted officials had come before him to assure him that, while their personal bonds to him were unbreakable, they preferred Akbar to take their lives rather than ask them to leave the religion of their birth. In response, Akbar assured them that there was no obligation upon anyone to join with him in what he described as a purely voluntary association. He also informed his courtiers that he would never depart from what was the Qur'an's injunction as well as his own conviction: there could be no coercion in religion.

Some orthodox Muslims, like Badauni, found it intolerable that the emperor seemed to countenance the criticism of Islam by Christians, and they disliked his apparent cultic behavior. In 1580, a revolt was launched to overthrow him. Badauni was not among the rebels. He held aloof from the conservative clerics and administrators opposed to Akbar's perceived departure from the traditionally close relationship between religion and the state, largely because he was true to much of Akbar's vision for the Mughal state. Badauni praised Akbar's commitment to intermarriage among the empire's elite ethnic groups and, although he was a strong critic of many of Akbar's Hindu officials, Badauni respected those who served the empire well. He also had no love for holy war, or even rebellion against a straying emperor like Akbar. It is likely that many conservatives shared those views. In any event, the 1580 revolt was easily quashed by Akbar's increasingly indigenized army, confirming Akbar's conviction that the legitimacy of the Mughal regime resided in its broad appeal.

Despite Akbar's acumen as a ruler and the popular support he enjoyed during his very long reign as Mughal emperor, he failed to achieve the fuller unification of Muslim and Hindu culture he desired. But he did succeed in establishing a multicultural and often syncretic governing ethos, which became a hallmark of Mughal rule down the generations. It is thus somewhat tragic that toward the end of his long life, he caught a glimpse of one cause of the instability and ultimate downfall of his empire as well as those of the Ottomans and Safavids to the west. This was the problem of succession. Akbar's God-granted son, Prince Selim, grew impatient for power during the long years of Akbar's reign. He waged an unsuccessful revolt that weighed heavily on Akbar's mind, but they reconciled; Akbar rose from his deathbed to place the royal turban on his son's head.

Ironically, Prince Selim's eagerness for power passed not long after his accession to the throne as Emperor Jahangir (ruled 1605–1627). Thereafter, he left many of the day-to-day affairs of the empire to his able wife, Nur Jahan (Light of the World), the daughter of a religiously conservative, politically astute Persian immigrant family. She conducted ministerial meetings and Jahangir directed that her name appear on imperial coins. However, Jahangir was not wholly absent from Mughal administration. He dealt effectively with the pretentions of the Portuguese, the first European state to project its power into the region in search of souls as well as spices.

The Portuguese sought a direct sea route that would allow them to gain a monopoly of the rich Indian Ocean trade system that was then in the hands of Venetians, Muslim Arabs, and Turks. These merchants acted as middlemen between Europe and Asia, trading in Indian pepper and cotton as well as the spices of Southeast Asia, which, while essential to preserving meat, also constituted the bulk of Western medicines (oil of cloves was the only anesthetic known to Europeans). This effort began with the rounding of the Cape of Good Hope in southern Africa in 1488 by the Portuguese Bartholomew Diaz. To exploit that achievement, an experienced Portuguese commander, Vasco da Gama, was given a small fleet that passed the Cape of Good Hope in 1497–1498.

As he continued his voyage northward along the coast of East Africa, he encountered multiethnic city-states managed by Africans and Muslim Arabs, who had created a hybridized language and culture known as Swahili (meaning "of the coast"). He was welcomed at the Swahili port of Mozambique because he disguised himself as a Muslim trader, but the poor gifts he offered to the local rulers betrayed the relative poverty of Europe and revealed him to be a Christian. When forced to flee the port, da Gama turned his guns on the city, setting it afire. He thereafter gained knowledge of the monsoon from local sailors and used its winds to cross the Indian Ocean to Calicut, south of today's Mumbai.

Calicut was a well-known port of call. It had been visited several times between 1409 and 1430 by the Chinese admiral and official envoy Zheng He (alternatively romanized as Cheng Ho), who offered rich presents and association with China.[5] At the time of da Gama's arrival, Calicut was ruled by a Hindu prince, called the Zamorin, who managed the affairs of local and transregional traders. Most of these were Arab Muslims, but among them were Jews, some who had settled on the western coast of the subcontinent from five hundred to one thousand years earlier and others who conducted trade there from their community in what is now modern Cairo. The Zamorin, like his Swahili counterpart, was unimpressed with the presents da Gama offered as an inducement to trade, especially as they included no gold, silver, or ivory (as was customary.) He directed da Gama to pay the same customs duty in gold as all other traders paid and refused da Gama's request to set up a warehouse to store goods. However, the Zamorin also denied Muslim requests to drive da Gama off (they contended he was a mere pirate) and permitted da Gama to trade in the port. Da Gama departed richer for the trade he did conduct—though, he kidnapped some local fisherman to serve as crew for his ships on their return to Portugal.

The Portuguese sent larger forces that eventually set up a network of fortress settlements from west of the mouth of the Indus River in Gujarat (Dui and Daman) down to the towns of Goa and Cochin. Others were set up on the eastern side of the subcontinent, just south of today's Chennai (formerly Madras) and in Bengal. They also set up pepper plantations in Sri Lanka. Touching on all corners of the subcontinent, these settlements were well placed to capture the region's oceanic trade. To make sure they did, the Portuguese established a pass system called the *cartaz* and began seizing all vessels traveling without evidence of license fees paid to them. Portuguese trade had one immediate, apolitical impact: they brought chilies from the Americas, which, within decades of their arrival, became a staple of South Asian cuisine and remain so to this day.

Though the Mughals were land-oriented, they took notice of Portuguese ambitions to control the seaborne trade of southern Asia. Akbar wished to curtail these ambitions, but found it more politic to secure compromises that, for example, gave free passage to ships leaving the Mughal's main international port at Surat in Gujarat (south of the long-lost port at Lothal), which were filled with pilgrims on their way to Mecca. The security of this passage was perhaps not a small thing to an emperor who needed to be seen protecting essential Muslim religious practices.

A few years before Akbar's death in 1605, captains of ships sailing from Protestant Britain and Holland began entering the Indian Ocean, seeking gold—but not souls, as had the Portuguese. They contested the Portuguese *cartaz* system both by force and by lodging appeals at the Mughal Court. The Dutch and English ("British" only after the union of Scotland and Ireland with England in 1707 created Great Britain) were no less troublesome than the Portuguese in interfering with international shipping in the Indian Ocean, but the Portuguese made the mistake of taking such aggressive actions in defense of their threatened monopoly that they lost any favor with Jahangir. Among those actions was the seizure of a ship owned by a former Rajput princess and still-practicing Hindu, Maryam-uz-Zamani, Jahangir's mother.[6] After the governor of Gujarat lodged a formal complaint that showed that this was no isolated action, Jahangir ordered an end to the Portuguese trade at Surat, the seizure of the Portuguese settlement at Daman in Gujarat, the shutting of the Jesuit church in Agra, and the suspension of all allowances to Portuguese religious leaders in Mughal India, even though a Portuguese friar was one of Jahangir's personal advisors.

Further, the Mughals and other local regimes in South Asia granted trade and other privileges to the English and Dutch merchant companies so that they might serve as a check on the Portuguese and stimulate competition for their own spices and fabrics. Both the English and the Dutch soon established strategically located coastal trading settlements on the Portuguese model. For the English, the opportunity to compete in South Asia was something of a lifesaver, as the Dutch had driven them out of the more lucrative trade of the spice-rich islands of Southeast Asia. With the Portuguese in decline and the Dutch focused on their trade in Southeast Asia, the English were well placed to dominate Europe's trade with India. The French, latecomers whose trading company was subordinate to the French throne, proved unable to out-compete English merchants.

Jahangir believed that his response to Portuguese aggression would be sufficient to defuse open warfare between Catholic and Protestant traders and preserve Mughal seaborne interests without a serious breach in his relations with Westerners, which he greatly enjoyed. To impress such visitors, and his own people, he lost no chance to incorporate Christian symbolism as part of his employment of the decorative arts to express Mughal eclecticism as well as to enhance his legitimacy as ruler. He ordered images of a crucifix, the Virgin Mary, and Saint Ignatius Loyola, the founder of the Jesuits, to be painted at the entrance to his father's tomb near Agra. His court produced a painting of a royal scene showing the Virgin Mary floating above the emperor's head in benediction, with *putti* (winged baby angels) decorating the edges of the image, as was then in vogue in the West. Perhaps inspired by European artistic style, Jahangir, like all the Mughal emperors, encouraged artists to create lifelike portraits of the members of the court as well as its emperors. Jahangir preferred to decorate existing courts rather than build new ones, so he was able to spend lavishly on such sumptuous paintings, as well as jewel-encrusted weapons, splendid court robes, and glorious gardens. European visitors were so impressed by the grandeur of Jahangir's Mughal imperial style that the term "mogul" became a synonym in English for an important or powerful person.

Western visitors, perhaps because of the repressive sexual environment in their own lands, were also impressed, if not always favorably, with the emperor's harem (from *harim*, "forbidden"). The harem was the private section of the emperor's apartments, which Westerners understood to be filled with hundreds of women ready at a moment's notice to serve him at his pleasure. In reality, while the harem was where the emperor sought to continue his line with his wives and concubines, it was also where aunts, female family members of his in-laws, widowed female relations, and all the children of the palace also lived— and, under Jahangir, lived well.

Unfortunately, Jahangir's love of pleasure and beauty led him away from more active pursuits and, eventually, to dependency on alcohol and opium. Jahangir even allowed his state to drift away from his father's policy of religious toleration, though he continued it in his personal life, such as by joining in festivities of the Hindu spring festival of Holi. His wife Nur Jahan, however, sought to dispose of such eclecticism entirely. As his health declined, Nur Jahan began to arrange for Jahangir's successor to be a much more observant Muslim. This path was made easier by the revolt of Jahangir's eldest son, Khusrau Mizra. As punishment for his rebellion, Mizra, the treasure of his grandfather Akbar's heart, who had grown to share Akbar's openness to all religious philosophy, was blinded, making him ineligible to be a ruler by Muslim tradition. He was also exiled for his attempt to usurp Jahangir's authority. Also exiled was another brother who had become a hopeless alcoholic. Jahangir's two remaining sons held more orthodox views than Khusrau Mizra. Of these two, Shah Jahan was the tougher warrior and more able administrator, but Nur Jahan supported Shah Jahan's less able but more malleable brother, Shahryar, as heir. This gambit failed, as upon Jahangir's death, Shah Jahan was able to seize power and execute Shahryar. Nur Jahan was forced to withdraw from public life, a fate easier to bear because she had earlier arranged for the new emperor to fall deeply in love with her niece, assuring that her family, and their orthodox views, remained influential.

Shah Jahan, like his father, led a brilliant court in which women exercised a great deal of authority. But beyond the palace walls, the position of women in both Muslim and Hindu society declined. Akbar's policy of raising the status of women by encouraging widow remarriage was in retreat, while child marriages and sati, which Akbar had virtually banned, grew in popularity. More women were secluded within the family home.

All Mughal rulers sought to expand their domains, but Shah Jahan (ruled 1628–1658) was more aggressive than most in pursuit of the Timurid lands in Central Asia and Afghanistan, lost during Mughal wars of secession to opportunistic Uzbeks and Persians. He was also determined to complete the conquest of the Deccan. Yet the enormously expensive northern campaigns he launched failed to achieve their objectives, and the Deccan was won only as a result of two costly campaigns by his third son, Prince Aurangzeb. These campaigns gave Aurangzeb an edge over Shah Jahan's eldest son and chosen successor, Dara Shikoh, whose activities at court were devoted to building upon the syncretic values and indigenizing precedents established by Akbar.

Despite these demands on the empire's finances, Shah Jahan reveled in new construction. He rebuilt the interior halls of Akbar's Red Fort at Agra in marble, but was not wholly satisfied with the result, so he then built an entirely new capital in Delhi, known as Shahjahanabad. This new city included the world's largest mosque at the time, the Jama Masjid, and a palace so opulent as to justify the inscription above its private chambers, "If on earth there be a paradise of bliss, it is this."

Shah Jahan then considered a suitable tomb for his beloved wife, Mumtaz, who perished while giving birth to her fourteenth child. This became one of the world's most recognizable buildings, the Taj Mahal. It took twenty-two years to build. It was made of the emperor's pre-ferred white marble, inlaid with precious and semi-precious stones, and inscribed with verses from the Qur'an. The entire tomb complex was set among lush gardens bisected by four watercourses meant to represent the Four Rivers of Paradise. These orthodox features were combined with *mughlai* elements such as an archway-pierced pediment or main floor, elongated domes, and umbrella-like *chatri*.

The graceful effect achieved by the Taj Mahal's melding of the subcontinent's diverse cultures was initially not much apparent in Shah Jahan's religious policy. Upon assuming the throne, Shah Jahan adopted a more orthodox view of the role of religion in an Islamic state. In 1632 he ordered Christian churches at Agra and Lahore to be demolished and all Hindu temples recently built or still under con-struction to be torn down. He also passed laws governing the marriage of Muslims to Hindus, mandating the conversion of the non-Muslim spouse. However, as he aged, Shah Jahan resumed the Mughal practice of giving Hindu scholars and artisans grants and stipends. This change may have been an expression of a growing awareness of his own indigenous status: he had a Hindu mother and a Hindu grandmother. His most favored poet, Abu Talib Khan, noted the custom of writing in praise of the cool, fresh, fruited valleys of Mughulistan, but wrote of Hindustan: "One can say it is a second paradise [after Heaven] in this respect; whoever leaves this garden is filled with regret."[7] Another factor in Shah Jahan's turn toward the values of indigenization may have been the influence of his eldest son, Dara Shikoh, who often acted as his deputy and exhibited Akbar's passion for exploring reli-gious philosophy.

Dara Shikoh sponsored Persian translations of Hindu texts, including the Upanishads, and wrote "Majma ul-Bahrain" ("The Mingling of the Two Oceans"), in which he sought to comprehend and reconcile the monism inherent in Sufi thought with that of the Upanishads. For these acts, and his willingness, like his grandfather, to favor Rajputs and indigenous Muslims over Persian Muslims and other foreigners at court, Dara Shikoh gained considerable personal popularity. Naturally enough, foreign-born *mansabdar*s (Persians, Central Asians, and Afghans) and orthodox Muslims disliked him, but he was seen by his foremost Sufi associate, Shah Muhibullah, as Rahmat-ul-lil-Alimin, "a blessing to all people." In what may be the highest expression of the spiritual message of Akbar as well as Dara Shikoh, Shah Muhibullah wrote:

> It does not matter if one is a believer or a non-believer. All human beings are the creatures of God. If one has such a feeling, he will not differentiate between a believer and non-believer and will show sympathy and consideration towards both. It is in the Qur'an . . . that the Prophet was sent as a mercy unto all mankind.[8]

Dara Shikoh brought Sufis into court, and may have convinced Shah Jahan to see the value of diverse views, enough at least to remove the last vestige of taxes on non-Muslims: the payment of the *jizya* by Hindu pilgrims to the holy Hindu city Prayaga, renamed Allahabad by its Muslim rulers. Fatefully, Shah Jahan also came to favor Dara Shikoh above his other sons. This may be the source of the softening of the tenor of his religious policy, but such royal favor also may have stirred resentment among Dara Shikoh's brothers. Shah Jahan's liberal shift in his religious policy did not immediately play a role in the course of his empire, but subsequent military adventures and building projects were so costly as to force a fateful reconsideration of the fiscal arrangements between the Mughal court and its vast network of alliances that sustained the empire and in which the tolerant Mughal religious policy played a key role. The man destined to preside over this reconsideration was not Dara Shikoh but Shah Jahan's third son, the supremely able, but self-admittedly unloved and puritanical Prince Aurangzeb.

Shah Jahan enjoyed the support of a multicultural court which favored Dara Shikoh's adherence to Chisti-style Sufi cultural openness, while Aurangzeb identified himself with the orthodox Naqshbandi Sufi order that, in the person of Imam Rabbani Shaykh Ahmad al-Faruqi al-Sirhindi, had long opposed Akbar's liberal view of the Islamic state. Naqshbandi influence grew in the Mughal court during the reigns of both Jahangir and Shah Jahan and, under Naqshbandi tutelage, Aurangzeb developed a deep respect for its version of Islamic orthodoxy, as well as an austere personality and a preference for the field of action over court life, which was dominated by Dara Shikoh. He spent much of his life fighting under his father's orders, and later under his own authority, expanding the empire in the south. During his reign as emperor, the empire reached its greatest territorial extent, occupying by direct rule or through traditional Mughal local alliances virtually the entire subcontinent.

Aurangzeb earned his subsequent formal title of Emperor Alamgir (World Burner) with all the ruthlessness that Mughal wars of succession had come to acquire. When Shah Jahan seemed to be near death in 1658, a struggle for the throne erupted during which Aurangzeb's military and diplomatic experience in the south stood him in good stead. He imprisoned his father and politically outmaneuvered, as well as outfought, his brothers until only a captured Dara Shikoh and his older brother Murad remained to be dealt with. Aurangzeb deliberately humiliated Shah Jahan's favorite son by marching Dara Shikoh and his son in dirty clothes through the streets of Delhi and convening a kangaroo court of nobles and orthodox clerics who had opposed Dara Shikoh's policies to serve as judges at his trial. They promptly declared Dara Shikoh an apostate to Islam for his intellectual engagement with the non-Muslim "other." Dara Shikoh was beheaded in front of his son; the head was sent to Shah Jahan, who had largely recovered his health but was condemned by Aurangzeb to spend the rest of his life as a prisoner in the Red Fort at Agra. The remaining brother, Murad, was executed after trying to escape from prison in 1661. Shah Jahan died in 1666, but not before forgiving Aurangzeb, much as Jahangir was forgiven by Akbar.

Aurangzeb then addressed the larger issue represented by Dara's alleged apostasy. Aurangzeb's interpretation of the precepts of political Islam followed the orthodox Naqshbandi religio-political outlook that may have inhibited the Delhi Sultanate from constructively addressing the essential question of diversity that confronted Muslim rulers of Hindustan before Akbar. Aurangzeb recognized that his empire was rooted in its diversity. He regarded Hindus as *dhimmi* and continued to appoint Hindu *mansabdar*s. However, his zealotry as an orthodox Muslim overrode his understanding of the limits to which the empire could endure his imposition of Islamic political principles in their orthodox form.

Aurangzeb's break with customary Mughal multiculturalism began with banning music and dance in his court. This ban drew some praise from the devout, but little public criticism because it was limited to the court itself. However, Aurangzeb next sought to enforce Islamic codes of public conduct via *mustasib*s (public censors). Aurangzeb also moved to halt construction of new Hindu temples, and then to attack established structures, even Somnath, once the target of the "Breaker of Idols," Mahmud of Ghazni. As in that case, it is necessary to consider Aurangzeb's actions in light of similar actions taken by Hindu rajas, who often destroyed the royal temples of rival Hindu rulers and rebels. However, Aurangzeb seems to have gone beyond Hindu and certainly common Muslim practice. Even the most orthodox of Delhi sultans, Firuz Shah Tughluq, had followed the practice of leaving unmolested existing houses of worship of all those enjoying the protection of the Islamic state as enjoined by the Qur'an, which the Delhi sultans applied to Christians and Hindus as *dhimmi*. With only a few initial exceptions, so had Shah Jahan, who went so far as to rescind an order by Prince Aurangzeb to destroy an existing Jain temple that had given no offense.

Of greater significance, Aurangzeb reimposed the *jizya* that had been abolished by Akbar and that was again rejected, perhaps tellingly, by Shah Jahan under Dara Shikoh's influence. Sibling rivalry aside, Aurangzeb may have merely wished to observe a passage in the Qur'an which referred generally to the need for non-Muslims to humble themselves before the supremacy of the revelation of Islam, as well as the *jizya* payment in lieu of state service, which was demanded of non-Muslims alone. Aurangzeb, however, took this "humbling" to an extreme level by ordering the *jizya* fees to be paid in person while standing before a seated collector of the tax and chanting the verse in the Qur'an referring to their inferior status as non-Muslims. While Aurangzeb exempted Hindu *mansabdar*s from the tax because they were engaged in service to the state, he also made it known that, in the future, he intended to oppose appointing Hindus to the highest ranks, which would be reserved for Muslims. Whatever the cause or actual extent of these actions, Aurangzeb was making enemies the empire could ill afford.

The emperor's subjects did not miss the negative implications of the reimposition of the *jizya*: throngs of people blocked Aurangzeb's movements through the streets of Delhi, begging him to reconsider his decision. Hindu courtiers and some court poets lamented that this act constituted a break in religious forbearance that could herald the demise of the empire itself. Hindu concerns deepened with developments arising from the rapid expansion of the empire. The huge weight of the expenses incurred by their wars of conquest forced first Shah Jahan and then Aurangzeb to take fiscal as well as political steps (the reimposition of the *jizya* was both) that may have fatally undermined the delicate web of personal, religious, ethnic, and economic ties that held the empire together.

At the beginning of Shah Jahan's reign, the finances of the empire were secured by the spread of cash-cropping (food for sale rather than local consumption) and continuing improvement in roads that stimulated commercial activity. This encouraged the Mughals to double their demand for revenue. Unfortunately for the empire, Shah Jahan's campaigns in the north and in the Deccan so surpassed those revenues that the empire had to economize. Shah Jahan slowly lifted Akbar's restraints on the *jagirdar* system to allow officials to gain income and thereby retain their loyalty, but with the same evil result that Akbar had sought to avoid by his reforms. The nobility were again free to rack-rent farmers and use the revenue to build independent bases of power—the very behavior that had aided in the disintegration of the Delhi Sultanate. The empire was also driven to give revenue-enhancing privileges to a host of local elites, such as zamindars (Mughal tax collectors), who faced off against local *mansabdars*, both of whom were acting in their own interests rather than the state's.

Aurangzeb ordered increases in land-tax revenue to meet expenditures so as to avoid internal political unrest among officials and merchant elites, but the increases fell heavily on the Hindu agricultural population in the north, particularly the Hindu Jats, a key productive group. Further, the financially strapped Aurangzeb had to keep the income from the richest of the newly conquered lands for the Mughal treasury, which reduced the quality of land granted to the local nobility, Muslim and non-Muslim, whom Aurangzeb had brought into the Mughal fold as a reward for their role in the empire's conquests. For the Hindu nobility among this group, things now looked bleak. With their incomes from grants of lesser value, and the Mughal court seemingly bent on reducing them to second-class status, the new recruits in the Deccan and in the south, numbering nearly 20 percent of all *mansabdars*, wondered why they had allied themselves to its cause.

One of the most able and most disaffected among these newly minted Hindu nobles in the south was Raja Shivaji Bhonsle. Shivaji had long been a chief in his own right among the Maratha people of the west-central section of the subcontinent before he had fought in support of Aurangzeb's conquest of the Muslim sultanates in the Deccan. The combination of anti-Hindu policy and sentiment at court and the reduction in the value of subsidies or land grants to Maratha *mansabdars* turned Shivaji into not merely a rebel but a rival. Upon escaping the court just ahead of orders for his arrest for criticizing Aurangzeb's policies, Shivaji purportedly sent the emperor a letter contrasting the excellent condition of the country under the rule of Akbar, Jahangir, and Shah Jahan with that of Aurangzeb, "where poverty and beggary" had become commonplace, and "the army in ferment." Why would Aurangzeb, he asked, sully the honor of Timurid rule by adding "the hardship of the *jizya* to this grievous state of things?"[9]

Upon fleeing the Mughal court, Shivaji was invested by the Marathas with the title of Chatrapati, a rank akin to the ancient *chakravartin*. From 1674 to 1680, he confronted the Mughals with one of the most sustained guerrilla campaigns in world history. This struggle forced Aurangzeb to squander more of the empire's dwindling wealth, which the emperor complained of even on his deathbed. Aurangzeb's campaigns against Shivaji spurred the Marathas to create an empire of their own in the south. Aurangzeb's own son, Prince Muhammad Akbar, opposed what he believed to be his father's misguided policies and aided the Marathas. After Shivaji's death (of natural causes) in 1680, Aurangzeb was able to capture Shivaji's able son Sambhaji (but not his own son, Prince Akbar, who fled to Arabia). Aurangzeb executed Sambhaji in 1689 after he refused to convert to Islam under torture, then set about laying claim to all the Maratha lands.

The following year, Aurangzeb had to address a dispute between agents of what would later be known as the British East India Company (hereafter referred to as the Company) and the cash-strapped Mughal governors at Surat and in Bengal over taxes that local officials were trying to impose on international merchants. Even though non-Company English merchants paid these local taxes willingly, in 1686 the Company's directors tired of what they saw as illegal exactions. They interpreted their Mughal firman (license to trade) to mean they only paid taxes to imperial officials at the main international port of Surat in Gujarat and nowhere else. In defense of this principle, the Company declared war on the Mughal Empire and sent ships and infantry to both Bengal and Surat to cut off the empire's trade until the local taxes were withdrawn. Aurangzeb, who had expected his provincial officials and the Company's agents to negotiate a settlement, retaliated by defeating the English forces on land, laying waste to or seizing the Company's factories and stopping its trade. The Company was subsequently able to force the Mughals to open peace negotiations by employing its naval forces to sink unarmed Muslim pilgrim ships bound for Mecca. The result of these negotiations was that the Company was forced to pay an enormous fine (£15,000) in return for being allowed to continue their exemption from the unwanted taxes. The war "seriously demoralized" the aggressive Company directors at home, while the members of the embassy they sent to arrange a peace agreement in 1691 were humiliated when ushered into the Mughal court "with their hands tied in front of them with sashes."[10] This experience forced the Company to realize that it lacked the strength to impose its will on Asian powers, a lesson driven home by the Chinese manipulation of their trade and the disastrous results of Company aggression in Borneo and Vietnam.[11]

By then, Aurangzeb was facing a perfect storm of revolt that ultimately helped alter the balance of power between Europe and South Asia. The north was ablaze. Most of the Mughal Empire's once most stalwart allies, the Rajputs, broke into open rebellion alongside the tax-resisting Jats. The Rajputs and Jats were joined by the Sikhs, whose ninth guru, Tej Bahadur, was executed for calling for a Sikh state if Mughal persecution of non-Muslims led to the forced conversion of Sikhs. Under his successor, Guru Gobind Singh, the Sikh community became an army of the KHALSA (pure) determined to free themselves from Mughal rule. In the South, Marathas slowly recovered from the death of Shivaji's son, Sambhaji, and their forces marched north to menace Delhi.

Aurangzeb was so great a field commander that he was able to stave off the enemies of his empire until his illness and death in 1707 at the age of ninety. In his last will and testament, he blamed his letting Shivaji escape from his court as the cause of much misery, but offered no remarks as to why he had lost the Maratha leader's support. He seemed to feel that his campaigns of conquest, particularly the twenty-six years he spent exhausting his army and treasury in the Deccan, had led him away, rather than toward, the divinely guided life he sought, but gave no sign he understood how this happened. If he sought to renew his faith through the Islamicization of his empire, whose religious pluralism he viewed as an offense against God, that purpose escaped him as death approached. To his son, he wrote, "I do not know who I am, nor what I have been doing."[12]

During the reigns of Aurangzeb's successors, wars of imperial succession and the resultant rise of regional states in much of South Asia hastened the empire's decline. The Marathas won control of so much Mughal territory that the empire's rulers were forced to pay them tribute. The Sikhs carved out an empire in the Punjab, taking the lands to the west of the Indus River from the Afghans and gaining influence over Kashmir. Mughal provincial governors in Bengal and in the hard-won Deccan took up the reins of power, though such was the remaining prestige of the Mughal Empire that they acknowledged the titular supremacy of the emperor by offering largely symbolic tribute.

As has often been the case in South Asian history, the subcontinent flourished in this less centralized condition. Regional empires, like that of the Marathas, redistributed wealth through their local courts. Entrepreneurial market towns flourished as industry was stimulated by the end of Mughal royal monopolies in the manufacturing sector. In the absence of a centralized court setting religious policy, new approaches to Muslim and non-Muslim relations could be advanced. The globally influential eighteenth-century Salafist Sunni philosopher Shah Waliullah, himself deeply influenced by the teachings of the Naqshbandi

Sufi Sirhindi, wished to purify Islam of all Hindu, Sufi, and Shi'a influences with an eye to internal reform. He denounced the then current craze among the wealthy for "jewelry, costly garments and the like," and opposed, on chiefly economic grounds, "expensive and un-Islamic ceremonies . . . except for . . . the post-wedding meal for guests."[13]

In the political and commercial arena, the decline of the Mughal court forced emerging or breakaway regional rulers to construct new relationships with local producers, administrators, and bankers. Bankers and merchants along the subcontinent's coastlines enlisted English, Dutch, French, and American trading companies as partners in extracting wealth from the interior and taking South Asian products, from cotton to opium, into an expanding global international market.

Several events then intervened to forestall South Asia's independent religious, political, and economic development. In 1739, the Persian emperor Nadir Shah, recognizing that South Asia was as rich in resources as its political cohesion was poor, launched an invasion of the northwest. The treasure lost to his raid included Shah Jahan's jewel-encrusted peacock throne. Other invaders to the northwest inflicted a serious blow to the prestige of the growing Hindu Maratha Empire. In 1761, Maratha forces rose to defend the subcontinent from an assault by Ahmed Shah Durrani, a former lieutenant of Nadir Shah's and the founder of modern Afghanistan, only to be crushed by Afghans allied with what remained of the Mughal nobility.

With the Marathas thus weakened, and the Mughal Empire a shadow of its former self, South Asia was vulnerable to the ambitions of the Europeans who had thus far been held at bay. In Bengal, where memories of the Anglo-Mughal War of 1686–1691 remained fresh, concern about European aggression was high, but there and among South Asia's other coastal regimes, local rulers were distracted by competition from their opportunistic neighbors and were threatened by internal rivals, both political (disgruntled relatives and heirs) and economic (opportunistic bankers and merchants). As a result, many South Asian princes entered into agreements with European merchants allowing them to profit from European trade in exchange for what seemed to be a marginal loss of sovereignty over small coastal enclaves, where they allowed Europeans to build fortress-warehouses to secure their goods against local unrest. In fact, Europeans were realizing that levying taxes on the inhabitants of these settlements and their surrounding lands might be as profitable as trade.

When local rulers saw the first signs heralding the transformation of these European settlements into bridgeheads for conquest, their response was fierce but blunted by their internal disunity and poor relations with their neighbors. Local rulers betrayed each other via what they thought would be limited alliances with the Europeans in order to gain the upper hand in their own regions. A lack of capital that a united polity might have made available to them rendered this disunity all the more dangerous. By the time a full-blown European threat materialized, Hindu, Muslim, and Sikh rulers were unable to acquire the number of advanced weapons necessary to turn it back.

But they did try. In the late 1700s, the Muslim ruler of much of the southern tip of the subcontinent, Tipu Sultan, had just enough funds to employ European military equipment and advisors to great effect against the Company. However, he raised that capital from revenues squeezed from Hindu cultivators, which undermined his legitimacy, while leaving him just short of enough weapons to ensure victory over the Company, whose hands were strengthened by their skillful turning of some of his Muslim and Hindu neighbors against him.

CHAPTER 6

From Company State to Crown Rule, 1757–1877

O n his ascension to the Mughal imperial throne in 1658, Aurangzeb took to task his boyhood tutor, Mullah Shah, for failing to inform him adequately about the world beyond his borders. Why, he asked, had his teacher dismissed the study of distant powers such as England on the mere assumption that foreign non-Muslim states could only be inferior to his own? Why had Mullah Shah failed to distinguish even between any of his empire's nearer neighbors?

> Was it not incumbent upon my preceptor to make me acquainted with the distinguishing features of every nation of the earth; its resources and strength; its mode of warfare, its manners, religion, form of government, and wherein its interests principally consist; and, by a regular course of historical reading, to render me familiar with the origin of States, their progress and decline; the events, accidents, or errors, owing to which such great changes and mighty revolutions, have been effected.[1]

That Aurangzeb had a command of world history and found his traditional education inadequate lends an air of tragedy to his troubled rule. As for the English, he was fortunate as emperor in being able to manage his relations with them to his own satisfaction. Yet these foreigners, of whom he recognized he knew too little, moved quickly to exploit the political divisions that followed his death. Most of South Asia became "British India" for almost two centuries, though the English began their conquest not as a nation but as a joint-stock company, the root of all modern corporations.[2]

In 1600, Queen Elizabeth granted a royal charter to the Governor and Company of Merchants of London Trading into the East Indies, which gave it a monopoly over England's trade with India ("India," after the region's age-old Greek designation "Indos"), China, and the lands of Southeast Asia lying between them. The queen had earlier paved the way for England's contact with the Mughal Empire. On February 12, 1583, the merchant John Newberry and a small party left London carrying a letter entreating Emperor Akbar to receive them "with kindness" and to offer "liberty and security" to any of her countrymen who may arrive in his dominions to enable them to conduct "mutual and friendly traffique of marchandize on both sides." While she was naturally concerned for the safety of her subjects in "places so distant," because of the glowing reports she received "of your imperial Maiesties humanitie in these uttermost parts of the world, we are greatly eased of that burden."[3] English traders prospered under Akbar and also under Jahangir, who gave the new Company a firman (license) providing the liberty and security Queen Elizabeth had sought. In view of this "laudable commerce," King James I sent an ambassador, Thomas Roe, to the Mughal court to formally negotiate conditions of trade.[4] Roe and Jahangir became friends, allowing Roe to gain insight into the strength of the Mughal Empire, which led him to advise his countrymen, in a letter to the Company's directors, that if they wished to prosper on the subcontinent they should respect Mughal authority and seek their profits not in territorial conquest but "at sea and in quiet trade."[5]

As early voyages of the Company's ships garnered returns of between 100 and 234 percent and thereafter could offer profits of well over 20 percent on their investment when other markets generated about 8 percent, the Company's directors had little reason to depart from Roe's advice until the revolts against Aurangzeb's regime in the later seventeenth century exposed the Company's merchants (and their profits) to anti-Mughal rebellions (the port city of Surat was sacked by Shivaji). The decline of power at the center also led to what the Company regarded as harassment by increasingly independent Mughal provincial governors and emerging Mughal successor states, who sought to squeeze revenue from European traders. The Company's futile military response, the lost Anglo-Mughal War of 1686–1690, led to a return to Roe's recommended course, but the Company's directors were beginning to see the value of converting its fortress-trading bases into sovereign territories to "procure us the liberty of collecting [from its inhabitants] such Duties as is consistent with our Methods and Rules of Government."[6] As struggles among Mughal successor states grew, the value of sovereign control of their fortress-bases and surrounding areas increased, providing a motive, or at least a rationale, for foreign conquest. By 1754, a European observer concluded "the country might be conquered and laid under contribution as easily as the Spaniards overwhelmed the naked Indians of America."[7] Fatefully, a series of conflicts fought between emerging European states during the eighteenth and early nineteenth centuries forced their trading companies into a race for dominance on the subcontinent that spurred competition for territory there. Of these struggles, the Seven Years' War (1754–1763) proved decisive.

The Seven Years' War (known as the French and Indian War in the Americas) included attempts by European states to seize their rivals' overseas colonies of settlement (such as in French Canada and the neighboring British thirteen colonies on the Atlantic) or territories in which their enemies' licensed traders held sway. In South Asia, under the leadership of Joseph-François Dupleix, the French East India Company, a royal rather than private enterprise, pursued a strategy of playing newly independent local rulers, the governors of breakaway Mughal provinces, and their competing local and internal rivals, against each other in order to gain control over them, after which they used their militaries to seize British trading bases along with British-Indian commerce. Fortunately for British interests, their own Company's agents, most famously Robert Clive, were able to turn this strategy against the French, and later used it to seize much of what today is southern India. In 1757, the richest province of the subcontinent, Bengal, fell victim to Company intrigues.

Over the next hundred years, the Company used Bengal's resources and the Company's European-trained and armed, but largely indigenous, army (recruited from the armies of the South Asian states they had bested) to gain control over much of South Asia. In the process, as much as 40 percent of the subcontinent, deemed lacking in commercial value, was left in the hands of politically subordinated rulers in what were called "Native" or "Indian Princely" States. After 1806, the Mughal emperor became no more than a nominal ruler supported by a Company pension. By 1818, the remainder of the subcontinent was under Company control, including Nepal and Sri Lanka.

On one level, this vast expansion of the Company's territory between 1757 and 1818 led to much less change than the massive loss of indigenous sovereignty would suggest. The Company held itself out as mere servants (and tax collectors) of the Mughal emperor. Its coinage featured the face of the emperor, and its administrators continued the Mughal practice of giving grants supporting Muslim and Hindu educational institutions. It even continued Mughal land assessment policies in many areas, though out of ignorance or convenience it often extracted the maximum tax permitted (as much as one-half of income), rather than employing a sliding scale downward (as in Akbar's day) to take account of poor local conditions. Company officials continued to work in partnership with Indians as bankers and brokers who served as middlemen between Company agents and the Indian producers of high-value commercial products, such as fine cotton textiles and, later, tea and opium. Company agents smoked tobacco in a hookah (water pipe) and lived in cottages adapted to the Indian climate called bungalows, which, along with other loan words such as *pajama* and *khaki* (dust-colored), passed into the English language.

The establishment of the British bridgehead in Bengal marked the beginning of a deeper process of mutual cultural discovery and exchange. It also led to a prolonged political debate that was to transform much of the subcontinent's intellectual life and expose both South Asians and the Company itself to the virtues and vices of Britain's evolution as a modern state.

The process of cultural discovery and exchange can be said to have begun with Warren Hastings, who, as the Company's first governor-general over all of its South Asian possessions, set the early tone and pace of the expansion of British authority after its conquest of Bengal. Arriving there in 1750 as a young Company clerk, Hastings had immersed himself in its languages. As governor-general (1773–1785), he supported Company scholar-administrators such as William Jones and James Prinsep, who through their study of Sanskrit discovered the existence of the Indo-European family of languages, linking Sanskrit to most European languages, including English. Further research led to the study of the sacred Upanishads, the philosophical treatise dating from the time before the rise of Buddhism. The Upanishads suggested that Hinduism possessed an underlying rationalism and a concept of a single divine spiritual consciousness. This idea helped offset prevailing British views of South Asia as a Hindu land dominated by morally debased polytheists. In time, the Upanishads would come to influence the writings of the transcendentalist poets Ralph Waldo Emerson and Walt Whitman in the United States and the philosophers Max Müller and Arnold Schopenhauer in Europe. Those scholars who engaged in East-West cross-cultural studies in the late eighteenth and early nineteenth centuries were known as Orientalists ("Orient" derives from the Latin word for east).

Given the decline of central Mughal authority and the subsequent political disunity that permitted the Company to gain dominion over the subcontinent, most Orientalists had reason to regard their own European cultures as superior to that of "India" in its current condition. But some Orientalists went further, holding that even if Europeans were presently superior to India materially, Indians were not and perhaps never had been inferior to Europe spiritually and philosophically. Charles "Hindu" Stuart, a major-general in the Company's army, who lived by Hindu customs and manners, saw parallels in the divine instructions given by Jesus and by Krishna, both of whom stressed love of God as the ultimate vehicle of salvation. Stuart concluded in his book *Vindication of the Hindoos* that "Hinduism little needs the meliorating hand of Christianity to render its votaries a sufficiently correct and moral people for all the useful purposes of a civilized society."[8] William Hodges, a well-known and well-traveled British painter living in Bengal, was a frequent visitor to mixed parties of British and Indians in Calcutta, the new capital of British-Indian enterprise. As he noted in his memoir, *Travels in India*, Hodges found it "highly entertaining to an inquisitive mind to associate with a people whose manners are more than 3,000 years old; and to observe in them that attention and polished behavior which usually marks the most highly civilized state of society."[9]

To the vast majority of South Asian leaders, both Hindu and Muslim, the Company's rise to power in the late eighteenth century constituted a direct threat to their traditional political and social dominance. However, elite businessmen, including landlords, merchants, and others benefiting from the wealth generated by commercial relations with the British, embraced the expanding Company presence in their society as they had in the past adjusted to Greek, Roman, and Arab traders and other would-be conquerors. Since Bengal was long accustomed to international trade and experienced the longest and most intense exposure to Company rule, it is not surprising that leading Bengali intellectuals, such Rammohan Roy, Henry Louis Derozio, and Ishwar Chandra Bandyopadhyay, were among the first South Asians to respond to Company raj (rule).

Like British Orientalists, Rammohan Roy saw the Upanishads as a meeting place between East and West. A social reformer as well as a philosopher, Roy saw the progressive ideas of the West (such as human equality and the stirrings of feminism) already present in the sacred tenets of Hinduism, and used that discovery to aid him in his effort to reject much of what he saw as backward Hindu customary beliefs which had no basis in divine scripture. These included the caste system, polytheism, polygamy, child marriage, dowry-giving, and sati, which was the relatively rare practice among high-caste Hindus (including his own Brahmin family) of inducing a young widow to place herself on her older husband's funeral pyre to prevent any subsequent behavior on her part that might bring discredit on his name. Roy, a patriot who foresaw the nationalist movement, was aware that admitting the backwardness of some tenets of his own religion would fuel claims of British superiority over Indians. However, he pragmatically argued, in a private letter written in 1828 to a European correspondent about the disabilities of caste, "The present system of Hindus is not well calculated to promote their political interests," making some changes were "necessary at least for the sake of their political advantage and social comfort."[10] Roy is today honored for charting a path between traditional and modern values that Mohandas Karamchand Gandhi would follow a century later in his effort to regain self-rule for the dispossessed in South Asia and elsewhere.

Henry Louis Vivian Derozio, a writer and charismatic teacher at Calcutta's Hindu College (founded in 1817), was more explicit in his concern over the weakness of "the present system of the Hindus." In the dedication to a collection of his poetry, he wrote: "My Country! In thy glory past/A beautiful halo circled around thy brow/And worshipped as a deity thou wast/Where is that glory, that reverence now?"[11] However, while Rammohan Roy sought parallels between Hindu and Western thought and defended Hinduism, but not polytheism, Derozio rejected Indian traditions and customs wholesale and espoused Western conceptions of rationalism, including atheism. He even exceeded in intellectual scope Roy's opposition to sati, arguing that "the philanthropic views of some individuals are directed to the abolition of widow burning, but they should first ensure the comfort of those unhappy women in their widowhood," which he likened to a living death:

> The most degrading and humiliating household offices must be per-
> formed by a Hindu widow; she is not allowed more food than will
> suffice to keep her alive; she must sleep upon the bare earth and suffer
> indignities from the youngest members of her family; these are only a
> few of her sufferings.[12]

Ishwar Chandra Bandyopadhyay was given the title of Vidyasagar (Ocean of Wisdom) for his great learning. He so admired the high quality of European rationalist thought that he introduced Francis Bacon and other British philosophers into the curricula of Calcutta's Sanskrit College (founded in 1824). His interest in social reform and in the abolition of sati was even deeper than Derozio's: he married his own son to a Hindu widow and successfully campaigned for a public law sanctioning the remarriage of Hindu widows. Roy, Derozio, and Vidyasagar represented a wide-ranging process of cultural reexamination and self-renewal similar to that of the European Renaissance, with Bengal serving in the role of Italy and Calcutta as Florence. Like innovative thinkers in Europe such as Galileo Galilei, imprisoned for arguing that the earth orbited the sun, both Derozio and Vidyasagar lost their teaching positions for taking their engagement with Western knowledge too far.

However, for British politicians in Parliament seeking to transform South Asia along Western lines, neither Orientalist bridge-builders nor even Derozio had gone far enough. The expansion of the Company's territorial acquisitions had from the first attracted the interest of these leaders. They accused Company agents, including Robert Clive, of wrongly enriching themselves with war booty and otherwise siphoning off the Company's profits. In his successful defense, Clive first reminded his critics of his own efforts to stem frauds against the Company that the Company itself refused to pursue. As to his alleged greed, he sought to make them understand how he felt in the aftermath of his decisive victory over the nawab (governor) of Bengal at Plassey in 1757 that

Sati *is the Sanskrit word for "good woman" or "true wife." It refers to Hindu widows who, according to tradition, allow themselves to be burned to death on their husbands' funeral pyres. This rare practice was largely suppressed in the nineteenth century, when paintings on this controversial subject were made to be sold locally for British buyers curious about the custom. Very isolated instances of* sati *still occur in South Asia today, though it is prohibited by law.* ©Victoria and Albert Museum, London, AL.8805 secured for the Company the richest lands on the subcontinent. At that time, the treasury of Bengal was thrown open to him. He then walked alone through its vaults "piled with gold and jewels on either hand." Given what he saw there and what he seized, he remarked, "I stand astonished at my moderation."[13] He was knighted by the king, though Parliament responded by giving more power, but with tighter controls, to Clive's successor, Warren Hastings, who was expected to curtail these abuses.

Warren Hastings, who admired Indian statecraft as well as its literature, succeeded in further securing the Company's interests, but Parliament accused him of acting too much like a ruthless Indian prince during his successful effort to destroy an almost overwhelming combination of local rulers and French forces arrayed against him. Thereafter, Parliament chose a very upright Englishman, Lord Charles Cornwallis, to succeed Hastings as governor-general (1786–1793) and charged him with running the Company's administration along more European lines. Cornwallis was a friend of the Orientalist Hastings. But in America, where his forces had been defeated by American revolutionaries, he established a reputation for obeying his orders, and did so in India. He ended corruption among the Company's agents by raising their wages. He created a solid base for British rule by securing the financial well-being of Bengal's zamindars (tax collectors), whom he mistook for high-ranking Mughal aristocrats. He was as crafty as Warren Hastings in expanding Company rule, but unlike his friend, he understood Parliament's desire to raise the moral tenor above what it believed were the low standards of Indian politics. He acted with utter disrespect for anything tainted with Indian customs, though these provided for "modern" concepts such as private property rights. To guarantee that the Company was free of that taint, he removed Indians from the Company's higher administration in Bengal.

The drive to impose British values over Indian customs was rooted in more than a perceived need to establish Parliament's control over the Company's possessions. Britain emerged from the wars of the later eighteenth century as the world's leading military power, but it was riven by internal divisions over the moral and political ideas that should guide the British state in the future. The clearest of these divisions was between two schools of thought, utilitarianism and evangelism. Utilitarianism was promoted by the philosopher and social reformer Jeremy Bentham. It was an anti-traditionalist, radically rationalist, scientific, and secular approach to social transformation. Its emphasis on social discipline was in tune with Britain's evolving industrial economy, while its emphasis on efficiency reflected Britain's emerging "modern" values. Evangelicals rejected the radicalism of utilitarianism, in part because its underlying rationalism and secularism were too much like the values of the chaotic and destructive French Revolution. They were more concerned with the conversion of Britons and their non-Christian subject peoples to God's true cause as they saw it.

The leaders of the British government were both too cautious and too secular to hastily adopt either utilitarianism or evangelical philosophy in their most uncompromising forms, but they were quite willing to permit their advocates to apply their views in South Asia. Parliament modified the Royal Charter (the Charter Act of 1813), under which the Company operated, to permit Christian missionaries to preach actively in its territories. Following the Benthamite preference for laissez-faire or free-market economics, Parliament also ended much of the Company's trade monopoly; henceforth the Company's profits were chiefly derived from land and other local revenue sources.

After 1818, the tenor of the Company's administration increasingly ran along the lines set by Jeremy Bentham's close friend and fellow utilitarian, James Mill. Mill sought to sweep away Orientalist ideas that respected traditional Indian customs and languages as an indirect means of attacking traditional culture in Britain. In his immensely influential three-volume *History of British India* (1818), Mill created a vision of Indian barbarian backwardness which he extended to Britons who held fast to traditional values. He made fun of Orientalists, like William Jones, who believed that Hindu autocratic government and Brahmanical authority had always been "limited by law" and by "artfully" constructed "checks and balances." Mill scoffed, "As if a despotism limited by law were not a contradiction in terms." He dismissed as misguided the thought that Indians had ever achieved anything of value in human history. He urged that Indians should be raised up by gradual exposure to European ideas, this being "the best option" next to importing vast numbers of Britons to the subcontinent via "colonization."[14]

The influence of Mill on Company policy became apparent at a dinner honoring the Company's new governor-general, William Bentinck, during which Bentinck gestured toward Mill and said, "I am going to British India; but I shall not be Governor-General. It is you that will be Governor-General."[15] True to his word, once in India, Bentinck condemned sati. In doing so, Bentinck wrote, "I feel as a good legislator for Hindus, and as, I believe, many enlightened Hindus think and feel." He brushed off wider Hindu public opinion opposed to the legislation when he outlawed the practice in 1829. Later, when the conqueror and chief administrator of Sindh, Sir Charles Napier, met with an Indian delegation complaining about this interference by one country in another's customs, he brusquely remarked, "You say that it is your custom to burn widows. Very well. But my nation has also a custom. When men burn women alive, we hang them and confiscate their property."[16] Bentinck and Napier understood that such means were authoritarian but were convinced that by helping India discard its "darker" traditions, they were paving the way for its "political liberty" and a European-style nationality, a belief that came to be called "liberal imperialism."[17]

Fatefully, by 1835, Bentinck had on his own governing council Thomas Babington Macaulay, who had a great flare for expressing his and Bentinck's liberal imperialist views. Macaulay was no less a utilitarian than James Mill, but questioned the rank imperial impulse inherent in both utilitarianism and evangelicalism. Previously, as a member of Parliament, Macaulay had successfully argued that the Company's compact (the Charter Act of 1833) be further amended to read that no subject of the Company would be "debarred from holding any office under the Company by reason of his religion, place of birth, descent or colour."[18] To his mind, this ruling established that evolving British ideas of free trade, freedom from government interference in commerce, and liberty should put an end to the idea "that [Indians] might continue to be our slaves. . . . To trade with civilized men is infinitely more profitable than to govern savages."[19]

But civilized they must be. Two years later, while Macaulay was serving in India with Bentinck, the two men agreed that the medium of the English language was the best vehicle for raising up the Indian character. Macaulay's "Minute on Education" (1835) aided Bentinck in securing legislation making English the official language of the Company's courts (replacing the Mughal customary use of Persian), and requiring that Company grants in support of higher education be devoted to English instruction. This approach, called "Anglicization," much like the abolition of sati, aroused Indian public opposition, but Macaulay was looking to the day when all Indians, led by "a class of persons Indian in blood and colour, but English in tastes, in opinions, in morals and in intellect . . . began to demand European institutions," which, he believed, "would be the proudest day in English history."[20]

The passage of the Charter Act of 1833 and the sponsorship by many wealthy Indians of English-language education and cultural exchange (Shakespeare's plays were performed by Indians in Indian languages by the 1850s) established important precedents in British-Indian cultural exchange. Yet Bentinck and Macaulay's vision of a future Europeanized sovereign India achieved through Macaulay's vision of a hybrid class of Indians sharing European values and its people as partners in commerce was judged far too liberal for the times.

From the 1770s to the 1850s, the Company, under the increasing control of Parliament, had regularized and expanded its administration in keeping with British needs and interests alone. By the 1840s, Orientalist and liberal ideas such as those embedded in the Charter Act of 1833 had been brushed aside. Aggressive military action was taken by governors general sent from Britain to secure territory in South Asia best suited to commercial exploitation by Britons for Britons. Sindh and all the lands along the Indus River were initially conquered under the false impression that this river was navigable by steamships. An exaggerated fear of Russian domination of Afghanistan, then unfounded, led to an invasion of that country that led to the massacre of an entire Company army during its retreat from Afghan territory (1839–1842). Coastal Burma was taken by force (1824–1826) in response to Burmese thoughts of expansion in South Asia, but that campaign, while ultimately successful, was nearly as disastrous as the Afghan War. A Second Burmese War (1852) expanded that foothold by "gunboat diplomacy," a term coined because that conflict was forced upon the Burmese by the provocative action of the Company's naval forces.

In the mid- to late 1850s, the British desire for a more rational exploitation of Indian lands led to their annexation of several Indian Princely States long allied with the Company via the employment of novel political theories, such as the "doctrine of lapse,"[21] which were developed solely to invalidate treaties long secured by Indian customary law. The underhanded means used to annex the Kingdom of Oudh in north central India (1854) were collectively described by its sympathetic British commissioner, Henry Lawrence, as "the most unrighteous act ever committed."[22] Such actions were accompanied by or added to previous assaults on local custom. The abolition of sati had been followed by a series of further regulations, such as the Hindu Widows' Remarriage Act (1856), which traditional leaders regarded as a deliberate effort to destroy caste and spur the conversion of Indians to Christianity. Henry Lawrence in Oudh was one of a number of officials who warned that Indians could not be expected to long endure such treatment, but most resident Britons were confident of their mastery over the subcontinent. As one British woman raised in Delhi later noted in her memoirs, "no anxiety or fear . . . ever entered anybody's mind, and we considered ourselves as safe there as if we were in London."[23]

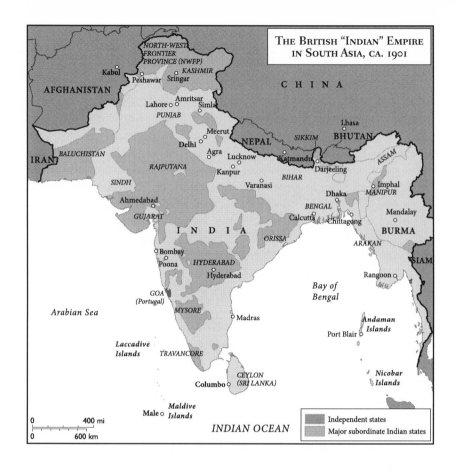

In May 1857, festering discontent broke into a massive and violent revolt that spread across most of the northern and central portions of the subcontinent. The British came to call this revolt "the Great Mutiny" or "the Sepoy Rebellion" because it was ignited by resistance among sepoys (Indian soldiers, from the Persian word *sepahi*) to biting the end off of newly issued paper rifle cartridges as part of a loading process that would maximize the efficiency of a new model of rifle. The soldiers believed—correctly, as it turned out—that the imported cartridges were coated in Britain with a greasy preservative derived from beef and pork fat. Hindu soldiers feared the loss of caste status associated with eating or touching beef to the lips, while the Qur'an prohibited Muslims from ingesting pork products. High-caste sepoys were now vulnerable to such insults as "What caste are you of, who bite pig's grease and cow's fat on your cartridges?"[24]

This was not the only grievance of the sepoys. Many were angered at a new regulation embedded in the recent General Service Enlistment Act (1856) which required recruits to serve overseas, despite a caste proscription against such travel, leading sepoys to join the growing number of Indians who believed that the British were out to degrade their religious practice and speed their conversion to Christianity. Further, many sepoys had been in the service of the deposed king of Oudh, and were angered at the injustice of the state's annexation. As one sepoy, Sita Ram, later remarked, the "seizing of Oudh filled the minds of the sepoys with distrust and led them to plot against the Government."[25]

The Company's overconfident administrators and army officers failed to defuse these concerns. The Company's army ordered mass dismissals of Indian troops unwilling to use the new cartridges. It was that act that helped spark a general rebellion, which was taken up by all those who had suffered, or were most threatened, by British rule, and also by those eager to use the resulting disturbed conditions to settle old scores among themselves. In the resulting malestrum, hundreds of

Accused Indian "mutineers" are summarily executed by being blown from cannons. Though showing events in 1857–1858, this image was painted in 1884, and the artist, Vassili Verestchagin, depicted British uniforms in use at that time.
Library of Congress LC-USZ62-117473

resident British officers and civilian men, women, and children were caught up in the violence and slain out of anger at the growing unsympathetic and invasive nature of British rule.

For a variety of reasons, this rebellion, now commonly called the War of 1857, failed to drive the British off the subcontinent. No leader emerged to unite Muslim and Hindu soldiery against British rule or to coordinate military operations. In the old Mughal capital of Delhi, an aged descendent of the Mughal line, Emperor Bahadur Shah Zafar, was persuaded to serve as a rallying point, but this had little effect, as neither Sikhs nor Hindus anticipated any benefits accruing from a revival of the long-decrepit Mughal state. Along the coast and near major port cities, India's commercial elites sufficiently benefited from the increased access to global markets that they remained loyal to Company rule, as did some Indian princes still on their thrones who sought to profit from the eventual defeat of their traditional princely enemies who had joined the revolt. For their part, the Company's British soldiery rallied quickly, backed by ethnic and religious minorities, such as the Sikhs, who had little to gain from Muslim or Hindu rule. The Company's forces also benefited from the diversion to India of a large British force sailing through southern Asian waters on the way to attack China. The British response was accompanied by terrifying reprisals. Hundreds of prisoners, many of whom were rounded up in the countryside on mere suspicion of being involved in the revolt, were formed into groups and hung from gallows or lined up and tied with their backs to the mouths of cannons and dismembered as the guns were fired off one by one.

In the aftermath of the revolt, which was quelled within a year, the British government blamed the Indian people for what they saw as a barbaric betrayal of British trust. They also blamed the Company for the disastrous policies Parliament's hand-picked governors general had pursued. The Company's affairs were wound up and the administration of British India, now including the subcontinent of India, the Maldives, Nepal, Sri Lanka, and much of Burma, became the responsibility of a secretary of state for India responsible to Parliament.

Fearing too great a backlash among loyal Indians, liberal politicians reasserted the right of Indians to have a voice in their own government (the Queen's Proclamation of 1858), as guaranteed in the Charter Act of 1833. They argued that the absence of these voices precluded an awareness of the depth of unrest that might have prevented the revolt of 1857. Yet again, this call went ignored; a few small advisory councils were created (the Indian Councils Act of 1861), but its members were not representative of Indian public opinion. The introduction of European science knowledge, administration, industry, and commercial development of resources continued apace with no consultation with and little regard for Indian sensibilities or interests.

By the mid-1860s, the development of South Asia's resources was being carried out in keeping with a growing belief among rapidly industrializing nations from Britain to Japan that national power lay in manufacturing at home, which required getting access to cheap raw materials abroad, or denying them to rivals. Europeans became convinced that an industrial economy required a colonial policy, and that view helped spur the conquest of new colonies and the consolidation of old ones. In British India and elsewhere, that process was facilitated by the development of the primary tools of modern empire-building: steamships, advances in tropical medicine, and, perhaps most important, the machine gun (invented by an American, Hiram Maxim).[26] This emerging "new imperialism" was justified by pseudo-scientific racial rationales. One of these was social Darwinism, according to which members of the human species were thought to be engaged in "a struggle for survival of the fittest," though most Europeans saw this struggle not in terms of natural selection but as "who had the Maxim gun and who had not."[27]

Accordingly, in the first decades following the War of 1857, the perceived needs of British industrial production, backed by the latest racial theories, were applied across the subcontinent to the detriment of most South Asians. Despite Britain's purported commitment to free trade, it sought to control commerce across the Indian Ocean as had the Portuguese, and in this and other ways it limited the subcontinent's access to its once-vibrant overseas trade. The Indian traders and entrepreneurs who had helped make the Company rich had insufficient capital to be seen as valued major partners in British commercial enterprises.[28] Self-interested factory owners in Manchester, Britain's manufacturing hub, secured the passage of humanitarian legislation designed to make rising Indian-owned factories less competitive (by shortening their hours of work and other measures), which led Indian mill hands to complain in a newspaper article that "Manchester is indeed, extremely kind to our work people, but it is the kindness that kills."[29] Together with other steps, such as flooding Indian markets with cheap British manufactured goods, including textiles made of Indian cotton, British rule ensured that some of the subcontinent's once most productive cities became depopulated due to the loss of local industry.

The British also managed the South Asian natural environment for their profit. In order to reserve India's forests for future commercial exploitation, the government of India criminalized the activities of the thousands of woodland people who depended upon them for their live-lihoods. To provide the infrastructure needed by the expanding British Empire, British agents used false promises of riches to be earned to lure thousands of poverty-stricken Indians to labor on railroad building pro-jects or plantations in Sri Lanka, Fiji, Trinidad, and East Africa. Few such workers would ever earn even the price of a return ticket. Thousands of British troops served on the subcontinent to guard against any further unrest, while South Asian soldiers were deployed in support of colonial wars from Africa to China, all at the Indian taxpayer's expense.

Also significant in terms of the subcontinent's long-term develop-ment was the doctrinaire introduction of the machinery of the modern state without consideration for Indian circumstances. The rigid applica-tion in India of the British census system fixed with the force of modern law what had been a more fluid caste hierarchy, thus reducing caste mobility and hardening caste identity and caste competition. It also deepened divisions between Hindus and Muslims. Moreover, British census categories and related population studies included European fads, such as phrenology, in which human intelligence and behavior were believed to be determinable by the shape of the human skull.

Pseudo-scientific theories combined with racial theories to place South Asians across the region outside of the social circle of the resi-dent British elite. British officials and their families increasingly lived apart from Indian communities in self-contained enclaves called "civil lines" replete with housing, clubs, and tennis courts, away from city centers and near to British military cantonments. This insularity was encouraged by the opening of the Suez Canal and the arrival of steam-ship travel in the Red Sea and the Indian Ocean in the 1860s, which swelled the numbers of British women traveling to India in search of husbands from among the well-paid British Indian civil servants. This "fishing fleet" was expected to instill British domesticity into the homes of resident officials. As a result, Britons in India increasingly saw them-selves bound to (temporary) exile, serving in only the dimmest and most distant of hopes of actually bringing civilization to Indians who had murdered so many of their predecessors, a view that served to justify near-apartheid British and Indian social relations until the end of British rule.

Despite the growing alienation between Britons and their subject peoples, the post-Mutiny expansion and consolidation of British rule inevitably required a vast bureaucracy that would be too expensive to staff with officials from Europe, so a small but increasing number of Western-educated South Asians were admitted into the lower ranks of government as judges and administrators. Haunted by living memories of the War of 1857 and now driven by fears that Indians might replace them, most British administrators and other British residents in India socially shunned these Indians, much to the latter's displeasure. After a brief sojourn in India, a British imperial handyman, Colonel Charles "Chinese" Gordon, criticized the British failure to better utilize the administrative skills of Indians and the racial antipathy they directed toward them. In a letter to his friend, Florence Nightingale, who was also deeply concerned over racism in India, he complained that Britons in India "know nothing of the hearts and minds of [their] subject people," who, having been excluded from the wealth generated by their rulers, "may hope to gain more from our disasters than our prosperity. . . . We are not far off losing [India] and the sooner the better."[30] His words proved prophetic.

Toward Freedom,
1877–1947

In 1877, Benjamin Disraeli, the British Conservative prime minister, arranged for Parliament to proclaim Queen Victoria as Empress of India in an attempt to strengthen the link between the British monarchy and Britain's imperial ambitions. The queen had long taken an interest in Indian culture. She studied Urdu and dined on Indian food prepared by a *munshi* (clerk) in her home at Windsor Castle. She also took an interest in the region's politically emasculated, but still colorful, indigenous royalty. In the wake of the celebration of the queen's new title, her son the Prince of Wales (Edward VII) made a tour of South Asia. He was impressed by his nation's material achievement there, particularly its railroads and modern ports, but was shocked by the "rude and rough manner" of British officials in advising its surviving aristocrats, his mother's favorites. He was also offended by the "disgraceful usage of nigger" by South Asia's British residents. In his view, just "because a man has a black face and a different religion from one's own, there is no reason why he should be treated like a brute."[1]

In a sense, the Prince of Wales had identified the reason why, at the very moment of Disraeli's celebration of India's place as the brightest jewel in the queen's imperial crown, the prospects of Britain's Indian empire were beginning to fade. Unwittingly, Britain's effort to consolidate its rule via increased transportation and communication was speeding the development of a national consciousness. Its post–Great Mutiny effort to lower the status of traditional South Asian leaders had created a political vacuum, clearing the way for the emergence of new leadership whose growing national identity undermined British authority. This new leadership arose out of a growing Western-educated Indian middle class called "New India"[2] by a few far-sighted officials willing to acknowledge the rise of indigenous political aspirations for self-rule. But British self-interest, compounded by racist values, made conflict between the British and their South Asian subjects inevitable.

South Asia's anti-colonialist and nationalist stirrings, among the first arising in Europe's overseas possessions, were stimulated by the work of a new generation of intellectuals. Among them was the Muslim intellectual Sayyid Ahmed Khan, the author of *The Causes of the Indian Revolt* (1858), who blamed the "Mutiny" on unethical British policy. He also championed Western-style scientific education, as did Sayyid Jamal ad-Din al-Afghani, who produced a synthesis of modernist and Salafist outlooks. Though born in Iran in 1838, al-Afghani studied in India in the years before and after the Great Mutiny to gain knowledge of modern European science. He then visited the Ottoman Empire, arguing that a return to the older forms and practices of Islam, together with the adoption of Western technological innovations, would enable the Islamic world to revive itself without sacrificing its religious convictions to secular modernization. "It is not," he wrote, "that religious beliefs are opposed to culture and material progress," but the false belief that they do, "which prohibits learning of sciences, earning one's livelihood and the ways of culture."[3] In 1866, followers of the Muslim Salafist philosopher Shah Waliullah created a madrasa (school) in Deoband, near Delhi, where they combined their resistance to religious pluralism (no compromise with Hindu and Christian ideas) with their opposition to British imperialism, which they believed oppressed Muslims globally.

In 1893, Swami Vivekananda, acting as a representative of Hinduism at the World's Parliament of Religions in Chicago, delivered an electrifying speech representing the Hindu faith, which he opened by saying, "I am proud to belong to a religion which has taught the world both tolerance and universal acceptance."[4] In 1876, Dadabhai Naoroji, a leading Parsi of Bombay (the Parsi were descendants of Zoroastrians who had fled Persia at the time of the Muslim conquest in 642–651 CE), gave a speech in Bombay that became an influential study, *Poverty and un-British Rule in India*, in which he championed the idea that poverty in India was not the result of overpopulation or even "the pitiless operations of economic laws, but . . . the pitiless action of British policy; it is the pitiless eating of India's substance in India and further pitiless drain [of its wealth] to England."[5] This "drain theory" of colonial underdevelopment (poverty among the colonized was due to the extraction of their fiscal and material resources by colonial powers) became a standard critique of imperialism in South Asia adopted by nationalist movements the world over. In 1909, Vinayak Damodar Savakar offered an analysis of the War of 1857 that attempted to prove that it was not a

"DISPUTED EMPIRE!"

The Indian famine of 1877–1878 was so horrific and so much a product of British economic policy that cartoons critical of British Indian policy appeared in the British press. Punch, vol. 72 (London: Bradbury, Agnew & Co., Printers, Whitefriars, 1877), 427 mere rebellion but the Indian War of Independence of 1857. This interpretation of that event was influenced by his study of the American and French revolutions and, like Naoroji's work, served as a useful nationalist critique of foreign rule.[6]

During the late nineteenth and early twentieth centuries, South Asians of all philosophic stripes asserted with increasing confidence that they were the moral, intellectual, and cultural equals of their British rulers and Western culture at large, reflecting the belief among its middle class that the achievement of a modern national identity, such as the one possessed by their colonial masters, was within their reach. This outlook was reinforced by their growing command of British political ideals and also by contemporary European developments, such as the demand for "home rule" in Ireland and the rise to nationhood of Italy, whose diverse population had not possessed a common identity until inspired by nationalists to join together to throw off their foreign masters.

Aggressive imperial policy on South Asia's frontiers by British Conservative Party politicians stimulated nationalist sentiment in India. Conservatives supported a second invasion of Afghanistan in 1878 and annexed what remained of independent Burma in 1885 in order to thwart what proved to be largely imagined expansionist thrusts by Russia and France, respectively. When Indian-owned newspapers complained about Indian taxpayers paying for such imperial adventurism, British administrators passed legislation muzzling the press and restricting other civil liberties that Western-educated Indians had enjoyed. These repressive actions backfired, raising the ire of the Indian-owned press and regional political associations. When members of these associations learned that the Indian government's Famine Fund had been emptied to cover the expenses of the final conquest and pacification of Burma, they joined to create the Indian National Congress (1885), which was to serve as the umbrella organization under which most South Asians began their quest for political freedom. It also served as the prototype for the African National Congress in South Africa.

Searching for a counterweight to the outspokenness of their largely middle-class, Western-educated Indian critics, the British began elevating the status of the traditional South Asian aristocracy, which they had shunned after the War of 1857. They showered these nobles with hollow awards, such as grand military honors, a process later labeled "ornamentalism."[7] The British also became more alert to ways in which they could benefit from traditional Hindu-Muslim divisions. They shunned overt divide-and-rule tactics: communal violence, once ignited, might be

This group photograph records the delegates at the first meeting of the Indian National Congress in 1885. In the center is Allan Octavian Hume, a cofounder of the organization and one of a few former British-Indian officials who embraced the Indian nationalist cause. H. P. Mody, *Sir Pherozeshah Mehta: A Political Biography* (Bombay: Times Press, 1921)

beyond their ability to control. However, they did little to resolve these divisions in the self-interested belief that nothing could resolve them.

A few liberal-minded British officials, some with ties to or experience of conditions on the subcontinent, and well known to each other, attempted to anticipate and even advance India's political development. Lord Ripon, secretary of state for India (1874–1880) and viceroy of India (1880–1884), established the building blocks of democracy at the local level (Resolution on Self-Government, 1882). He also introduced legislation giving Indian judges jurisdiction in areas in which they could judge crimes of Europeans against Indians (the Ilbert Bill).[8] Lord Lansdowne, a parliamentary undersecretary to Ripon (1880) and viceroy (1888–1894), after consulting with Ripon, championed the expansion of British India's existing small advisory provincial and imperial legislative councils via the election of Indian members and giving them the power to debate British administrative policies (the Indian Councils Act of 1892).

Lansdowne's grandfather had helped draft the Company Charter Act of 1833, promising that Indians would be eligible for government employment. That promise, Lansdowne believed, had been so long unfilled in any meaningful way as to become a danger to the British Raj.

Correctly gauging the frustrations of Western-educated Indians seeking "a greater role in the governing of their own country," Lansdowne warned in his correspondence with the secretary of state for India that unless these aspirations were met, Britain faced political agitation in India that "would likely gain strength" and would inevitably lead to reforms being "extorted from us."[9] Lord Minto (viceroy 1905–1910), an aide-de-camp to Lansdowne in Canada, helped secure a major expansion of the 1892 reform scheme and the appointment of two Indians to the secretary of state for India's own council in London (the Indian Councils Act of 1909).

All three reformers met overwhelming opposition among British officials in India, which, Minto admitted in a letter to the secretary of state for India, was rooted in "our own inherent prejudice against another race."[10] That opposition was supported by the dominant Conservative Party in Parliament, guided by its prime minister, Lord Salisbury. Upon learning that Dadabhai Naoroji was planning to run as a Liberal Party candidate in the next British elections, Salisbury declared in a speech that he would "never countenance the seating of a Black Man" in Parliament.[11] This opposition succeeded in so weakening Ripon's reforms and the Councils Acts of 1892 and 1909 that they proved, as Lansdowne feared, to be too little and too late to meet the rising political aspirations and economic concerns of Western-educated Indians.

In an attempt to break the opposition to Indian political reform in Britain, the Indian National Congress made alliances with Irish home-rulers in the British Parliament and also gained strength from the outcome of the Russo-Japanese War, in which an Asian power defeated a European imperial state in 1905. Nationalist-minded Indians faced opposition not only from the British imperial state, but also from within their own movement. They were aware that most of their movement's leaders were drawn from a Western-educated middle class arising from the most privileged social orders, which Lansdowne's predecessor as viceroy, the Marquis of Dufferin and Ava, dismissed in a dinner speech as a "microscopic minority."[12] However, their numbers were growing rapidly and the benefits they derived from British rule, such as Western education, rail transportation, and other trappings of modern technology, had both encouraged a sense of national unity and provided the means of communication to rally their people to recover their lost sovereignty. If they initially addressed issues of concern, such as admission to places in government, mostly to the Western-educated elite, the Indian National Congress's attacks on British economic policy and its criticism of the use of the British Indian Army as an engine of imperialism elsewhere in the empire won public support and laid the foundation for mass political action.

The Indian National Congress also had to confront the traditional ethnic and religious divisions among Indians. Many Muslims and other minority groups saw little future in a new Hindu-majority nation whose policies were decided by "one man, one vote." Further, in the first decade of the twentieth century, moderate Congress leaders who sought increased power through gradual and peaceful constitutional change faced stiff competition from more extreme nationalist factions who sought immediate *swaraj* (self-rule) and encouraged the action of assassins and suicide bombers, both men and women, who killed British officials at work or in their racially exclusive clubs. The ablest representative of these factions, the ardent Hindu nationalist Bal Gangadhar Tilak, imprisoned from 1908 to 1914 for encouraging such violence, denied he had done so but thereafter won fame for his declaration that "*Swaraj* is my birthright, and I shall have it!"[13]

The outbreak of the First World War in 1914 forced the British to take a "different angle of vision"[14] toward Indian political affairs such that implied support for the postwar movement toward Tilak's goal of self-government. They had little choice but to do so, as Britain desperately needed Indian troops to blunt the early German offensive in Belgium and northern France and to use against the Ottoman Empire when the Ottomans decided to ally themselves with the German and Austrian cause. It also needed to forge a united war effort among its major colonies, all of which were populated by white settlers and all of which, save India, were self-governing. Angered by such patent inequality, Tilak and Annie Besant, a firebrand, sari-clad longtime resident and newspaper editor in India, founded Home Rule Leagues, which demanded self-government within the empire, not in return for their loyalty, but in recognition of India's place as an equal partner in empire. Their efforts won the support of many Hindus and Muslims, including a rising young Muslim leader, Muhammad Ali Jinnah. However, criticism of the British administration in India, at least initially, was tempered by the belief that Britain's touted new angle of vision would lead to a major advance toward the desired goal at the end of the war. Most Indians, regardless of their status or political affiliation, would support the transfer of Indian revenue to Britain to aid in the war and help recruit the approximately one million Indian troops that eventually fought on all fronts, of whom fifty thousand were killed and seventy thousand were wounded.

Indian Muslim soldiers guard the Mosque of Omar in Jerusalem in 1917. Approximately one million Indian troops served in virtually every theater of combat in the First World War. Library of Congress LC-DIG-ppmsca-13291-00042

The first of 28,500 Indian soldiers arrived on the western front in September and October 1914. They served to blunt the initial German advance through Belgium and into France, having arrived "just in time" to save the British position in Flanders, where British troops were heavily outnumbered by German forces.[15] They fought in the battles of Ypres, Loos, and Neuve Chapelle, among others, winning the first two Victoria Crosses issued to Indians in the war. In addition to being among the first to encounter modern trench warfare, Indian sepoys were compelled to serve under officers who could not speak their languages, as their own British Indian army officers were killed in the war's initial bloody campaigns. When these conditions began to eat away at their efficiency, they were shifted to Africa and the Middle East to join Indian units fighting there and once again performed superbly, even in defeat, as much of the Indian Expeditionary Force deployed to Mesopotamia under British army command was destroyed at the First Battle of Kut in 1915–1916 due to the British government's over-eagerness to take Baghdad. However, the highest casualty rate among Indian forces committed to battle was at Gallipoli, where 1,624 of the 3,000 Indian combatants were killed or wounded. Indian letters written on the battlefield described "poisonous gases, bombs, machine guns which fire 700 bullets per minute, large and small cannon throwing [huge] cannon balls . . . Zeppelins, large and small flying machines which throw bombs from the air . . . liquid fire that causes the body to ignite." One Punjabi soldier wrote home: "No man can return to the Punjab whole. Only the broken limbed can go back." Another Indian soldier wrote, "In one hour 10,000 men are killed. What more can I write?"[16]

On the Indian home front, the Indian National Congress and the Muslim League's united support of the war helped effect a subsidence of domestic terrorism. There was limited violent extremist action in Bengal, and there was the small but active revolutionary Ghadar (Mutiny) Movement, which rallied Indian opposition to British rule in California, Singapore, and the Punjab. However, British administrators publicly attributed these signs of discontent to anarchists in the pay of Germany (which did attempt to supply them with arms). There was no stoppage in the export of strategically vital food and war materiel for the Allied war effort. However, while South Asia itself emerged virtually unscathed physically from the war (some coastal shipping was sunk and coastal cities were briefly bombarded by the German cruiser *Emden*), millions of Indian civilians endured a reduced standard of living, and some areas experienced famine due to food shortages and high prices driven by wartime exports and the diversion of public and private money to the war effort.

By the autumn of 1916, with no end of the war in sight and its costs to Indians rising, the Indian National Congress, the Muslim League, and leading Indian nationalist newspapers began asking for some sign that the British intended to make good on their promises of postwar political reform. When these requests were rebuffed, Hindu and Muslim nationalists agreed in Lucknow in northern India to promote a proposal of their own—the Joint Congress-Muslim League Scheme—that overcame past political divisions over majority-minority representation between the two communities. It also introduced a plan that would result in elected majorities of Indians in the legislatures of their own country (the Lucknow Pact—destined to be the high wartermark of Hindu-Muslim political accord). Indian nationalists went on to establish this scheme as the vehicle for eventually securing Indian autonomy within the empire and the bare minimum they would accept with regard to postwar reforms.

In the face of such pressure, the viceroy, Lord Chelmsford (1916–1921), and his executive council were willing to introduce some degree of reform but would not agree to the elected Indian majorities in India's legislatures. They viewed elected Indian legislative majorities as bringing an early end to British rule, which many of Chelmsford's colleagues believed was premature given India's need for at least a generation of further British tutelage. Sir Afsar Ali Baig, the only Indian on a committee advising the secretary of state in London on the Chelmsford administration's reform policy, accurately observed that this view—when taken to its extreme, as some members of the viceroy's council were determined to do—would mean that "India may be effectively shut out from any reasonable prospect, proximate or remote, of ever becoming a self-governing unit of the Empire."[17]

Yet, much to Chelmsford's frustration, he found the government in London too preoccupied by the war to allow them to seriously consider any reform scheme they developed. Handcuffed by this decision and embarrassed by increasingly virulent Indian criticism of its failure to act on the issue of political reform, the Indian government decided in June 1917 to crack down on Indian unrest in order to preserve its authority. This included the internment without a hearing of the then seventy-year-old Annie Besant, an act that some British officials recognized beforehand would only raise her political profile and that of her own and Tilak's Home Rule Leagues. They were right. Soon-to-be leading figures in the nationalist movement, including Tej Bahadur Sapru, C. R. Das, Sarojini Naidu (the remarkable nationalist poet who would one day become the first woman to be the governor of an Indian state), and Rabindranath Tagore (the first South Asian winner of the Nobel Prize, for literature), then formally joined the leagues. Besant was elected president of the Congress later that year.

With the political situation in India fast deteriorating and India's support for the war still vital, the secretary of state for India, Edwin Samuel Montagu, announced in Parliament on August 20, 1917, that henceforth the aim of British policy was "the increasing association of Indians in every branch of the administration and the gradual development of self-governing institutions, with a view to the progressive realization of responsible government in India as an integral part of the British Empire."[18] Much to the delight of Indian moderates and extremists alike, Montagu followed these remarks by coming to India at the head of a delegation that would meet with Indian leaders across the subcontinent, as well as the viceroy and other officials "on the spot" in an effort to draw up legislation designed to further that goal. At the start of these discussions, Besant, who was released from internment on Montagu's order, read a welcoming address. Tilak, having been released from jail in 1914, but closely watched, placed the traditional Indian welcome of a garland of flowers around Montagu's neck. Not everyone present at these acts of mutual respect and accommodation was pleased by them. Sir Malcolm Seton, an adviser to the secretary of state for India who was opposed to political reform in India, composed a letter after witnessing these events in which he bitterly remarked, "That I would live to see a Secretary of State garlanded by Bal Gangadhar Tilak!"[19]

In fact, even before Montagu's arrival, members of his own delegation, like Seton, were prepared to join with high officials in India and conservative politicians in Britain to undermine Montagu and Chelmsford's progressive efforts, much as these factions had undermined the liberal spirit of the Council reforms of 1892 and 1909. They achieved this goal. When the Montagu-Chelmsford (or Montford) reforms eventually passed into law as the Government of India Act of 1919, it came as an embarrassment to both moderate and extremist Congress leaders who had believed that British pledges would be redeemed with more substantial postwar reforms, which even British officials in India admitted was a reasonable assumption. The reforms offered only very limited power-sharing at the provincial level and continued the British practice of providing separate electorates for Hindus and Muslims that threatened the unity that Hindu and Muslim leaders had forged during the war. It left nationalists divided into a variety of factions over how best to respond to them: to reject the scheme outright was ungenerous, given the genuine effort Montagu had made to overcome official opposition to reform, but to accept proposals that fell so far short of their own wartime proposals was a bitter pill to swallow. In a speech made at the special session of the Indian National Congress held in 1918 to consider the options, Tilak expressed the view of Annie Besant and many other leaders of Congress that the reforms were "disappointing and unsatisfactory." He saw them, as had Sir Afsar Ali Baig, as reflecting the views of diehard British Indian officials who would delay real progress toward self-government for at least a decade and perhaps a generation.[20]

The strength of the conservative backlash against the reform proposals was so pervasive that, despite the admission of key officials that Indian unrest was at its lowest point in decades, the Indian government followed the passage of the reforms into law with the near-simultaneous passing of the Rowlatt Act, which contained unprecedented restrictions on Indian personal and political freedoms.

The Congress and leading Indian newspapers called this step "monstrous" and "a gigantic blunder which would arouse the worst passions of peaceful, law-abiding people."[21]

Frustration over the betrayal represented by the 1919 reforms, the harshness of the Rowlatt Act, and the divisions among nationalist political parties over how best to respond to the new act led younger nationalists to seek a fresh approach that would take them beyond the gradualist posture of moderate leaders but would also avoid violent extremist acts that might provoke the British to even greater acts of repression. They would find that fresh approach in the strategy of nonviolent civil disobedience developed by the charismatic Mohandas Karamchand Gandhi, who became known as Mahatma (Great-Souled One).

Like many Western-educated Indians, Gandhi was from childhood prepared to go to any length to resist British rule. As a boy in the early 1880s, he once ate meat on the advice of a mentor, Mehtab Singh, who argued that it was this dietary habit that gave Britons their advantage over South Asians. "We are a weak people," he told the young Gandhi, "because we do not eat meat. The English are able to rule over us, because they are meat-eaters . . . Try it and see the strength it gives."[22] He did try it but abandoned the effort at the behest of his father, a modern man but one who valued tradition—as did Gandhi himself. After training in England to become a lawyer in the family-run law firm in Bombay, he was as well versed in the work of Western political theorists as in the texts of the classical Indian philosophical political tradition. His chosen course of political action would combine elements of each.

After earning his legal qualifications in London and a brief return to India, Gandhi journeyed to South Africa as a lawyer serving the needs of Indian merchants who had gone there to supply the needs of Indians working on railway projects. It was there, after experiencing the racism of white South Africans, that he began his experiments with satyagraha (holding fast to the truth), an active, courageous, nonviolent approach to social as well as political change that drew on the textual centerpiece of modern Hinduism, the Bhagavad Gita, with its evocation of selfless action in pursuit of righteousness. It also drew on the Sermon on the Mount's evocation of the transformative power of love, the American philosopher Henry David Thoreau's practice of civil disobedience against government-sponsored injustice, and the Jain-Buddhist philosophy of nonviolence (ahimsa) that had permeated Gandhi's birthplace in western India. Through a synthesis of these and other philosophies of human transformation, Gandhi created a vehicle for nonviolent political action designed to persuade the oppressor to accept the "truth" that injustice was the denial to others of that which one desired for oneself.[23]

In Gandhi's view, violence against the oppressor merely enabled him or her to justify their own violent behavior. Nonviolent resistance not only removed this path of escape, but offered open arms to the oppressor, thus creating space for reconciliation. As for the campaign to end British rule in India, he wrote in *Non-Violence in Peace and War* that "a non-violent revolution is not a program of seizure of power. It is a program of transformation of relationship, ending in a peaceful transfer of power."[24] Gandhi enjoyed only limited success from his practice of satyagraha in South Africa, but what he did achieve made him a renowned figure in the fight against racial discrimination and a hero upon his return to India in 1915.

One of Ghandi's first political acts was to provide leadership for peasant resistance to conditions imposed by a British-owned indigo plantation system, for which he was briefly jailed. This action garnered support for his leadership that reached beyond Congress's traditional following among the Hindu urban middle class. He also sought to broaden the nationalist movement by lending his support to the Muslim Khilafat Movement that had emerged to protest the breakup of the Ottoman Empire at the end of the First World War. Muslims across the globe had risen in protest against what was perceived as a European-led assault on the Ottoman Empire's role as the symbol of the unity of the Islamic world. Indian Muslims joined in the Khilafat struggle, though they needed no transnational movement to convince them that the British were among those determined to divide and rule the Middle East, as they believed the British had already done so in South Asia. Gandhi identified himself with the Khilafat Movement because he hoped to employ local Muslim opposition to Britain's interference in the Islamic world as a means of binding Indian Muslims more closely to the Indian freedom movement. He needed to do so because his employment of traditional Hindu religious symbols and tactics (such as ahimsa) did not have the same appeal to Muslims as it did to Hindus.

Nonetheless, the Muslim leader Abdul Ghaffar Khan, an anti-colonialist hero of the Pashtun-speaking Indo-Afghan borderlands, became known as the "Frontier Gandhi" for his adoption of satyagraha. He was impressed that Gandhi strove to live his principles through patience and humor and afforded respect to all whom he encountered. In the final analysis, Gandhi's personal character attracted many to the nationalist cause, while the power inherent in his mass boycotts and campaigns of civil disobedience won over all those who sought to benefit from the end of British rule. Among the latter were many of South Asia's leading entrepreneurs, such as the Tata (in steel) and Birla (in jute and cotton) families, whose financial contributions fueled the independence movement. Few Indian businessmen shared Gandhi's belief that private wealth was a public trust, but they came to see satyagraha as the best means of liberating themselves from British imperial control and unfair British competition.

Gandhi's opposition to immoral activities, such as alcohol consumption, which destroyed many Indian families, and his commitment to the advancement of women attracted many social reformers and women, including Madame Bhikhaiji Rustom Cama, a firebrand nationalist, who had earlier made history by unfurling an Indian national flag on foreign soil for the first time (Germany, 1907), and Sarojini Naidu, a poet and president of the Indian National Congress (1925). Gandhi's assault on racism rallied to the nationalist cause even many of the pro-British Parsi of western India. This shift in allegiance to the nationalist cause was noticed by an American financier, Robert Drennan Cravath, traveling in India in 1924 and again in 1930. When he asked a junior British official to explain this, the answer was, "Because they want to be members of the Bombay Yacht Club and we will not let them in." In his 1931 memoir of that visit, Cravath judged that "the young man was not far from right."[25]

Despite the support of Abdul Ghaffar Khan and a few other leading Muslims, Gandhi proved unable to develop close ties with the traditional Muslim elite or to sustain Hindu-Muslim unity on a mass level. In December 1906, a group of Muslim leaders drawn from a small circle of conservative nawabs, religious leaders, and intellectuals, such as Sayyid Ahmad Khan, formed the All-India Muslim League, which courted the favor of British administrators in the hope that they might serve as a counterweight against what they perceived as a rapidly mobilizing majority-Hindu polity. When the end of the caliphate in 1922 alienated many Muslims from British rule, the Muslim League shifted its stance and joined the nationalist mainstream, a transition aided by Mohammad Ali Jinnah, who had joined the League in 1913. Jinnah, like Gandhi, was a British-trained lawyer with exceptional political skills. At that time, he shared Gandhi's vision of a united and independent nation, though to protect the interests of the subcontinent's largest minority, he sought to reserve for Muslims one-third of the seats in any future national assembly. However, in the 1930s and 1940s, Jinnah and the Muslim League took an increasingly separatist stance, which gained popularity and strength among many Muslims who were increasingly alienated by Hindu extremists. These extremists were perhaps the greatest force that impeded the consensus Gandhi sought to build. They not only ramped up their campaign to seek the "reconversion" of Indian

Muslims to Hinduism, but they also opposed the political secularism, as well as the religious syncretism, that Gandhi preached.

Gandhi's campaigns were also hampered by poor mass communication resources, which made it difficult for him to achieve the level of discipline necessary to ensure nonviolent behavior among the millions of freedom campaigners required to appeal to the hearts of the oppressors. This problem was revealed during Gandhi's first major political campaign, an effort in 1919 to repeal the Rowlatt Act via an India-wide *hartal* (work stoppage). In the Punjab, a local official so feared the possibility of another great Mutiny that he called in the local military commander, who, to demonstrate British resolve in the face of that threat, gave orders that led to a massacre of hundreds of unarmed demonstrators at a peaceful rally in Amritsar on April 13, 1919. Gandhi blamed himself for the incident, as his followers had not been able to prevent a riot sparked by the sudden and unexplained British seizure of local leaders in the days preceding the massacre. He ended another campaign in 1922, when a single act of deadly violence against a police headquarters marred an otherwise peaceful national protest.

The British arrested Gandhi in the belief that his confinement would reopen the divisions within the Indian nationalist movement, which it did. Moreover, the nationalist movement had a new foe, Winston Churchill. Churchill rarely strayed from the prevailing post-Mutiny view that British India would need generations more of British rule before the subcontinent was ready for self-rule and that this development depended on crushing the dominance of its landlord class and other traditional elites: Britain itself had only just achieved those goals shortly before the First World War. Nonetheless, during a short stint of military service in India, he had participated in a campaign on the northwestern frontier of India against communities that he recognized were merely fighting because of "the presence of British troops in lands the local people considered their own."[26] He also regretted the Amritsar massacre of 1919, remarking in Parliament that "collisions between troops and native populations have been painfully frequent in the melancholy aftermath of the Great War . . . [and] the Amritsar crowd was neither armed nor attacking."[27]

However, his commitment to the imperial idea was total. Within a decade, Churchill was the leading opponent of the devolution of power in South Asia. In 1931, he condemned the efforts that the then-viceroy, Lord Irwin, to negotiate with Gandhi, who attended these meetings dressed as always in a common dhoti (a seamless cloth worn about the body). Churchill, when addressing a conservative political meeting in

February 23, 1931, declared, "It was alarming and also nauseating to see Mr. Gandhi, a seditious . . . lawyer of the type well-known in the East, now posing as a fakir (a holy man), striding half naked up the steps of the Viceregal palace to parley on equal terms with the representative of the King-Emperor." Gandhi successfully turned the tables on Churchill, saying that he was merely "trying to identify with India's naked millions."[28] In fact, Churchill's concerns were perhaps more economic than political or even racial. He remarked in a speech that India was so important to the British economy that if its troops ever marched home from the subcontinent, "they would bring famine in their wake."[29] He was wrong. The subcontinent would, as Macaulay suggested, be a better trading partner when freed of its imperial yoke.

In January 1930, Gandhi was no longer in prison and had recovered from the ill health he had experienced while there. He revived nationalist aspirations with a national declaration of independence and shortly thereafter launched the civil disobedience campaign of 1930–1934, during which he began a 241-mile walk culminating in a symbolic making of salt from the sea that violated the spirit, if not the letter, of the long-standing retrogressive British levy on salt. Gandhi was immediately arrested for this act of defiance, even though salt made this way was not taxed and was inedible. But this Salt March, in which thousands joined Gandhi, drew worldwide attention to the British reliance on a tax that fell most heavily on those who could least afford it. The rich needed little salt for survival and their income was hardly dented by the tax, while it was a heavy blow to poor farmers sweating in the fields, as the tax took a large portion of their meager earnings. Many Indians who had in the past mistrusted Gandhi rallied to him, providing the leverage he eventually used to force the colonial government to make significant political concessions, including provincial autonomy, direct elections, and a template for an All Indian Federation (the Government of India Act of 1935).

Believing that the achievement of full independence was now inevitable, Gandhi focused on sarvodaya (the uplift of all) in an effort to heal the divisions of religion and caste within South Asia via satyagraha at the grass roots; unless these divisions were resolved, political independence would have no meaning. He addressed caste discrimination on the local level by encouraging young satyagrahis (practitioners of satyagraha) to use nonviolent techniques such as sit-ins to open up Hindu temples and village wells that denied access to the lower orders. Parallel efforts were aimed at building Hindu-Muslim unity. As Gandhi argued in his weekly newspaper, *Young India*, "Everybody knows that without unity between Hindus and Mussulmans no certain progress can be made by the nation."[30] But nothing he did could change the divisive tenor among both Hindu and Muslim leaders. Many members of the Indian National Congress had by then spent much of their lives in political struggle, and Muhammad Ali Jinnah, newly elected as president of the Muslim League, was determined to prove himself on the national stage. Neither party could take their eyes off the now inevitable prize of complete independence. Their subsequent actions led to Gandhi's worst nightmare: communal violence and partition of the subcontinent along religious lines.

In 1937, national elections mandated by the Government of India Act of 1935 were carried out. These were largely swept by candidates put forward by the Indian National Congress, now a political party as well as a movement. Congress interpreted this victory as confirmation of their claim to represent all Indians and, as a result, refused to share power with the Jinnah-led Muslim League, which had not put up candidates in key areas, but expected a power-sharing agreement to emerge. This lack of generosity may have sprung from the Congress's long struggle to establish itself as the sole voice of India against British rule, but it did nothing to reduce Muslim fears of a Hindu-dominated government.

Two years later, the region was once again embroiled in a world war. Once again, Britain called on Indian troops, eventually numbering over 2.5 million men, to fight in Africa, Europe, and the Middle East. As they had thirty years before in Flanders, the British Indian army helped turn the tide of a world war, defeating a Japanese invasion of India in the jungles of Manipur State in eastern India in a battle from which Japanese imperial forces in south and southeast Asia never recovered. However, where thirty years before Indians fought with the blessings of the most politically advanced among their own leaders, this was not to be the case in the sequel to the Great War.

Britain had granted a sufficient degree of freedom to India in 1935 to ensure the loyalty of most Indians, including soldiers in the British Indian army, many of whom were from professional soldiering communities who remained beyond the reach of Gandhi's political agitation. At the commencement of hostilities, Britain again made unspecified pledges of postwar reforms, but as in 1914, it had also unilaterally declared India at war against Germany in 1939. The Congress was furious at Britain's presumption to again act without any consultation with Indian leaders and eventually adopted a stance of non-cooperation as a means of securing complete autonomy for India to avoid a repetition of the betrayal of political promises the British had made at the beginning of the First World War.

With the Indian army and India's resources central to the British war effort and the astute political use by Japan of Indian prisoners of war captured early in the conflict to create an Indian National Army under the command of Gandhi's chief Hindu rival, Subhas Chandra Bose, Britain had no choice but to negotiate with Indian nationalists. Sir Stafford Cripps, a Labour Party leader supportive of the independence movement, was dispatched to India to help resolve this situation. Yet the "Cripps Mission" of 1942 was thwarted by Winston Churchill, who had become Britain's wartime prime minister. He made his stance clear in a famous address at Mansion House in London: "I have not become the King's First Minister in order to preside over the liquidation of the British Empire."[31] What is less well known was his determination not only to hold on to the British Indian Empire but to expand it in postwar Asia by linking Burma to Malaya through the annexation of Thai territory that separated these two British possessions.[32]

These self-interested visions of British postwar imperial expansion only served to strengthen Churchill's lifelong opposition to Indian nationalism. Without a moment's reflection on the realities of Britain's class system, which until just before the First World War had long reserved the highest political offices for aristocrats and only grudgingly raised taxes on the wealthy to support the needs of commoners, Churchill would tell Parliament that it was Britain's duty to continue to protect India from "its political parties and classes [that] do not represent the masses.[33]

Consistent with these views, Churchill undermined the work of the Cripps Mission, further alienating the Congress. In response, the Congress launched the "Quit India" movement. Although it was intended as a strident, but still peaceful campaign, growing frustration among nationalists led to murderous attacks on European civilians, some of whom were dragged from trains and slaughtered. Congress leaders were then rounded up and imprisoned for the duration of the war, as the British blamed them for this explosion of violence.

The Muslim League had by then positioned itself as the vehicle for achieving autonomy for areas with a Muslim majority—or outright independence, should the decolonization process endanger Muslim interests. The Muslim League profited from the imprisonment of Congress leaders by impressing British leaders with their loyal support. This stance yielded dividends at the war's end. In 1946, a British Cabinet Mission sent to India offered a groundwork for future Indian independence. This plan met the Muslim League's desire in that it permitted some areas, such as those with a Muslim majority, to opt out of a proposed Indian federal state. Congress rejected this formula in part because they were unable to accept that Britain, so proud of its vast South Asian empire, would simply divide and quit the subcontinent. Yet postwar economic decline at home and the consequent need to draw down its garrisons overseas and put them to work rebuilding their own country was driving Britain to extricate itself from its South Asian quagmire created by the intractability of Congress and the Muslim League.

The Muslim League helped push the British to exit the subcontinent when it called for a "Direct Action Day," a *hartal*, on August 16, 1946, which may have been an act of brinksmanship designed to force Congress to accept the Cabinet Mission's plan, and thus providing Muslims a means of exiting the federal union if it threatened Muslim interests. It may also have been an effort by the Muslim League's leadership to reject the Cabinet Mission's plan and directly engage the masses in a unilateral effort to establish a separate state composed of Muslim-majority areas. Neither the Muslim League nor Congress anticipated what followed: waves of communal violence that left four thousand dead and one hundred thousand homeless in Calcutta alone. Moreover, the possibility of violence and political impasse convinced the rulers of the fading British Empire that they could not and would not try any longer to control events on the subcontinent. On August 15, 1947, after a seventy-two-day marathon of final negotiations, Britain granted independence to India and Pakistan, via a partition made so hastily as to bequeath the two states only sketchily drawn common borders, and granting the rulers of the semi-autonomous Princely States the right to determine the future national identities of their subjects.

It will never be possible to take the full measure of the psychological as well as material damage done to those South Asians who crossed the Indo-Pakistani border or who remained where they were, only to find themselves socially, politically, and economically marginalized in the land of their ancestors. Moreover, the number of lives lost in conflicts directly arising from Britain's hasty departure from the subcontinent, such as in post-partition Kashmir, continues to mount. An estimated ten million to fifteen million people left their homes seeking a safer national haven, with Hindus and Sikhs traveling to India and Muslims to Pakistan. In so tense an atmosphere, rumors of massacres, often all too true, spread among the affected communities. As many as one million perished in revenge killings. A survivor remarked in an interview that "Nobody imagined that such a holocaust would take place," as

Hindus, Muslims, and Sikhs had often engaged in each other's society and culture. "You have played with them, you have lived with them, you have eaten together," he said, but as independence loomed, "the same people are coming and burning your houses and looting."[34]

Many Muslims, either unsafe in their own districts or unable to get to Pakistan (or both), gathered in Delhi in search of protection. Gandhi then undertook a fast-unto-death, a gesture of self-sacrifice he rarely employed, but usually to great effect. His intent was to move the new government of India to divert some of its hard-pressed resources to protect this gathering of its most vulnerable population. G. D. Khosla, an official returning from a visit to the main Muslim refugee camp in Delhi, reported to Gandhi that these refuges told him "they wanted to go to Pakistan anyway," implying that they should be encouraged to do so as "our own people are without houses and shelter." He asked Gandhi, "What should I do?" Gandhi replied, "When I go there, they say they do not want to go to Pakistan . . . They are also our people. You should . . . protect them."[35] A few days later, on January 30, 1948, Gandhi was slain by a Hindu fundamentalist who considered providing succor to Muslims an act of treason.

South Asia and the World, 1947 to the Present

At the stroke of midnight on August 14, 1947, Jawaharlal Nehru, a serious student of world history and South Asia's place within it, announced the independence of India via a radio broadcast. He referred to a tryst or date with destiny that the nationalist movement made when it committed itself to the achievement of complete independence more than twenty years earlier. He spoke of the "soul of India" being released from its colonial bonds and referred to the purpose the new nation might serve in redeeming the sacrifices that had been made to achieve its liberation:

> It is fitting that at this solemn moment we take the pledge of dedication to the service of India and her people and to the still larger cause of humanity. The service of India means . . . the ending of poverty and ignorance and disease and inequality of opportunity. The ambition of the greatest man of our generation [Gandhi] has been to wipe every tear from every eye. That may be beyond us, but as long as there are tears and suffering, so long our work will not be over.[1]

Not all Indians shared Nehru's vision of India as an exemplar of universal social justice and human development, but most did. The search for an equitable socioeconomic order, left incomplete at the time of Gandhi's death, would become one of the chief concerns of post-independence South Asia. During their own Independence Day celebrations, most leaders of the other new states of postcolonial South Asia also spoke of a higher purpose associated with what they considered their national destiny. Pakistanis expected to achieve a ground-breaking blend of secular constitutional government and Islamic law. In Burma and Sri Lanka, the engine of that pursuit was to be a dynamic, indigenized democratic socialism. All such hopes sprang from a near-universal postcolonial conviction, given clearest voice by Ghana's Kwame Nkrumah, who declared, "Seek ye first the political kingdom, and all things shall be added unto you,"[2] meaning that once the colonized were free to engage in building their own nation, the human potential so long held back by colonial chains would burst forth and carry all before it. In South Asia, postcolonial thinking clearly determined how that human potential would be managed. Most South Asian leaders were British-educated and sought to channel politics and public administration through a parliamentary system, with a strong executive office, because postwar development theory argued that only such a state could raise capital and coordinate economic activities.

Nehru was foremost among those leaders of the developing world who placed the state at the "commanding heights" of the national economy. Under Nehru's leadership, the Republic of India initially sought to guarantee a level economic playing field in the style of socialist regimes, but he still pursued mixed economic policies that provided opportunities for private-sector entrepreneurs, many of whom had financed the drive for independence. Perhaps the strongest of all postcolonial mindsets arising from the Western education of South Asian leaders was that the path to world-power status lay in rapid industrialization, as it had in America, Britain, Japan, and the Soviet Union.

In the first blush of independence, few emergent nations in South Asia or elsewhere anticipated how traditional political and social divisions, combined with the burdens of postcolonialism (the persistence of colonial-era models of thought and policy) and, later, the accelerating forces of neoliberalism and globalization, would come to influence their efforts to eradicate poverty and inequality. Fewer still were able to manage the burdens of the Cold War on their own terms or overcome the obstacles posed by ethno-nationalism in their internal relations or in their relations with each other.

The Republic of India's passage through the late twentieth century is representative of most South Asian nations facing the multiple obstacles of postcolonialism: the Cold War, neoliberalism, globalization, and ethno-nationalism. Jawaharlal Nehru began his term as independent India's first prime minister amid the great tragedies of partition and the death of Gandhi, but with resources well beyond those available to most decolonizing societies. Despite British efforts to limit Indian competition in manufacturing, by the 1930s Indian industrialists had wrested away much of Britain's trade with Asia. India's supplying of British needs during the Second World War, especially ammunition and jute for sandbags, ensured that India achieved independence with a favorable balance of trade.

Gandhi had told the British that India would be a better partner free than enslaved, the same point made by Thomas Babington Macaulay in the 1830s. They were both right. Post-independence, India became a major British trading partner. India also benefited from the continuation of the British colonial tradition of civilian control over the military. This allowed its constitution-building process to engage controversial issues without fear of a coup, helping Nehru to secure passage of Article 15 of the Indian Constitution (1950), which prohibited discrimination based on caste or religion and against certain minority ethnic communities. An amendment to that constitution (1993) protected women in rural areas and opened the way for women's rights, whose expansion has erased many barriers to women's employment. Yet actions taken to protect the rights of all women have floundered, in part due to the need to avoid reserving opportunities for wealthy, high-caste women who do not need such protections. Such efforts were criticized then and to this day by the elites whose power these policies are designed to limit. While not without flaws, these programs have successfully secured admissions to public universities for poor Muslims and descendants of outcastes formerly known as untouchables and now called Dalits (those who are beaten down).

What legislation has yet failed to do, self-help organizations attempted to do. One of these organizations, the Self-Employed Women's Association (SEWA), founded in 1972 by Ela Bhatt, has 1.8 million members. When asked in an interview if her movement was inspired by Gandhi, who, like Ram Mohun Roy almost two centuries before, had supported women's rights, Bhatt replied, "I am not a Gandhi scholar, nor a devotee. I am a Gandhian practitioner."[3]

Unlike Gandhi, but like many leaders of former European colonies, Nehru pursued highly centralized, state-led social and economic policies. Nehru was aware of Gandhi's views as to the dehumanizing nature of modern industrial society, and he was opposed to uneven development. However, he saw modern Western-style factories, along with massive dam projects, as examples of modern progress. He thus took major steps toward building up India's industrial sector, but critics argue that it was hamstrung by too many government restrictions.

Nehru eventually turned to agricultural reform, which included redistribution of land to poor rural farmers, who at that time made up the vast majority of India's citizens. Yet by the time the rural question was addressed in the form of Panchayati Raj (a Gandhian idea for using village self-governments—panchayats—as a tool for development), India's village councils, dominated by landlords and high-caste individuals, had learned how to obtain political influence over local governments and administrative officers to ensure that they continued to have greater access to land, water, and education than those on the margins of Indian society. A later land redistribution program, which was based on an attempt to place a cap on the size of an individual's landholdings, was thwarted by wealthy families who cloaked the extent of their properties to defeat the program's purpose.

Nehru's pioneering leadership of the "Green Revolution" led to a tripling of crop production, but, as elsewhere around the world, Green Revolution farming required costly genetically manufactured seed, equally expensive fertilizers, and economies of scale that favored those with large landholdings and mechanical harvesting equipment. As Nehru's reforms fell short of their grandest expectations, the most saintly of Gandhi's lieutenants, Vinoba Bhave, walked from village to village asking landowners to give a "gift of land" to the less fortunate. The results were not spectacular, but validated Gandhi's belief in the potential of local satyagraha to motivate people to act for the common good through what he called "soul-force."

Nehru acted much closer to Gandhian principles in announcing India's adherence to the principles of *panchshila* (Five Virtues or Principles of Peace) in foreign policy, which Sri Lanka also supported. These included mutual respect for each other's territorial integrity and sovereignty, mutual nonaggression, mutual noninterference in each other's internal affairs, equality and mutual benefit in bilateral relations, and peaceful coexistence. These were later absorbed into ten principles of international conduct advanced by the heads of states representing twenty-nine countries and colonies from Asia and Africa who met April 18–24, 1955, at the Asian-African Conference at Bandung in west Java. The meetings at Bandung laid the foundation of the Non-Aligned Movement. That movement was more than mere evidence of much of the world's anger at being forced to take sides in the bipolar US-USSR world. For Asia and Africa, it constituted a declaration of their desire to make their own contribution to world affairs.

Panchshila was also incorporated into a 1955 accord between India and China over Tibet. Nehru considered good relations with China as paramount, given their long common frontier, which over the centuries had been a conduit for peaceful cultural and commercial exchange. He hoped that the fact that both countries were forced to accept their current common frontiers set by European powers would serve to draw them together rather than become the source of conflict not of their own making. Unfortunately, China was determined to act more aggressively in Tibet and in the Indian province of Assam, part of which China calls Southern Tibet, a territory reaching south of the recognized China-India border onto the plains of northeast India. In 1962, perhaps angered that Nehru offered safe haven to the fleeing Tibetan leader, the Dalai Lama—or, more likely, as part of a desire to flex its muscles in the region—Chinese Communist forces attacked and routed ill-prepared Indian army units at several places along the border before withdrawing back toward, but always short of, the former frontier, thus seizing territory claimed by India, embarrassing Nehru, and damaging Indian national pride. Nehru had developed a close friendship with the American president John F. Kennedy and maintained good relations with the Soviets, which served him in good stead in the aftermath of the Chinese attack, but he was deeply wounded by India's defeat at the hands of its hoped-for Asian ally. Until his death of a heart attack in 1964, Nehru represented India as he wished it to be seen: tolerant, pacifist, and progressive.

After Nehru's death, the Congress Party faltered. Nehru had masterfully negotiated political compromises between its many factions, which included Gandhians, varieties of communists and socialists, social conservatives, trade unionists, and anti-unionist business leaders. In his absence, the Congress Party naturally began to lose momentum. Ironically, Nehru's daughter, Indira Gandhi (no relation to Mohandas K. Gandhi) was named prime minister in 1966 because she was the one candidate all contending factions judged to be the easiest to manipulate. They were wrong. Identifying herself with the most progressive among Congress leaders and backed by leftist parties, Indira Gandhi cut a wide swath through Indian politics. She began a nuclear program in answer to China's detonation of a nuclear device, abolished the privileges of India's former princes, nationalized the banking system, and rendered her father's Green Revolution initiatives more productive. She also defeated Pakistan's effort to hold its eastern provinces by force of arms in 1971, which led to the creation of Bangladesh. Her triumph over Pakistan produced a resounding victory for the Congress Party in the national elections of 1972.

Nonetheless, there were those within Indira Gandhi's own alliance who were concerned that her concentration of political power in the office of the prime minister was having a corrupting influence. In 1975, the High Court validated her opponents' claims that she had used government resources to wage her personal political campaigns. The court ordered her removal from office, but she refused to leave and extended her rule under a state of emergency. The public took great offense at

This campaign poster declares that Indira Gandhi's Indian National Congress Party "can bring about unity and prosperity of the country; vote for the Congress Party." The image of two yoked bullocks is the electoral emblem of her party. Library of Congress, Yanker poster collection yan.1a36965

her apparent belief that she was above the law, but Gandhi arrested her political opponents and directed her son Sanjay Gandhi to institute slum clearances and a forced sterilization program to limit population growth, steps that no previous government had had the courage to undertake. Yet Sanjay's programs were structured to increase his own power and were flawed, as the pressure to meet quotas led to men over seventy years old being offered inducements for sterilization (usually a transistor radio). Self-deceived into thinking her popularity was restored by her leadership, she called for early national elections, and lost.

A coalition government, the Janata Party, took office in 1977 with great expectations, but the old fissures within Congress erupted again, with communists, socialists, trade unionists, pro-business leaders, and Hindu fundamentalists jockeying for power with no hope of creating a common social or economic policy. Frustrated by this, Indian voters returned a seemingly chastened Indira Gandhi to power in 1980, but she had the misfortune to be faced with a challenge to her authority from which she felt she could not back down.

States emerging in the late twentieth century struggled to retain the allegiance of people who had been bound together by colonial rather than local ties. This led to long and bloody civil wars that often had genocidal overtones, as in Africa (Biafra, Rwanda). After independence, several regions threatened to leave the Indian federal system over issues of local control. In the mid-1950s, Nehru bought his new country some time in which to weave its pieces together by dividing the nation into linguistic provinces. However, subregional movements developed separatist agendas, from Kashmir in the north to Andra Pradesh in the south.

In the Punjab, separatism followed a global pattern now found in Scotland (in the United Kingdom), Antwerp (in Belgium), and Catalonia (in Spain), where desires for a more local, responsible government and management of their economies has led these mostly better-off areas to rethink the idea of nationhood. In the 1980s, politicians in the Punjab, the most productive of India's provinces, began to question why its taxpayers were supporting poorer regions such as Bihar. They ignored the fact that the Punjab's vast irrigation systems and public works were built from taxes collected even from Bihar by British and post-independence officials.

But the Sikh Akali Dal separatist party in the Punjab possessed a unique complaint that went beyond mere economic privilege. Their members were angered at past divisions of the Punjab into new states, each of which had Hindu majorities, thus creating a situation in which Sikhs were the majority population in the region but in the majority in no single state. Concerns about this undemocratic situation grew into a demand for the creation of an independent Sikh nation (Khalistan). Sikh militants subsequently occupied the holiest place in the Sikh religion, the Golden Temple complex in Amritsar. Militants turned this religious center into an armed base and coordinating center for the assassination of local government officials and rival Sikh leaders and for terrorist attacks on Punjabi Hindus. Arms were stacked in the precinct's hallways, against Sikh custom. Sikh activist Sant Janail Singh Bhindranwale is reputed to have said, "I don't fear for a physical death, but when my conscience dies, that is a real death."[4] He spoke these words as the government of India launched Operation Blue Star (June 1–10, 1984), which ended the occupation with great loss of life among Sikh militants (including Bhindranwale) and innocent Sikhs who rushed to defend what they saw as an attack on their shrines.

Thereafter, Indira Gandhi was warned not to trust her Sikh body-guard unit, which had provided security to British viceroys and all of India's prime ministers, but she refused to listen. On October 30, 1984, in a speech that mirrored Bhindranwale's commitment to his cause, she responded to threats against her life by saying:

> I do not care whether I live or die. I have lived a long life and I am proud that I spend the whole of my life in the service of my people. . . . I shall continue to serve until my last breath and when I die, I can say that every drop of my blood will invigorate India and strengthen it.[5]

The next day, two of her Sikh bodyguards riddled her with bullets. Her death did galvanize the nation as never before, but the shedding of her blood had immediate and horrific consequences for the Sikh community, with at least five thousand innocent Sikhs killed in riots in Delhi alone.

Into this tumult stepped Indira Gandhi's elder son, Rajiv, an airline pilot who had earlier been called on to run for Parliament after the death of his brother Sanjay in a stunt-flying accident in 1980. Raised to the office of prime minister in the wake of his mother's death, he seemed unready for this task. However, it soon looked as if the Nehru dynasty was in good hands.

Rajiv Gandhi is credited with turning India away from its mixed economy and toward the neoliberal or free-market-driven economies gaining traction in the West. Rajiv Gandhi began this shift by lifting import and export restrictions and attempting to end what was called License-Permit Raj, a system of government-issued permits and licensing requirements that slowed economic activity. At the same time, he championed the development of high technology and service industries, which he backed with tariff reforms. In an address to a joint session of the United States Congress, he said, "Due to colonialism, India missed the Industrial Revolution. We must not miss the computer revolution."[6]

Whereas elsewhere in the world free-market reforms were accompanied by the retreat of the state from the social sector, Rajiv Gandhi founded a system of free basic rural education and spoke eloquently of the need to address cultural and economic globalization through policies that yield economic development while preserving a sense of community cohesion as well as India's cultural tradition. Yet he stumbled when addressing corruption arising from his mother's centralization of power, which led to a scandal over a military procurement contract that touched him as well as other senior members of government and saw Congress temporarily driven from office.

Before his ouster, Rajiv Gandhi was making some progress toward ending separatist divisions that plagued South Asia. He ultimately lost his life due to his unsparing efforts to bring stability to Sinhalese-Tamil relations in neighboring Sri Lanka. Tamil speakers from the subcontinent had lived on the island of Sri Lanka as early as 200 BCE, where they predominated in the central highlands and in the north. Their numbers increased in the nineteenth and twentieth centuries as a new wave of Tamil speakers were recruited to work in British coffee, tea, and rubber plantations in what was then known as Ceylon. After independence, Tamils were subject to a degree of harassment by the Sinhalese that reduced them to the status of second-class citizens. Tamil resistance led to a civil war and fueled a demand for independence. Radical Tamil separatists so distrusted Rajiv Gandhi's past decision to militarily intervene in Sri Lankan affairs to enforce a political settlement that they assassinated him via a suicide bomber during the 1990 elections that returned the Congress Party to power. His Italian wife, Sonia, then took over the party's leadership, though she did not seek political office.

As India entered the twenty-first century, it did so with the Congress Party in disarray, without a Nehru holding the leading strings, with the emergence of the first economic dislocations attendant upon the "liberalization" of its markets, and engaged in a nuclear arms race with Pakistan. Rajiv Gandhi's death, the global recession of the 1990s, and a series of government scandals set the stage for a revived pro-business but devoutly Hindu fundamentalist movement (generically called Hindutva), under the direction of the Bharatiya Janata Party (BJP). During the ministry of Atal Bihari Vajpayee (1998–2004), the BJP promised to clean up corruption and restore the economy, but corruption continued unabated as the BJP embraced free-market economic principles. Moreover, BJP politicians sough to undermine India's extensive affirmative action program by turning its chief beneficiaries, poor Muslims and Dalits, into scapegoats for the nation's shortcomings. This tactic led to attacks on those the BJP sought to marginalize, including deadly anti-Muslim riots in 1992, 1993, and again in Gujarat in 2002, for which two senior and thirty other BJP officials were held criminally liable.

The BJP platform was rejected in elections in 2004 and 2009, leading to a Congress-led coalition (the United Progressive Alliance, or UPA) which espoused managed growth and social justice. This was no easy task. More than three hundred million Indians, a number roughly equivalent to the population of United States or the entire European Union, enjoyed the same standard of living as citizens of those wealthier nations. Yet three times that number lived in dire poverty with little access to education or other means of social or material improvement: more than three hundred million lacked access to electricity and half of its people lacked access to clean water and basic sanitation measures.

The United Progressive Alliance was led by the Congress Party's former chief economic adviser, Manomohan Singh, who had previously designed India's first economic liberalization scheme. Under Singh's leadership, a social contract was drawn up with rural Indians through guaranteed work as part of a balanced approach to market reform, and the economy enjoyed rapid, if still uneven, growth, with a booming service sector. Amid growing criticism that the government was, in fact, failing the interests of the poor in favor of economic development, Manomohan Singh addressed the nation, saying that "no government likes to impose burdens on the *aam admi*, the common man."

> At the same time, it is the responsibility of the government to . . .
> protect the long term future of our people. This means that we must
> ensure that the economy grows rapidly, and that this generates enough
> productive jobs for the youth of our country . . . The challenge is that
> we have to do this at a time when the world economy is experiencing
> great difficulty. . . . Even China is slowing down.[7]

The United Progressive Alliance met that challenge through a program of economic expansion that was on a par with China's, without the latter's authoritarianism, and without its aging, shrinking labor force. The once stolid, heavily regulated car manufacturing sector took off. Tata Industries, which had become an industrial giant despite colonial efforts to stunt the growth of local manufacturing, purchased the British Land Rover and Jaguar nameplates and will soon be manufacturing

Jaguars in India, while also developing the "nano-car," one that the less-than-affluent Indian will be able to afford. In recent years, Chennai has become India's new motor city, with BMW, Ford, and Nissan factories already in place.

Contributing to India's general growth has been the influx of highly skilled Indians returning from education and jobs in North America and Europe. For centuries, economic forces ranging from South Asia's traditional role in transregional trade to colonial-era overseas labor policies propelled its people take up residence in every corner of the world. Many young Indians educated in the West (nicknamed NRIs, non-resident Indians) have returned with enhanced professional expertise to live and work in India, where lower labor costs offer opportunities for new business startups with higher profit margins, and an ease of living no longer available to middle-income entrepreneurs in the West, such as low-cost domestic servants (often desperate migrants from Nepal and other weaker regional economies).

Ultimately, with the deepening of the global recession, the United Progressive Alliance was forced into austerity measures. It also sought to boost the economy by permitting the entry of "big box" foreign retailers and allowed a rise in diesel prices. Both of these measures directly undercut small businesses and proved so unpopular as to weaken Singh's administration. The global recession also exposed a series of business scandals born of the deregulation that has accompanied Congress-backed neoliberal reforms, the most famous connected to the deregulation of the coal mining industry. Santosh Hegde, a former Supreme Court justice, had once conducted an investigation of a coal mining scandal in southern India, by which the government doled out the rights to undeveloped coal fields to prominent businessmen and politicians via a process that, if not criminal, certainly lacked transparency. Hegde was nonetheless shocked in 2012 by the scale of what became known as "Coalgate," a scandal which the *New York Times* reported as revealing "a brazen style of crony capitalism that has enabled politicians and their friends to reap huge profits by gaining control of vast swaths of the country's natural resources, often for nothing. Hegde remarked to reporters, "Today in India, politicians are so powerful . . . All together, they are looting the country."[8] This is a global phenomenon. Chinese Communist Party insiders have exploited free-market reforms to control sectors of their economy, while much of post-communist Russia's economy initially fell into the hands of an insider elite, some of whom were proud to call themselves "oligarchs" in their postings on the blogosphere.

Frustrated by the United Progressive Alliance austerities and corruption scandals, the Indian electorate returned the BJP to power in 2014, hoping that its charismatic "up from tea-cart pusher" leader, Narendra Modi, would set aright the Indian ship of state. As governor of Gujarat, Modi cut government red tape and effected a turnaround of the local economy; he promised to do the same on a national scale. His opponents have voiced concern that the BJP has a poor record of curbing "crony capitalism" (it has the largest number of wealthy supporters of any Indian political party), and Modi's promises to expand the economy seem to offer employment for many, but at very low wages. There is also some fear that if Modi's neoliberal program fizzles, the ultra-Hindu fundamentalist BJP will look for scapegoats among Muslims as they have done in the past. As governor of Gujarat in 2002, Modi displayed a much-criticized lack of energy in quelling one of the worst outbreaks of communal violence since independence.

Neither of India's major political parties has recently done much to halt the growing gap between the richest and poorest citizens. In search of basic infrastructure, including electricity, so many of India's poor have relocated themselves to its cities that for the first time the urban population exceeds the rural population. Many who live in the cities are slum dwellers without access to escape routes from poverty (sometimes offered by contests, as in Danny Boyle's buoyant if fantastical 2008 film, *Slumdog Millionaire*), while those in rural areas are exposed to the vagaries of the marketplace as never before. Global shifts in the price of sugar have led to scores of suicides among sugar farmers because market contracts were made deliberately vague to protect marketers or inadequately spelled out in terms farmers could understand. Massive water projects, such as the damming of the Narmada River, have led to the forced displacement of indigenous populations via inadequate and mismanaged compensation schemes. This and most other water projects are designed to supply power to cities. Few actually address the needs of farmers, who are depleting the aquifers of India by overuse of wells to maintain their lives and livelihoods.

Growing numbers of India's wealthy see no future for the immediate post-independence dream of India as a beacon of peace, tolerant of differences, restrained in its regional ambitions, and an exemplar of socially responsible economics, which they feel was an unrealistic construct of a nationalist movement with socialist leanings. They understand that humanism, not socialism, was behind Gandhi's view that development should not come at the cost of the dignity of the laboring classes. Yet they see concern for the *aam admi* (the common man) as an obstacle to development in a world driven by market forces, despite rising labor unrest in South Asia and elsewhere that brings the free market into question as a governing ethos.

The task of managing elite demands and the expectations of the masses in South Asia is made more difficult by disputes along South Asia's long land borders. These have their origins not merely in boundary disputes with origins in the European colonial era's "great game" for the control of South Asia, but from problems arising from poverty-stricken settlers from India and Bangladesh (and also illegal loggers) encroaching on the lands of forest dwellers who live on the margins of both countries. There also has been outright warfare between India and Pakistan, which, like India itself, has been buffeted by internal as well as international forces.

Pakistan's national history opened in 1947 with a heroic effort to create an Islamic democracy, which floundered over the meaning of "Islamic" in view of its many minority sects, and "democracy" as interpreted according to shari'a law. These conflicts reach back to the earliest days of Islam in South Asia, but had deepened due to the self-interested unwillingness of the British to develop democratic institutions in the Punjab, Sindh, and the northwest frontier provinces. The inhabitants of these regions were perceived as members of "martial races," from which the British recruited much of their army in South Asia, but they also believed that such people were unsuited to political development that might lessen their fighting spirit and their loyalty to the British Raj. The resulting weakness of democratic institutions there helped open the door to intolerance, self-interest, and corruption among many Pakistani politicians, which in turn paved the way for military rule after independence (1958–1971, 1977–1988, and 1999–2008). Pakistan's military leaders routinely promised stability and prosperity, which competing civilian political parties had failed to deliver. In this task, the military had the support of the United States, which shifted its development aid from democratic India to the military dictatorships in Pakistan because of India's leadership of the non-aligned movement. Yet, as with past US aid in support of authoritarian rule globally, little US funding for nation-building programs in Pakistan reached the average citizen.

Pakistan's military leaders proved as capable of corruption and misrule as any of the civilian governments, enabling civilian politicians to unseat them periodically. In 1979, infighting among political parties led to the overthrow and execution of Pakistan's longest-serving civilian prime minister, Zulfikar Ali Bhutto, for his reputed personal corruption and alleged complicity in the murder of a political rival. His daughter,

Benazir Ali Bhutto, who twice held her late father's post, was also driven from the office by her opponents' charges of corruption. She was assassinated in 2007, perhaps as part of an effort by her rivals to thwart her expected victory in the coming national elections, which did return her democratic, center-left party to power in January 2008.

Since then, Western observers fear Pakistan's future may be as an unstable nuclear-armed Islamic power, but its leaders face more immediate problems. One is the challenge posed by the Pashtun nationalism of the Taliban on both sides of the Afghan-Pakistan border. This could lead to a further partition of Pakistan, with Pashtun-speakers on the western bank of the Indus uniting with a Pashtun-dominated Afghanistan. While not a popular idea among most Pashtun speaking Pakistanis, it is a long-standing goal of the Taliban in Afghanistan. For this reason Pakistan's intelligence services attempted to infiltrate and control the Taliban movement. The Taliban has some of its roots in South Asian Salafism, but became sufficiently connected to rising international Salafist movements, such as the Muslim Brotherhood and Al Qaida, that it was displaced from power in Afghanistan by the United States after Al Qaida's strikes on its soil in 2001. Pakistan also turned on the Taliban after Taliban politicians began openly urging Pashtun speakers on Pakistan's always turbulent frontier with Afghanistan to join their fight for a greater Afghanistan that would include all of western Pakistan. However, by then the Talban had infiltrated the Pakistan military itself, further complicating the relationship between secularist parties, religious parties, and the military and civilian authorities, many of whom vigorously oppose the Taliban's often violent efforts to prevent women from seeking an education and otherwise controlling their own lives.

Pakistan's struggle with civilian and military rule only exacerbated an age-old problem for South Asian Muslims: how to define the role of, and acceptable behavior among, those outside prevailing Muslim orthodoxy. This issue, still unresolved, led to the harassment of Hindus who remained in Pakistan after partition. It also spawned increasingly deadly attacks on minority Muslim sects marginalized by the orthodox ulama. The apparent use of Pakistani territory by Muslim terrorists to stage attacks on India (such as in Mumbai in 2008) is but the most recent driver of the region's conflicts. As a result, Pakistan, and the similarly nuclear-armed India, have devoted much of their budgets to military expenditure designed to protect each from the other.

Pakistan's and India's often bellicose stance toward one another has led to several military conflicts between them. Few of these have had much international significance, apart from the war that led to the repartition of Pakistan, which had Cold War dimensions. In 1971, during early discussions leading to President Nixon's ground-breaking 1972 visit to China in which Pakistan played a supporting role, West Pakistan's civilian and military elites sought to use force to maintain their dominance over their country's distant, more populous, and asset-rich eastern province after the results of a nationwide election suggested national power might pass to East Pakistanis. Such a transfer of power was intolerable to many West Pakistanis, as they regarded East Pakistani lifestyles as far too influenced by Bengali culture and language, as opposed to the Middle Eastern culture West Pakistanis favor. When the degree of force used by the Pakistani military to assert its control over its eastern province reached horrific levels, India intervened, which eventually enabled East Pakistanis to break with their former compatriots and create their own nation, Bangladesh. Coming to the aid of its ally, President Nixon threatened India with attack if it entered into what the United States considered Pakistan's internal affairs. This led India to sign a defense pact with the Soviet Union, greatly complicating affairs between the United States, Pakistan, and India, particularly after the Soviet invasion of Afghanistan (1979–1989), which threated the common national interests of all three nations.

Currently, conflict between India and Pakistan centers on Kashmir. The British ensured that the semi-autonomous rulers of the Indian States would be allowed to choose whether to join India or Pakistan at partition. This permitted Kashmir's Hindu maharaja to opt to join his mostly Muslim state to a majority-Hindu India. Periodic conflicts there have effectively partitioned Kashmir between Pakistan and India along a cease-fire line that pleases no one, least of all the Kashmiris. While the struggle over Kashmir initially focused on the right of its majority-Muslim population to join with Pakistan, it is now focused on the rights to the dwindling glacier melt into rivers flowing through Kashmir to India. That struggle became complicated by the efforts of Al Qaida to become the champions of Muslim Kashmir in place of Pakistan. Thus, postcolonialism, self-determination, climate change, and global terrorism all bedevil Indo-Pakistani relations.

In recognition of the growing confluence of so many troubling trends in world history, Pakistani and Indian officials are calling for a normalization of relations between the two countries, from trade to the need for Pakistan to "expeditiously bring the perpetrators of the Mumbai attack to justice."[9] Such efforts have failed in the past, but the number and scale of the mutual problems the two countries now face have lent such discussions a new urgency. Both sides have admitted, "We must learn from the past, recognize we cannot change our neighbors, and no longer be held hostage to history."[10] This view seemed to be confirmed in 2014 when the avowedly Hindu fundamentalist Narendra Modi invited Pakistan's prime minster, Nawaz Sharif, to attend his installation as India's prime minister.

After its birth, Bangladesh began to suffer from the same ill that troubled Pakistan from its inception: the struggle between civilian and military rule. This was further complicated by a power struggle between the military and Islamists, and between Islamists and potent socialist parties, such as the Awami League. The head of the Awami League and the first president of Bangladesh, Sheikh Mujibur Abdur Rahman, attempted to subordinate party politics to the national interest, as did his successor, a retired general turned reformist, President Ziaur Rahman. Both were assassinated. Succeeding governments supported a shift toward Islamic orthodoxy that ran against the grain of Bengal's moderate Sufi-influenced culture: illustrations of Bengali folk stories gracing the backs of rickshaws were replaced by Islamic themes.

In recent years, guided by two female prime ministers (Sheikh Hasina, daughter of Sheikh Mujibur Abdur Rahman, and Khaleda Zia, widow of General Zia) and aided by a series of peaceful, parliamentary elections since 2009, Bangladesh's economy has improved, with per-capita income doubling since 1975. A small part of that growth may be ascribed to the moral example set by Muhammad Yunus' Grameen Bank, which pioneered microfinancing as a means of instilling dynamism into economies whose people have little economic opportunity. Much more of the country's export-driven economy relies on foreign-investment-backed factories that have proven so shoddy as to lead to devastating building collapses and fires, with great loss of life among its low-wage workers.

Bangladesh also faces threats concerning water that may be beyond the power of a single nation to resolve. The melting of glacial ice in the Himalayas, related to global warming, is a long-term threat to its water security. Water diversion by dam construction in India and China is another. Both developments have led to the overuse of local tube wells (as in India) to cope with the resulting water shortages. Another threat is the encroachment of seawater from the Bay of Bengal, also related to climate change. It is little wonder that Bangladesh annually tops the Global Climate Risk Index.

The chief problems faced by Nepal and Sri Lanka are more directly man-made, and potentially more amendable to solution, than those posed by climate change. Nepal, an ancient hereditary monarchy under

British control from the early nineteenth century, recovered full sovereignty in 1923. It remained a monarchy, though reforms in 1990 led to a multi-party system. In 2004, the country was shaken by the murder of much of its royal family by one of its own. This crisis weakened the government's decade-long struggle against a long-simmering and violent Maoist-inspired movement practicing people's war, one of the last of its kind after the decline of the Shining Path (Sendero Luminoso) in Peru in 1992. However, the government proved just strong enough to persuade the Maoists to join in a power-sharing agreement and sign a Comprehensive Peace Accord (2006) with the support of the United Nations. This agreement included the disarming of Maoist forces and a Truth and Reconciliation Commission, on the post-apartheid South African model, to address human-rights abuses on both sides of a Nepalese civil war that took over fifteen thousand lives.

Divisions between Maoist factions, one of which wishes to restart the civil war, have prevented Nepal from being ruled under doctrinaire communist ideology—which was failing elsewhere in the communist world. The end of the civil war has helped keep Nepal from falling any lower on the Human Development Scale (145 out of 187 countries as of 2014), but a massive earthquake (as strong as 8.1) in April 2015, combined with a 6.7 aftershock, killed over twenty thousand people; destroyed much of Nepal's capital city, Kathmandu; and left infrastructure in shambles. One year later, as many as six hundred thousand residents remained homeless.

Since then, movement toward progressive constitutional change has been stymied amid the return of the old political order, committed to democracy but caste-based and representing the interests of only 30 percent of the population. As elsewhere in the world, many Nepalese are angry at the slow pace of economic recovery but find that their anger alone, currently expressed in street protests, is not enough to triumph over politics as usual.

Though situated at one of the most geologically stable places in the world, Sri Lanka has experienced both environmental and political catastrophes since independence. The effects of a devastating tsunami in 2004 that claimed thirty-five thousand lives still linger, and the country has endured a decades-long civil war between indigenous Sinhalese and Tamils, descendants of generations of southern Indian plantation workers imported by the British. This conflict ended in 2009 with the crushing defeat of Tamil militants and near-genocidal postwar mopping-up operations by the Sinhalese army (which in 2009 killed over forty thousand Tamil noncombatants). Reconciliation between these two peoples

after violence on this scale seemed unlikely. However, when the leading Tamil political party battling discrimination at the hands of the
Sinhalese majority withdrew its demands for a separate state, a "Lessons
Learnt and Reconciliation Commission" (2010) was established, holding out hope of recovery from war. It remains to be seen whether spo-
radic attacks by ultranationalists on Sri Lankan Muslims in 2015 will
subside before its human costs rise to higher levels.

Few would have predicted that any sort of democratic political
progress, let alone peace, was possible in Myanmar (formerly Burma).
In 1947, while negotiating the final steps of its march to independence
from Britain, its popular leftist leader, Aung San, was assassinated by
political rivals. This event released ethnic separatist passions once held
in check by colonial rule and provided a rationale for the creation of
a military junta, which banned opposition parties and rarely held elections. In 2010, the pro-junta results of the first elections held in twenty
years were judged to be fraudulent by the international community,
strengthening the hand of a pro-democracy movement led by Aung San
Suu Kyi, Aung San's daughter, who had been under house arrest for the
previous fourteen years. Buoyed by international public opinion in her
favor, she employed Gandhian civil disobedience to weaken the authoritarian regime in her country, only to be rearrested that same year. The
combination of the resulting international boycott and the refusal of
the democracy movement to relent or abandon its commitment to non-
violence ultimately forced the government to change tack. Aung San
Suu Kyi was soon released, a National Human Rights Commission
was established, labor unions and strikes were allowed, and press cen-
sorship was relaxed. In 2012, by-elections took place in which Aung
San Suu Kyi's National League for Democracy Party won forty-three
of the forty-five seats in the National Assembly that the junta allowed
it to contest. Another round of elections in 2015 swept her party into
power, enabling it to control all major offices. Though a clause in the
nation's constitution, deliberately created by the military to keep her
from serving as president (due to the foreign birth of her British husband and children), denied her the title of prime minister, her victorious
party immediately created a new post for her, state counsellor, which
placed her at the head of the government.

Since then, Aung San Suu Kyi has been struggling to hold
Myanmar's larger ethnic divisions in check. To do so, she appears to be
at best ignoring, at worst condoning, the oppression of the small resident Muslim population in her Buddhist nation, which regards them
as illegal immigrants. Nonetheless, she has helped her country achieve

multi-party elections, a relatively free press, the right of association under the law, and limited devolution of some government functions to fourteen state and regional governments and six autonomous zones. Under her leadership, Myanmar has peacefully negotiated the transfer of power from a dictatorship to a democracy and established the institutional stability necessary to keep the reform process moving, investors coming, and the economy growing.

The current place of Aung San Suu Kyi in Myanmar calls to mind a paradox of gender in South Asia. She numbers among several powerful South Asian women, such as Benazir Bhutto, Indira Gandhi, Sheikh Hasina, and Khaleda Zia, who are the daughters or wives of famous men. Their success is often attributed to a common belief that the strength of a powerful male resides in his offspring or near relations, even if they are women. Yet the region's people—Hindu and Muslim,

male and female—take great joy in the victories of their female athletes and have engaged in widespread protests in response to a recent rise in gang rapes, honor killings, and the attempted execution of a Pakistani girl by the Taliban for speaking out in favor of women's education. These developments suggest that the place of women and gender in politics is far more complex than common wisdom recognizes. It may also be taken as evidence of slowly improving gender relations, despite the recent global rise in patriarchy, driven perhaps by male economic and social insecurity in the face of globalization, for which patriarchal religious fundamentalism offers an antidote. The Taliban's view of the place of women, as well as gays, lesbians, and transgendered persons, is unique only in the means with which they pursue the most conservative and punitive injunctions of divine law found in many other creeds as well.

It is remarkable how many themes in world history have played across South Asia during its long history. The most recent include the cost of partition as a vehicle for decolonization (Ireland and Palestine, as well as South Asia) and the failures of postcolonial development efforts driven by a wide range of political and religious ideologies. It is even more remarkable how clearly such themes have been illuminated by South Asian writers of both fiction and nonfiction. Kuswant Singh (*Train to Pakistan*) made the agony of partition palpable to non–South Asian readers. The works of V. S. Naipaul and Jhumpa Lahiri have explored the struggle for identity in diasporic and immigrant communities. The late Kamala Purnaiya Taylor, writing as Kamala Markandaya, provided an intimate view of the global impact of industrialization and urbanization (*Nectar in a Sieve*). Maryse Jayasuriya's study of Sri Lanka's ethnic conflict, *Terror and Reconciliation*, has expanded our understanding of ethnic violence, while Salman Rushdie's *Satanic Verses* sparked global controversy over his exploration of the boundaries of faith and religious ideology in India and the world. Vandana Shiva and Arundhati Roy are among many South Asians writers who have raised global awareness of the potentially unsustainable nature and pace of global economic development. Siddhartha Mukerjee's *The Emperor of All Maladies: A Biography of Cancer* has illuminated this universal threat to human health, while the global plague of corruption is likened to a form of lunacy in Bano Qudsia's now classic Urdu novel, *Raja Gidh* (King of the Vultures).

Among some nationalists, the many prizes won by South Asia writers writing in English or benefiting from English translations of their works are not prizes at all, merely signs of the triumph of globalization over the subcontinent's local, mostly Sanskrit-based languages. Such concerns over the cost of cultural globalization in South Asia are particularly clearly expressed in a current trend threatening the Indian film industry, often called "Bollywood" for the location of most Indian film studios in the city formerly known as Bombay. Though Bollywood has long beaten the West in the number of films produced and distributed globally, it now fears that market forces will compel it to abandon its distinctive qualities as an Indian cinema. Many producers fear that the defining characteristic of their *filmi* (film culture), the chaste romance, will be replaced by the more sexually explicit action typical of Western films. Bollywood products have long been seen as a haven for global customers seeking to defend traditional conservative values, but if current market forces prevail, Bollywood films may give way to the demands of the global marketplace, undermining both diversity and local cultural values. Certainly, over the past decade, media commentators have noted how "Indian film producers are under pressure to push at the boundaries," and that their films are becoming more "raunchy."[11]

South Asia's media and the arts, as well as its politics, clearly lend themselves to the examination of the capacity of its people for innovation, synthesis, and inspiration identified throughout this study of the region's journey through world history. Recent developments in one of the smallest of South Asia's nations, Bhutan, perhaps offer the most expansive and the most positive measure of that capacity.

Bhutan is a modern state, organized on the lines of a traditional hereditary Buddhist monarchy. From the early 1900s, Bhutan's foreign policy was controlled by Britain and, after 1949, by India. However, since 1971, Bhutan has strengthened its sovereign status. In 2003, its king, Jigme Singye Wangchuk, began promulgating a constitution (completed in 2008) featuring decentralized, democratic governance, even though his subjects were satisfied with the old regime. The government then committed itself to achieving a high measure of "gross national happiness." This effort is exemplified by the country's new hydroelectric power plants buried in its steep mountains, next to reservoirs whose creation did not displace humans or disturb the beauty of their surrounding natural environment. The funds accruing to the government for selling this energy to China and India are being directed to education and to raising the general standard of living. Naturally, increased education and wealth and the freedom of choice that flows from them have already begun to undermine the traditional Buddhist values of the state. Access to television and the Internet have seen to that. Bhutan

Bhutanese children play soccer. Friends of Bhutanese indigenous culture are concerned that young Bhutanese children will be negatively influenced by the spread of Western culture. Photo by Hung Chung Chih/Shutterstock 375981034

recognizes this and has not been above taking harsh measures to keep the nation on an even keel. Thousands of Nepalese migrant workers and longtime residents were expelled to maintain the cultural cohesion of, and economic opportunities for, the Bhutanese, though some have since been permitted to return.

Bhutan seems to be taking the line that the challenges that flow from what the world calls modernization are just that—challenges—and that good government, in Buddhist practice, rests with the people's engagement with each other and the world. Of course, as the Buddha taught, things do change. Without abundant water resources, what might be the fate of Bhutan's experiment in "Taking the Middle Path to Happiness?"[12] However, at present, Bhutan is seen as an example of sustainable development conducted on a national scale. The recent dramatic growth in the world's population, the consequent over-fishing of the oceans, and the depletion of clean water and other natural resources due to a variety of seemingly irreversible factors have led some observers to believe that sustainable development must replace the concept of economic growth at any price. Bhutan is a case study on how sustainable development might be achieved.

Bhutan's recent history is in keeping with the history of South Asia and its place in the world. All nations are increasingly challenged by the demands of diversity, as well as the homogenizing/polarizing forces of modernization and globalization. All nations are struggling to blend traditional ethical values with modern economic theories. All nations are increasingly aware of their vulnerability to shifts in the natural environment. Bhutan's recent experiences may thus serve to remind us that, looking back over five millennia of South Asian history, it can be said of South Asia what has been said of its great epic poem, the *Mahabharata*: "There is nothing in it that cannot be found elsewhere in the world, and nothing in the world that cannot be found there."[13]

Chronology

7000–3300 BCE
Neolithic Era; beginnings of agriculture in the Indus valley; craftspeople make stone beads and bangles; artisans make pottery and copper and bronze tools; potters place identification marks on their work; potter's wheels appear; first writing at Harappa

2800–1900 BCE
Peak years of Harappan civilization; trade with Sumer; Harappans build drains and some houses of baked brick; after 1900 BCE urban complexes in the Indus Valley begin to decline

c. 1500–1200 BCE
Four Vedas are composed as an oral tradition

c. 800–500 BCE
Upanishads are composed

599–527 BCE
Life of Mahavira

563–483 BCE
Life of the Buddha

326 BCE
Alexander the Great in South Asia

321 BCE
Chandragupta Maurya overthrows the Nanda dynasty and establishes the Mauryan Empire

c. 268 TO 232 BCE
Reign of Ashoka

200 BCE–200 CE
Height of Buddhist influence in South Asia

185 BCE
End of the Mauryan Empire

78 BCE—150 CE
Kushans arrive in South Asia; rule of Kaniska; Indo-Greek art flourishes in Gandhara; Buddhist sects emerge; trade with Rome flourishes

320 CE–500 CE
Era of the Guptan Empire; science, the arts, and literature flourish

399 CE–412 CE
Chinese monk Faxian travels to and from South Asia

454–467, 495
Hunas (Huns) invade, are initially repelled, but return to set up states that undermine Guptan authority

476–550
Astronomer Aryabhata at work describing the solar system

629–645
Chinese monk Xuanzang journeys to India and returns to China bringing Mahayanist Buddhist teachings and texts to China

711–712
Muslim Arab conquest of Sindh

1192–1198
Delhi Sultanate established

1221–1337
Mongol invasions of the subcontinent

1398
Timur sacks Delhi

1498
Portuguese arrive in Calicut

1526
First Battle of Panipat; the Mughal Empire is established by Babur (r. 1526–1530), followed by Humayun (r. 1530–1540 and 1555–1556)

1540–1555
Afghan interregnum

1556
Second Battle of Panipat reestablishes Mughal rule; era of the Great Mughals: Akbar (r. 1556–1605), Jahangir (r. 1605–1627), Shah Jahan (r. 1628–1658), and Aurangzeb (Alamgir I) 1658–1707, last powerful Mughal ruler

1600
London Company of Merchants Trading to the East Indies (later, the British East India Company) is founded

1737–1761
Raids and battles between Afghans and Marathas; Marathas are defeated and confederation broken up after Afghan sack of Delhi in 1761 at Third Battle of Panipat

1757–1858
Era of British East India Company rule

1857–1858
The variously named War of 1857, Sepoy Rebellion, the Great Mutiny, or Indian War of Independence of 1857

1858–1947
Era of British Crown rule

1877
Parliament confers upon Queen Victoria the title of Empress of India

1885
Indian National Congress formed

1906
Muslim League founded

1915–1919
Home Rule Movement forces the British to address promises made to Indians of political reforms in recognition of their support during the Great War; results in the Montagu-Chelmsford reform scheme and Government of Indian Act of 1919

1919
Rowlatt Act extends wartime restrictions on Indian liberties; Amritsar Massacre

1919–1922
Khilafat Movement

1930
Gandhi's Salt March to the Sea

1935
Government of India Act

1942
Cripps Mission fails; "Quit India Movement," imprisonment of most of the leadership of the Indian National Congress

1946
"Direct Action" call by Muhammad Ali Jinnah

1947
Partition accompanying the independence of India and Pakistan amid communal massacres

1948–1949
Burma (now Myanmar) achieves independence, followed a year later by Sri Lanka

1955
India and Sri Lanka help spearhead the Non-Aligned Movement

1958–1971, 1977–1988, 1999–2008
Military coups periodically interrupt civilian government in Pakistan

1964–1966
Nehru dies; two years later, his daughter, Indira Gandhi, becomes prime minister

1971
Indo-Pakistan conflict, leading to the creation of Bangladesh

1977
Indira Gandhi driven from office

1983
Sri Lankan Civil War begins, continues to 2009

1984
Indira Gandhi returns as prime minister; she is assassinated in the wake of Operation Blue Star; her son Rajiv Gandhi succeeds her as prime minister

1984–1991
Rajiv Gandhi begins the process of economic liberalization, lends support

to the development of a high-technology and service economy

1989
Aung San Suu Kyi is first sentenced to house arrest; she will spend much of the next fifteen years under government detention

2003
The BJP is ascendant in the Indian government, ruling with a coalition of parties of the National Democratic Alliance from 1998 to 2004

2003
Bhutan begins development policy promoting "gross national happiness"

2004–2014
India is governed by the India National Congress Party–led coalition (the United Progressive Alliance); beginning of 8 percent annual growth rate

2007
Benazir Bhutto, who served nonconsecutive terms as prime minister of Pakistan (1988–1990 and 1993–1997), is assassinated days before elections that would have returned her to power

2010
Bangladesh begins its run at top of the Global Climate Risk Index

2012
"Coalgate" scandal in India

2014
Slowing economic growth leads to the election of a BJP government led by Narendra Modi

2015
Delhi achieves the status of the world's most polluted capital city

2016
China pledges to expand cooperation with India to fight global terrorism

Notes

PREFACE

1. F. Max Müller, *India: What Can It Teach Us? A Course of Lectures Delivered Before the University of Cambridge* (London: Longmans, Green, and Co., 1892), 15.

2. Romain Rolland, *Prophets of the New India*, trans. E. F. Malcolm-Smith (London: Cassell and Company, 1930), 4.

3. William Shakespeare, *Henry IV, Part I*, act III, scene 1, line 1710, and *The Merchant of Venice*, act II, scene 2, line 1626.

4. Jawaharlal Nehru, *The Discovery of India* (Delhi: Penguin, 2010), 562.

CHAPTER 1

1. See the discussion of this trade in Mark Kenoyer and Kimberly Heuston, *The Ancient South Asian World* (New York: Oxford, 2005), 64–65.

2. Mortimer Wheeler, *The Indus Civilization and Beyond* (New York: McGraw-Hill, 1966), 37–41.

3. Sargon's scribes quoted in Noah S. Kramer, *The Sumerians: Their History, Culture and Character* (Chicago: University of Chicago Press, 1963), 281–284.

CHAPTER 2

1. Raimon Panikkar, trans., *The Vedic Experience: Mantramañjarī: An Anthology of the Vedas for Modern Man and Contemporary Celebration* (Berkeley: University of California Press, 1977), 123.

2. Manusmṛti, 3.55–57 quoted in William Theodore DeBary, ed., *Sources of Indian Tradition* (Delhi: Motilal Banarsidass, 1988), 237.

3. Ralph T. H. Griffith, trans., *Hymns of the Rigveda*, 3rd ed. (Benares: E. Lazarus and Company, 1926), 1:43–44.

4. Devi Chand, trans., *The Yajur Veda* (Hoshiapur, India: All India Dayanand Salvation Mission, 1959), 296.

5. Ralph T. H. Griffith, trans., *Hymns of the Artharvaveda* (Benares: E. Lazarus and Company, 1916), 1:214.

6. Griffith, *Hymns of the Rigveda*, 2:365.

7. A balanced assessment of the "Aryan Invasion theory" and its associated arguments can be found in Edwin Bryant, *The Quest for the Origins of Vedic Culture: The Indo-Aryan Migration Debate* (London: Oxford University Press, 2001).

8. Johannes Adrianus Bernardus van Buitenen, ed. and trans., *The Mahabharata* (Chicago: University of Chicago Press, 1981), Book 2, 2:122.

9. Krishna Dharma, *The Mahabharata: Retold by Krishna Dharma* (Nadia, India: Torchlight, 2008) at http://www.vedabase.com/en/mbk/2/7, accessed January 8, 2016.

10. Hari Prasad Shastri, trans., *The Ramayana of Valmiki: The Complete Modern English Translation* (London: Shanti Sadan, 1952), 3:40–41.

11. Jiotty Kausahl, *A Son, a Prince, a Husband, a King: Ramayana, an Interpretation*, 2nd ed. (Gadalming, Surrey, UK: Busbridge Publishing, 2012), 236.

12. Griffith, *Hymns of the Rigveda*, 1:86.

13. Robert Ernest Hume, trans., *The Thirteen Principal Upanishads Translated from the Sanskrit with an Outline of the Philosophy of the Upanishads and an Annotated Bibliography*, 2nd rev. ed. (London: Oxford University Press, 1931), 128.

14. Hume, *The Thirteen Principal Upanishads*, 248.

15. Ibid., 209–210.

16. *Ācharanga Sutra*, Book 1, Lecture 4, Lesson 1, trans. H. Jacobi, quoted in Michael W. Fox, *The Boundless Circle: Caring for Creatures and Creation* (Wheaton, IL: Quest Books, 1996), 262.

17. In the first book of the *Acharanga Sutra*, the elements of nature are described as living beings and thus to be protected; consequently, there "should be no waste, no overuse, no abuse, and no polluting." Remarks of R. P. Chandaria, Chairman of the Institute of Jainology, August 15, 2008, at the Alliance on Religions and Conservation, http://www.arcworld.org/faiths.asp?pageID=7, accessed on January 8, 2016.

18. Manpreet Singh, "Buddha Statues Destroyed Completely," *Buddhism Today News Service*, October 3, 2001, at http://www.buddhismtoday.com/english/world/facts/091-destruction.htm, accessed on January 8, 2016.

19. Thomas W. Rhys Davids and Hermann Oldenberg, trans., *Vinaya Texts, The Sacred Books of the East* (Oxford: Clarendon Press, 1879–1910), 13:94–97.

CHAPTER 3

1. Plutarch, *Plutarch's Lives, The Translation Called Dryden's Corrected from the Greek by A. H. Clough, in Five Volumes* (Boston: Little, Brown and Company, 1906), 4:239; Plutarch, *Plutarch's Lives: Demosthenes, Cicero, Alexander and Caesar*, trans. Bernadotte Perrin (Cambridge, MA: Harvard University Press, 1958), 403.

2. Megasthenes, *Ancient India as Described by Megasthenes and Arrian*, ed. and trans. J. W. McCrindle (Calcutta and Bombay: Thacker, Spink, 1877), 30–33.

3. Winthrop Lindsay Adams, *Alexander the Great: Legacy of a Conqueror* (New York: Pearson, 2005), 143. See also Upinder Singh, *A History of Ancient and Early Medieval India: From the Stone Age to the Twelfth Century* (New York: Pearson, 2008), 331.

4. "13th Rock Edict of Ashoka," in Ananya Vajpeyi, *The Righteous Republic: The Foundations of Modern India* (Cambridge, MA: Harvard University Press, 2012), Appendix B, 255.

5. Alexander Cunningham, *Inscriptions of Asoka* (Calcutta: Office of the Superintendent of the Government Press, 1877), 140.

6. Ibid.

7. Thomas Christie, ed., *The Analytical Review; or, History of Literature, Domestic and Foreign, on an Enlarged Plan 9* (January–April 1791): 484.

8. *The Periplus of the Erythrean Sea: Travel and Trade in the Indian Ocean by a Merchant of the First Century*, trans. Wilfred H. Schoff (New York: Longmans, Greem and Co., 1912), 42.

9. P. Meile, "Le Yavananadans l'Indetamoule," *Journal Asiatique* 232 (1940): 85–123.

10. See Faxian, *The Travels of Fa-hsien (399–414 A.D.); or, Record of the Buddhistic Kingdoms*, trans. Herbert Allen Giles (Cambridge: Cambridge University Press, 1923), 69.

11. Arthur W. Ryder, trans., *Translation of Shakuntala and Other Works, Translated by Arthur W. Ryder* (London: J. M. Dent, 1912), 39–50.

12. Barbara Stoler Miller, trans., Barry Moser, illus., *The Bhagavad-Gita: Krishna's Counsel in Time of War* (New York: Columbia University Press, 1986), 32.

13. Ibid.

14. Ibid.

15. Quoted in Tansen Sen, "The Travel Records of Chinese Pilgrims Faxian, Xuanzang, and Yijing: Sources for Cross-Cultural Encounters Between Ancient China and Ancient India," *Education about Asia* 11, no. 3 (2006): 29–30.

CHAPTER 4

1. The Greeks mistook the Sanskrit term for a river (*sindhu*) as the name of the river they mispronounced as Indos, later Latinized as Indus, with the region and its people called India and Indian. The Muslim world follows the Persian pronunciation of sindhu, which drops the *s* in favor of an *h*, describing the region as al-Hind or Hindustan, from which English speakers derived the words Hindu, Hinduism, and Hindustani (Hindi).

2. The Holy Quran, Sura 42 (Ash-Shura), Ayah 13, quoted by Michael Oren Fitzgerald, "Universal Foundations of Islam," in *Universal Dimensions of Islam: Studies in Comparative Religion*, ed. Patrick Laude (Bloomington, IN: Wisdom, Inc., 2011), 25.

3. See Edmund Burke, "Islam at the Center: Technological Complexes and the Roots of Modernity," *Journal of World History* 20, no. 2 (June 2009): 165–186.

4. Edward Sachau, ed., *Alberuni's India: An Account of the Religion, Philosophy, Literature, Geography, Chronology, Astronomy, Customs, Laws and Astrology of India about A.D. 1030, Edited, with Notes and Indices* (Delhi: S. Chand, Indian reprint, 1964), 22.

5. Domingos Paes, "Narrative of Domingos Paes of Things Which I Saw and Contrived to Learn Concerning the Kingdom of Narasimga," in Robert Sewell, *A Forgotten Empire (Vijayanagar), a Contribution to the History of India*, 2nd Indian ed. (New Delhi: National Book Trust, 1970), 247–248.

6. C. Defrémery and B. R. Sanguinetti, eds. and trans., *Voyages d'Ibn Batoutah* (Paris, Imprimerie Nationale, 1853–58), 3:145.

7. Fīroz Shāh Tughlaq, Futūhāt-i-Fīroz Shāhī, in H. M. Elliott and John Dowson, eds. and trans., *The History of India as Told by Its Own Historians: The Mohammadan Period* (Allahabad, Bombay, Delhi, Calcutta, Jaipur and Patna: Kitah Mahal Private Ltd., 1964), 3:374–381.

8. Malfuzat-I Timuri in H. M. Elliott and John Dowson, eds. and trans., *The History of India as Told by Its Own Historians: The Mohammadan Period* (Allahabad, Bombay, Delhi, Calcutta, Jaipur and Patna: Kitah Mahal Private Ltd., 1964), 3:446.

9. See Douglas E. Streusand, *Islamic Gunpowder Empires: Ottomans, Safavids, and Mughals* (New York: Perseus Books Group, 2010).

10. These and related Sufi views can found in English translation in Khaliq Ahmad Nizami, *Supplement to Elliot and Dawson's History of India by Its Own Historians, Muslim Polity in India during the Fourteenth Century* (Delhi: Idarah-i Adabiyat-i-Delli, 2009), 3:6, 11, and in both Urdu and English at Khaliq Amad Nizami, "The Contribution of Indian Sufis to Peace and Amity," a website maintained by the Indira Gandhi National Centre for the Arts, New Delhi, at http://ignca.nic.in/cd_09019.htm, accessed Jannuary 8, 2016.

11. Rabindranath Tagore, trans., *Songs of Kabir* (New York: Macmillan, 1915), 100, 122.

12. Dadu's Prayer is quoted in "Dadupantis," at http://www.philtar.ac.uk/encyclopedia/hindu/devot/dadup.html, accessed on January 8, 2016.

CHAPTER 5

1. J. Horton Ryley, *Ralph Fitch, England's Pioneer to India and Burma: His Companions and Contemporaries, with His Remarkable Narrative Told in His Own Words* (London: T. F. Unwin, 1899), 98.

2. Ibid., 98n1.

3. Quoted in R. P. Karkaria, "The Religion of Akbar," *The Imperial and Asiatic Quarterly Review and Oriental and Colonial Record*, 3rd Series, 5, nos. 9 and 10 (1898): 167.

4. "Letter of Akbar to Philip II of Spain, Fatehpur Sikri, c. March 25–April 23, 1582," reproduced in Jorge Flores and Antonio Vasconcelos de Saldanha, eds., Richard Trewinnard and Mário Semião, trans., *Os Firangis na Chancelaria Mogol: Copias Portuguesas de Documentos de Akbar, 1572–1604* (New Delhi: Embaixada de Portugal, 2003), 87.

5. Fei Hsin, *Hsing-ch'a-sheng-lan: The Overall Survey of the Star Raft*, ed. Roderick Ptak, trans. J. V. G. Mills (Wiesbaden: Harrassowitz, 1996), Part 1, 31–32, 67–69.

6. Ellison B. Findly, "The Capture of Maryam-uz-Zamānī's Ship: Mughal Women and European Traders," *Journal of the American Oriental Society* 108, no. 2 (1988): 227–238.

7. Quoted in Patnaik Naveen, *A Second Paradise: Indian Country Life, 1590–1947* (New York: Doubleday, 1985), 55.

8. Nizami, *Supplement to Elliot and Dawson's History of India*, 3:18.

9. Letter from Shivaji to Aurangzeb, quoted in J. N. Sarkar, *Shivaji and His Times*, 2nd rev. ed. (London and New York: Longmans, Green and Company, 1920), 366–370.

10. Letter from Colonel Mill to the German Emperor, in William Bolts, *Considerations on Indian Affairs* (London: J. Dodsley, 1771–75), 2:xv–xvi.

11. Marc Jason Gilbert, "The Collapse of the English Trade Entrepôts at Pulo Condore and Banjarmasin and the Legacy of Early British East India Company Urban Network-Building in Southeast Asia," in *The Growth of Non-Western Cities: Primary and Secondary Urban Networking, c. 900–1900*, ed. Kenneth R. Hall (Lanham, MD: Rowman and Littlefield, 2011), 205–239.

12. Letter from Aurangzeb to Muhammad Azam, his third son, quoted in Waldemar Hasen, *The Peacock Throne* (New York: Hot, Rinehart, and Winston, 1972, 1972), 485.

13. Shah Wali-ullah, Al-Tafhimat al-Ilahiyya of Shah Wali-ullah, quoted in Saiyid Athar Abbas Rizvi, *Shāh Walī-Allāh and His Times: A Study of Eighteenth Century Islām, Politics, and Society in India* (Canberra: Marifat Publishing, 1980) 312–313.

CHAPTER 6

1. Report of a speech Aurangzeb addressed to his former tutor, Mullah Shah, c. 1658, given to François Bernier then in Delhi, in François Bernier, *Travels in the Mogul Empire*, A.D. *1656–1668*, 2nd ed. (London: Oxford University Press, 1916), 155–157.

2. The joint-stock system provided for buying and selling shares in a company, which diversified risk for its many investors. It was developed by the Dutch as well as the British and applied to their Asian trade in 1600–1602.

3. "Queenes Majestie to Zelabdin Echebar, King of Cambaia, and sent by John Newbery. In February Anno 1583," in Richard Hakluyt and Edmund Goldsmid,

The Principal Navigations, Voyages, Traffiques and Discoveries of the English Nation, Vol. X Asia Part III (Edinburgh: E & G Goldsmid, 1889), 9–10.

4. "The King's Letters Sent to Selim Shagh, the Great Mughal, in the Year 1614 by Thomas Roe," in C. U. Aitchison, A Collection of Treaties, Engagements, and Sunnads Relating to India and Neighboring Countries (Calcutta: Foreign Department at the Government Press, 1892), 356–358.

5. "Sir Thomas Roe to the East India Company, November 24, 1616," in The Embassy of Sir Thomas Roe to India: 1615–1619, ed. William Foster (London: Hakluyt Society, 1899), 2:342–352.

6. General Letter from Bengal to the Court of Directors, December 14, 1694, in C. R. Wilson, Old Fort William in Bengal: A Selection of Official Documents Dealing with Its History (London: John Murray, 1906), 1:15.

7. William Bolts, Considerations on India Affairs: Particularly Respecting the Present State of Bengal and Its Dependencies. With a Map of Those Countries, Chiefly from Actual Surveys. By William Bolts, Merchant, and Alderman, or Judge of the Hon. Mayor's Court of Calcutta (London: printed for J. Almon in Piccadilly, P. Elmsley in the Strand, and Richardson and Urquhart under the Royal Exchange), 2:xv–xvi.

8. Charles Stuart, Vindication of the Hindoos: Part the Second, in Reply to the Observations of the Christian Observer; of Mr. Fuller, Secretary to the Baptist Mission (London: Black, Parry, and Kingsbury, 1808), 105–106.

9. William Hodges, Travels in India During the Years 1780, 1781, 1782, & 1783 (London: Printed for the author and sold by J. Edwards, Pall-Mall, 1793), 60.

10. Sophia Dobson Collet and Hem Chandra Sarkar, eds., The Life and Letters of Raja Rammohun Roy, 2nd ed. (Calcutta: R. Cambray and Company, 1914), 124.

11. Henry Louis Vivian Derozio, The Fakeer of Jungheera, a Metrical Tale: and Other Poems (Calcutta: Samuel Smith, Hukaru Library, 1828), unnumbered page following the Dedication.

12. Ibid., 124.

13. Remarks made during a 1772–1773 Parliamenty Committee (House of Commons) inquiry into the Company affairs, in Alexander J. Arbuthnot, Lord Clive: The Foundation of British Rule in India (New York: Longmans, Green, 1899), 207.

14. James Mill, The History of British India, abridged by William Thomas (Chicago: University of Chicago Press, 1975), 225–226, 232–237, 272–273, 545–549, 582.

15. Letter from Jeremy Bentham to Colonel Arthur Young, December 28, 1826, in Jeremy Bentham, The Works of Jeremy Bentham, Published under the Superintendence of His Executor, John Bowring (Edinburgh: William Tait, 1843), 10:577.

16. Comments of Sir Charles Napier upon addressing a delegation of Brahmans in Sindh in 1843 as related by his brother William, in William Napier, History of General Sir Charles Napier's Administration of Scinde (London: Chapman and Hall, 1851), 35.

17. Ibid., and John Rosselli, Lord William Bentinck: The Making of a Liberal Imperialist, 1774–1789 (Berkeley: University of California Press, 1974), 210.

18. Government of India Act, 1833 (3 & 4 Will. 4 c. 85).

19. Thomas Babington Macaulay, Speech on July 10, 1833, Great Britain, Parliamentary Debates (hereafter referred to as Hansard), 3rd series (Commons), vol. 19, cols. 535–536.

20. Thomas Babington Macaulay, "Minute by the Hon'ble T. B. Macaulay, dated the 2nd February 1835," in Bureau of Education Selections from Educational Records,

Part I, ed. H. Sharp (Calcutta: Superintendent, Government Printing, 1920; reprint, National Archives of India, Delhi, 1965), 107–117.

21. The Doctrine of Lapse abrogated the ancient custom of rulers adopting an heir to inherit a throne. Under this doctrine, the British gave themselves the right to veto such a succession and annex the state should it wish to do so.

22. Lady Selina Inglis, *The Siege of Lucknow: A Diary* (London: James R. Osgood, McIlvaine and Co., 1892), 11.

23. M. M. Kaye, ed., *The Golden Calm: An English Lady's Life in Moghul Delhi* (New York: Viking Press, 1980), 212.

24. This was a riposte aimed at a sepoy who would not share water with a lower-caste passerby, quoted in Charles Creighton Hazewell, "The Indian Revolt," *The Atlantic Monthly* 1, no. 2 (December 1857): 217–222.

25. Sita Ram quoted in "Indian Voices from the 1857 Rebellion: The Indian Mutiny and Rebellion, Which Broke out 150 Years Ago This Month, Was the Greatest Revolt against British Imperialism of Its Century, Joseph Coohill Uncovers Some Indian Accounts of What Happened and Why," *History Today* 57, no. 5 (May 2007): 48.

26. See Daniel Headrick, *Tools of Empire: Technology and European Imperialism in the Nineteenth Century* (New York: Oxford University Press, 1981).

27. This is a paraphrase of a line from Hilaire Belloc and Basil Temple Blackwood, *The Modern Traveler* (Edwin Arnold, 1898), 41; its meaning here is supported by Michael Adas, *Machines as the Measure of Men: Science, Technology and Ideologies of Western Dominance* (Ithaca, NY: Cornell University Press, 1989).

28. Robert Travers, "Imperial Revolutions and Global Repercussions: South Asia and the World, c. 1750–1850," in David Armitage and Sanjay Subramanyam, eds., *The Age of Revolutions in Global Context, c. 1760–1840* (New York: Palgrave/Macmillan, 2010), 165.

29. The *Din Bandhu*, January 9, 1889, British Library, London, India Office Records, Indian Newspaper Reports, L/R/5/136.

30. Charles Gordon to Florence Nightingale, April 25, 1881, British Library, London, Additional Manuscripts, 45806, fos. 136–137. For the full text of this and other correspondence between Gordon and Nightingale, and her interest in Indian politics, see Marc Jason Gilbert, "Florence Nightingale and the Indian National Congress," in Reeta Chowdhari Tremblay, et al., eds. *Interfacing Nations: Reflections on the 50th Anniversary of India's Independence* (Delhi: B. R. Publishing Corporation for the Canadian Asian Studies Association, 1998), 17–48.

CHAPTER 7

1. Quoted in Christopher Hibbert and Hugh Thomas, *Edward VII: The Last Victorian King*, 2nd ed. (New York and London: Palgrave Macmillan, 2007), 138.

2. For the use of the term "New India," see Henry James Steadman Cotton, *New India or India in Transition* (London: Kegan, Paul, Trench, and Trubner, 1909). For the Indian "middle class," in both South Asian and global contexts, see A. Ricardo López and Barbara Weinstein, eds., *The Making of the Middle Class: Toward a Transnational History* (Durham: Duke University Press, 2012), 36–63.

3. "Aqidah (Belief)," quoted in Anwar Moazzam, *Jamāl Al-Dīn Al-Afghānī, a Muslim Intellectual* (New Delhi: Concept Publishing Company, 1984), 13.

4. John Wesley Hanson, ed., *The World's Congress of Religions: The Addresses and Papers Delivered Before the Parliament and an Abstract of the Congresses Held in the Art Institute, Chicago, Illinois, U.S.A, August 25 to October 15, 1893* (Chicago: International Publishing Company, 1894), 39.

5. Dadabhai Naoroji, *Poverty and un-British Rule in India* (London: Winckworth and Folger, 1888), 191.

6. Vinayak Damodar Savakar, *The Indian War of Independence of 1857* (London: n.p., 1909).

7. See David Cannadine, *Ornamentalism: How the British Saw Their Empire* (London: Allen Lane, 2001).

8. See Edwin Hirschmann, *The "White Mutiny": The Ilbert Bill Crisis and the Emergence of Indian Nationalism* (Delhi: South Asia Books, 1980).

9. Lansdowne to Cross, June 12, 1889; February 12, 1889, British Library, London, India Office Records, Eur. MSS D. 558/2, and "Note" by the viceroy, July 4, 1889, British Library Eur. MSS 558/58. For Ripon's, Lansdowne's, and Minto's policies, see Marc Jason Gilbert, "Insurmountable Distinctions: Racism and the British Response to Indian Nationalism," in *The Man on the Spot: Essays on British Empire History*, ed. Roger Long (Westport, CT: Greenwood Press, 1995), 161–181. The most liberal elements of the 1892 reform have been mistakenly attributed to Lord Dufferin, the viceroy who served between Ripon's and Lansdowne's administrations.

10. Lord Minto to Sir John Morley, July 11, 1906, in Mary, Countess Minto, *Minto, Morley and India 1905–1910: Compiled from the Correspondence Between the Viceroy and the Secretary of State by Mary, Countess of Minto: With Extracts from Her Indian Journal* (London: Macmillan, 1934), 98.

11. "Lord Salisbury's Black Man," British Library, London, India Office Records, Tract 682.

12. The Marquis of Dufferin and Ava, "St. Andrew's Day Dinner Speech, November 30, 1888," in *Speeches Delivered in India 1884–1888 by the Marquis of Dufferin and Ava*, ed. D. M. Wallace (London: MacMillan, 1890), 229–248.

13. N. G. Jog, *Lokmanya Bal Gangadhar Tilak* (New Delhi: Indian Ministry of Information and Broadcasting, Publications Division, 1962), 193.

14. The first to employ this phrase was Charles Henry Roberts, speaking in Parliament on November 24, 1914, in his official capacity as undersecretary of state for India (1914–1915). Others who did so included the British prime minister Herbert Henry Asquith. See St. Nihal Singh, "Constitutional Reforms for India," *Fortnightly Review* 109 (New Series), no. 627 (May 1, 1918): 775. Roberts was fully committed to such an advance, but he and other British leaders in Parliament did not consider its ramifications at the time, and Asquith's Liberal Party dominated ministry was forced to admit Conservative Party leaders into Asquith's War Cabinet in May 1915. See also Valentine Chirol, *India Old and New* (London: Macmillan, 1921), 149.

15. Charles Hardinge, 2nd Viscount Hardinge, 1st Baron of Penshurst, *My Indian Years, 1910–1916: The Reminiscences of Lord Hardinge of Penshurst* (London: John Murray, 1948), 99.

16. Quoted in Dajit Nagra, "Last Post: Letters Home to India During the First World War," February 21, 2014, at http://www.theguardian.com/books/2014/feb/21/found-translation-indias-first-world-war, accessed January 6, 2016.

17. "Note by Mr. A. A Baig C.S.I," in the "Report on Government of India Despatch Home Department, No. 17 Political of 24 November 1916," copy in the Duke Committee Report, British Library, London, India Office Records, IOR/L/PO/6/1.

18. A. B. Keith, ed., *Speeches and Documents on Indian Policy, 1750–1921* (London: Oxford University Press, 1922), 2:133–134.

19. Malcolm Seaton, "Diary," Entry of November 26, 1917, British Library, India Office Records, MSS Eur. E. 267/66/1, 99.

20. Balgangadar Tilak, *His Writings and Speeches with an Introduction by Babu Aurabindo Ghose*, enlarged ed. (Madras: Ganesh & Co, 1919), 369–372. For other negative opinions, see press reports included in Telegram Viceroy to the Secretary of State, May 2, 1919, British Library, Indian Office Records, Mss Eur. E. 264/8.

21. Mohinder Singh Pannu, *Partners of British Rule: Liberators or Collaborators?* (Lucknow: Allied Publishers, 2005), 316.

22. Mohandas Karamchand Gandhi, *Autobiography: The Story of My Experiments in Truth.* 2nd ed. (Ahmedabad: Navajivan Publishing House, 1940), 13–14.

23. See Ronald J. Terchek, "Conflict and Nonviolence," in *The Cambridge Companion to Gandhi*, ed. Judith M. Brown and Anthony Parel (Cambridge and New York: Cambridge University Press, 2011), 118, 218.

24. Mohandas Karamchand Gandhi, *Non-Violence in Peace and War* (Ahmadabad: Navajivan Publishing House, 1949), 2:8.

25. Robert Drennan Cravath, *Letters from the Far East and Russia* (Garden City, NY: Country Life Press, 1931), 9.

26. Winton Churchill, *A Roving Commission: My Early Life* (New York: Charles Scribner's Son, 1930), 127–128.

27. Winton Churchill, Speech on July 8, 1920, *Great Britain, Parliamentary Debates (Hansard)*, 5th series (House of Commons), vol. 131, col. 1725.

28. R. R. James (ed.), *Winston S. Churchill: His Complete Speeches, 1897–1963*, (New York: Chelsea House, 1974), 5, 4985.

29. As related by Gandhi's grandson and biographer Rajmohan Gandhi in Rajmohan Gandhi, *Revenge and Reconciliation: Understanding South Asian History* (New York: Penguin, 1999), 205, 218.

30. "Comments on Hindu-Muslim Unity," *Young India*, July 28, 1921, in *The Collected Works of Mahatma Gandhi* [electronic book] (New Delhi: Publications Division Government of India, 1999), 24:18, at http://www.gandhiserve.org/e/ cwmg/cwmg.htm, accessed January 8, 2016.

31. "A Speech at the Lord Mayor's Day Luncheon at the Mansion House, London, November 10, 1942," in Winston S. Churchill, *The End of the Beginning* (London: Cassell, 1943), 264.

32. See Gerhard Weinberg, *Visions of Victory: The Hopes of Eight World War II Leaders* (New York and London: Cambridge University Press, 2007), 143.

33. Winston Churchill, Speech on March 6, 1947, *Great Britain, Parliamentary Papers (Hansard)*, 5th series (House of Commons), vol. 434, cols. 663–678.

34. Interview with Ravi Chopra, participant in an oral history of the Partition, reported in "Oral History Project Races to Record Voices of Partition Survivors in India and Pakistan," in *IndiaRealtime*, August 12, 2014, at http://blogs.wsj.com/ indiarealtime/2014/08/12/oral-history-project-races-to-record-voices-of-partition- survivors-in-india-and-pakistan/, accessed January 8, 2016.

35. Gopal Das Khosla, *Memory's Gay Chariot: An Autobiographical Narrative* (Delhi: Allied, 1985), 175.

CHAPTER 8

1. Jawaharlal Nehru, "A Tryst with Destiny," August 14–15, 1947, in Sarvepalli Gopal, ed., *Selected Works of Jawaharlal Nehru*, 2nd series (New Delhi: Orient Longman, 1972), 3: 135. For context, see Stanley Wolpert, *Nehru: A Tryst with Destiny* (Oxford: Oxford University Press, 1996), 406.

2. Kwame Nkrumah, *Ghana: The Autobiography of Kwame Nkrumah* (New York: International Publishers, 1957), 164. For a critique of this assumption, see Ali Al'Amin Mazrui and Christophe Wondji, eds., *UNESCO General History*

of Africa, vol. 8, Africa since 1935 (Berkeley: University of California Press, 1993), 105.

3. Ela Bhatt, interview with Tom O'Neill, "In the Footsteps of Gandhi," *National Geographic* 228, no. 1 (July 2015), 106.

4. Cynthia Keppley Mahmood, *Fighting for Faith and Nation: Dialogues with Sikh Militants* (Philadelphia: University of Pennsylvania Press, 1996), 40.

5. Indira Gandhi, *Selected Speeches of Indira Gandhi: January 1, 1982–October 30, 1984* (New Delhi: Government of India, Publications Division, Ministry of Information and Broadcasting, 1986), 495.

6. Rajiv Gandhi, "Address to the 99th Joint Session of the United States Congress, June 13, 1985," in *Foreign Affairs Record* (Ministry of External Affairs: External Affairs Division, Government of India) 31, no. 6 (June, 1985): 207.

7. "Dr. Manmohan Singh's Address to the Nation," September 21, 2012, at http://www.ndtv.com/india-news/full-speech-prime-minister-manmohan-singhs-address-to-the-nation-499920, accessed January 8, 2016.

8. Vikas Bajaj and Jim Yardley, "Scandal Poses a Riddle: Will India Ever Be Able to Tackle Corruption?," *New York Times*, September 16, 2012, A6, 8.

9. Kanwal Sibal, "India-Pakistan Dialog: An Anatomy," *Indian Defence Review* 25, no. 3 (July–September 2010), 46.

10. India's Prime Minister Asif Ali Zadari, quoted in Salman Masood, "India and Pakistan Sign Visa Agreement, Easing Travel," *New York Times*, September 9, 2012, A12.

11. "Bollywood Changes," *BBC World Edition*, June 13, 2003, at http://news.bbc.co.uk/2/hi/programmes/newsnight/archive/2987328.stm, accessed January 8, 2016.

12. Tom Vendetti, director, *Bhutan: Taking the Middle Path to Happiness* (Wailuku, HI: Vendetti Productions, 2007).

13. A common axiom evoked, for example, in *The Mahabharata: What Is Not Here Is Nowhere Else*, ed. T. S. Rukmani (Delhi: Munishiram Manoharlal Publishers, 2005).

Further Reading

GENERAL WORKS

Anderson, Benedict. *Imagined Communities: Reflections on the Origin and Spread of Nationalism*. London: Verso, 1985.

Aung-Thwin, Michael, with Maitrii Aung-Thwin. *A History of Myanmar Since Ancient Times: Traditions and Transformations*. London: Reaktion Books, 2012.

Bertz, Ned. *Diaspora and Nation in the Indian Ocean: Transnational Histories of Race and Urban Space in Tanzania*. Honolulu: University of Hawai'i Press, 2015.

Bose, Sugata, and Ayesha Jalal. *Modern South Asia: History, Culture, Political Economy*. Abington, UK: Taylor & Francis, 2011.

Charney, Michael. *A History of Modern Burma*. Cambridge: Cambridge University Press, 2009.

Das, P. K. *The Monsoons*. New Delhi: National Book Trust, 1968.

Dehejia, Vidya. *Indian Art*. London: Phaidon, 1997.

Doniger, Wendy, trans. *Hindu Myths: A Sourcebook Translated from the Sanskrit*. New York: Penguin, 2004.

Embree, Ainslie Thomas, Stephen Hay, and William Theodore De Bary. *Sources of Indian Tradition*. New Delhi: Penguin, 1992.

Gombrich, Richard. *Theravada Buddhism: A Social History from Ancient Benares to Modern Colombo*. 2nd rev. ed. London: Routledge, 2006.

Hill, Christopher V. *South Asia: An Environmental History*. Santa Barbara, CA: ABC-CLIO, 2008.

Long, Roger D., comp. *History of Pakistan*. Karachi: Oxford University Press, 2015.

Madan, T. N., ed. *Muslim Communities of South Asia: Culture, Society, and Power*. Rev. ed. New Delhi: Manoharlal, 1995.

Mills, Margaret, Peter J. Claus, and Sarah Diamond. *South Asia Folklore, an Encyclopedia: Afghanistan, Bangladesh, India, Nepal, Pakistan, Sri Lanka*. New York: Routledge, 2003.

Schmidt, Karl. *An Atlas and Survey of South Asian History*. Armonk, NY: M. E. Sharpe, 1995.

Schwartzberg, Joseph E., ed. *A Historical Atlas of South Asia*. Oxford: Oxford University Press, 1992.

Talbot, Ian. *India and Pakistan*. New York: Bloomsbury, 2000.

Tharu, Susie J., and Ke Lalita, eds. *Women Writing on India, 6000 BC to the Present*. New York: Feminist Press at the City University of New York, 1990.

Wolpert, Stanley. *A New History of India*. 8th ed. New York: Oxford University Press, 2008.

SOUTH ASIA AND THE WORLD TO 1500 BCE

Allchin, Raymond. *The Archeology of Early Historic South Asia: The Emergence of Cities and States.* New York: Cambridge University Press, 1995.

Aronofsky, Ilona, and Sujata Gopinath. *The Indus Valley.* Chicago: Heinemann, 2005.

Aruz, Joan, ed. *The Art of the First Cities: The Third Millennium* BC *from the Mediterranean to the Indus.* New Haven, CT: Yale University Press, 2003.

Basham, A. L. *The Wonder That Was India.* New York: Grove Press, 1967.

Deraniyagala, Siran. *The Prehistory of Sri Lanka: An Ecological Perspective.* Colombo: Archaeological Survey Department of Sri Lanka, 1992.

Huntington, Susan L. *Art of Ancient India.* Boston: Weatherhill, 1985.

Kenoyer, Jonathan Mark. *Ancient Cities of the Indus Valley Civilization.* New York: Oxford University Press, 1998.

Kenoyer, Jonathan Mark. "Uncovering the Keys to Lost Indus Cities." *Scientific American* (July 2003): 67–75.

Lal, B. B. *The Earliest Civilization of South Asia: Rise, Maturity and Decline.* New Delhi: Aryan Books International, 1997.

Marshall, John Hubert. *Mohenjo-daro and the Indus Civilization.* Delhi: Indological Book House, 1973.

Possehl, Gregory L. *The Indus Civilization: A Contemporary Perspective.* London: Altamira Press, 2002.

THE VEDIC AGE, 1500–500 BCE

Bhagarva, Puroshattam Lal. *India in the Vedic Age: A History of Aryan Expansion.* 3rd ed. New Delhi: DK Printworld, 2011.

Bowden, Rob, and Richard Spilsbury. *Settlements of the Ganges River.* Chicago: Heinemann, 2004.

Jamison, Stephanie W. *Sacrificed Wife/Sacrifice's Wife: Women, Ritual, and Hospitality in Ancient India.* New York: Oxford University Press, 1996.

Müller, F. Max, and H. Oldenberg, trans. *Vedic Hymns.* 2 vols. Oxford: Oxford University Press, 1891–1897.

O'Flaherty, Wendy Doniger, ed. *Karma and Rebirth in Classical Indian Traditions.* Berkeley: University of California Press, 1980.

Thapar, Romila. *Early India: From the Origins to* AD *1300.* Berkeley: University of California Press, 2003.

Trautmann, Thomas R. *Aryans and British India.* Berkeley: University of California Press, 1997.

Trautmann, Thomas R. *Dravidian Kingship.* Cambridge: Cambridge University Press, 1981.

Trautmann, Thomas R. *Languages and Nations: The Dravidian Proof in Colonial Madras.* Berkeley: University of California Press, 2006.

Trautmann, Thomas R., ed. *The Aryan Debate.* New Delhi: Oxford University Press, 2005.

Wasson, R. Gordon. *Soma: Divine Mushroom of Immortality.* New York: Harcourt Brace Jovanovich, 1968.

Witzel, Michael, ed. *Inside the Texts, Beyond the Texts: New Approaches to the Study of the Vedas.* Cambridge, MA: Harvard University Press, 1997.

Auboyer, Jeannine. *Daily Life in Ancient India: From 200 BC to 700 AD*. Translated by Watson Taylor. London: Phoenix Press, Orion Publishing Group, 2002.

Basham, A. L., and Kenneth G. Zysk. *The Origins and Development of Classical Hinduism*. Boston: Beacon, 1989.

Chattopadhyaya, Debiprasad. *History of Science and Technology in Ancient India: Astronomy, Science and Society*. Columbia, MO: South Asia Books, 1996.

Coomaraswamy, A. K. *The Dance of Shiva*. Rev. ed. New Delhi: Sagar, 1968.

Davis, Richard. *The Bhagavad Gita: A Biography*. Princeton, NJ: Princeton University Press, 2015.

Faxian. *The Travels of Fa-hsien (399–414 a.d.); or, Record of the Buddhistic Kingdoms*. Translated by Herbert Allen Giles. Cambridge: Cambridge University Press, 1923.

Hinds, Kathryn. *India's Gupta Dynasty*. New York: Benchmark Books, 1996.

Kramrisch, Stella. *The Hindu Temple*. Reprint. Delhi: Motilal Banarsidass, 1976.

Kulke, Hermann. "India's Impact on Southeast Asia: Causes and Consequences." In *A History of India*, edited by Hermann Kulke and Dietmar Rothermund, 151–161. London: Routledge, 1990.

Lahiri, Nayanjot. *Ashoka in Ancient India*. Cambridge, MA: Harvard University Press, 2015.

Liu, Xinru. *Ancient India and China: Trade and Religious Exchanges, AD 1–600*. New Delhi: Oxford University Press, 1988.

Megasthenes. *Ancient India as Described by Megasthenes and Arrian*. Translated by J. W. McCrindle. 2nd ed. Calcutta: Chuckervertty, Chatterjee, 1960.

Miller, Barbara Stoler. *The Bhagavad Gita: Krishna's Counsel in Time of War*. Barry Moser, trans. New York: Columbia University Press, 1986.

Narain, A. K. *The Indo-Greeks*. Oxford: Clarendon Press, 1962.

The Periplus of the Erythrean Sea: Travel and Trade in the Indian Ocean by a Merchant of the First Century. Translated by Wilfred H. Schoff. New York: Longmans, Greem and Co., 1912.

Ray, Himanshu Prabha. *The Archaeology of Seafaring in Ancient South Asia*. Cambridge: Cambridge University Press, 2003.

Sen, Tansen. *Buddhism, Diplomacy and Trade: The Realignment of Sino-Indian Relations, 600–1400*. Honolulu: University of Hawai'i Press, 2003.

Thapar, Romila. *Asoka and the Decline of the Mauryas*. Oxford: Oxford University Press, 1961.

Thapar, Romila. *Early India: From the Origins to AD 1300*. Berkeley: University of California Press, 2003.

Wilkinson, Phillip. *Buddhism*. New York: Dorling Kindersley, 2001.

Wood, Francis. *The Silk Road: Two Thousand Years in the Heart of Asia*. Berkeley: University of California Press, 2004.

Xuanzang. *Si-yu-ki: Buddhist Records of the Western World*. Translated by S. Beal. Delhi: Oriental Books Reprint Corp., 1969.

Young, Gary K. *Rome's Eastern Trade: International Commerce and Imperial Policy 31 BC–AD 305*. London: Routledge, 2001.

Zimmer, Heinrich, and Joseph Campbell. *Myths and Symbols in Indian art and Civilization*. New York: Pantheon Books, 1946.

ISLAM IN SOUTH ASIA, 711–1556

Ali, Daud. *Courtly Cultural and Political Life in Early Medieval India*. Cambridge: Cambridge University Press, 2004.

Asher, Catherine B. *Architecture of Mughal India*. New York: Cambridge University Press, 1993.

Asher, Catherine B., and Cynthia Talbot. *India Before Europe*. Cambridge: Cambridge University Press, 2006.

Aziz, Ahmad. *An Intellectual History of Islam in India*. Edinburgh: Edinburgh University Press, 1969.

Burke, Edmund. "Islam at the Center: Technological Complexes and the Roots of Modernity." *Journal of World History* 20, no. 2 (June 2009): 165–186.

Decker, Michael. "Plants and Progress: Rethinking the Islamic Agricultural Revolution." *Journal of World History* 20, no. 2 (June 2009): 187–206.

Eaton, Richard Maxwell. *The Rise of Islam and the Bengal Frontier, 1204–1760*. Berkeley: University of California Press, 1993.

Eaton, Richard Maxwell, ed. *India's Islamic Traditions, 711–1750*. New Delhi: Oxford University Press, 2003.

Ewing, Katherine P., ed. *Shari'at and Ambiguity in South Asian Islam*. Berkeley: University of California Press, 1988.

Gilmartin, David, and B. B. Lawrence, eds. *Beyond Turk and Hindu*. Gainesville: University Press of Florida, 2008.

Hollister, John Norman. *The Shia of India*. 2nd ed. New Delhi: Oriental Books Reprint, 1979.

Hurani, George Faldo. *Arab Seafaring in the Indian Ocean in Ancient and Medieval Times*. Revised and expanded by James Carswell. Princeton, NJ: Princeton University Press, 1995.

Jackson, Peter. *The Delhi Sultanate: A Political and Military History*. Cambridge: Cambridge University Press, 1999.

Khandalavala, Karl, and Saryu Doshi, eds. *An Age of Splendour: Islamic Art in India*. Bombay: Marg Publications, 1983.

Kumar, Sunil. *The Emergence of the Delhi Sultanate, 1192–1286*. New Delhi: Permanent Black, 2007.

Mujeeb, M. *The Indian Muslims*. London: G. Allen & Unwin, 1967.

Wink, Andre. *Al-Hind: Early Medieval India and the Expansion of Islam, 7th–11th Centuries*. Boston: Brill, 2002.

THE GREAT MUGHALS, 1556–1757

Beach, Milo Cleveland. *Mughal and Rajput Painting*. New York: Cambridge University Press, 1993.

Eaton, Richard Maxwell, ed. *India's Islamic Traditions, 711–1750*. New Delhi: Oxford University Press, 2003.

Gommans, Jos. *Mughal Warfare: Indian Frontiers and Highroads to Empire, 1500–1700*. London: Routledge, 2002.

Hambly, Gavin. *The Cities of Mughal India*. New York: HarperCollins, 1968.

Hasan, Farhat. *State and Locality in Mughal India: Power Relations in Western India, c. 1572–1730*. Cambridge: Cambridge University Press, 2006.

Richards, John F. *The Mughal Empire*. Cambridge: Cambridge University Press, 1993.

Rizvi, Saiyid Athar Abbas. *Shāh Walī-Allāh and His Times: A Study of Eighteenth-Century Islām, Politics, and Society in India*. Canberra: Ma'rifat Publishing, 1980.

Schimmel, Annemarie, and Burzine K. Waghmar. *The Empire of the Great Mughals: History, Art and Culture*. London: Reaktion Books, 2004.

Sharma, Sri Ram. *The Religious Policy of the Mughal Emperors*. Columbia, MO: South Asia Books, 1989.

Singh, Khushwant. *A History of the Sikhs*. 2 vols. Princeton, NJ: Princeton University Press, 1963, 1966.

Streusand, Douglas E. *Islamic Gunpowder Empires: Ottomans, Safavids, and Mughals*. Boulder, CO: Westview Press, 2010.

Subrahmanyam, Sanjay. *The Portuguese Empire in Asia, 1500–1700: A Political and Economic History*. London: Longman, 1993.

Willis, John, Jr. *The World from 1450–1700*. New York: Oxford University Press, 2009.

FROM COMPANY STATE TO CROWN RULE, 1757–1877

Armitage, David, and Sanjay Subramanyam, eds. *The Age of Revolutions in Global Context, c. 1760–1840*. New York: Palgrave/Macmillan, 2010.

Bowen, H. V. *The Business of Empire: The East Indian Company and Imperial Britain, 1756–1833*. Cambridge: Cambridge University Press, 2007.

Chaudhuri, Kirti Narayan. *The Trading World of Asia and the English East India Company*. Cambridge: Cambridge University Press, 1978.

Hawley, John Stratton, ed. *Sati, the Blessing and the Curse: The Burning of Wives in India*. Oxford: Oxford University Press, 1994.

Marshall, Peter. *Bengal, the British Bridgehead: Eastern India 1740–1829*. Cambridge: Cambridge University Press, 2006.

Moon, Prenderel. *Warren Hastings and the British East India Company*. London: Macmillan, 1949.

Pearson, Michael. *The World of the Indian Ocean, 1500–1800: Studies in Economic, Social and Cultural History*. Burlington, VT: Ashgate Publishing, 2005.

Robertson, Bruce Carlisle. *Raja Rammohan Roy: The Father of Modern India*. New Delhi: Oxford University Press, 1995.

Schrikker, Alicia. *Dutch and British Colonial Intervention in Sri Lanka, 1780–1815: Expansion and Reform*. Leiden and Boston: Brill, 2007.

Sivasundaram, Sujit. *Islanded: Britain, Sri Lanka, and the Bounds of an Indian Ocean*. Chicago: University of Chicago Press, 2013.

Stern, Philip J. *The Company-State: Corporate Sovereignty and the Early Modern Foundations of the British Empire in India*. Oxford: Oxford University Press, 2011.

TOWARD FREEDOM, 1877–1947

Basu, Sharbani. *For King and Another Country: Indian Soldiers on the Western Front 1914–18*. London: Bloomsbury, 2015.

Dalton, Dennis. *Mahatma Gandhi: Nonviolent Power in Action*. New York: Columbia University Press, 1993.

Davis, Mike. *Late Victorian Holocausts: El Niño Famines and the Making of the Third World*. London: Verso, 2001.

Gandhi, Mohandas K. *An Autobiography or the Story of My Experiments with Truth*. 2nd ed. Ahmedabad: Navajivan Publishing House, 1940.

Greenwood, Anna, and Harshad Topiwala. *Indian Doctors in Kenya, 1895–1940: The Forgotten History*. New York: Palgrave Macmillan, 2015.

Hardy, Peter. *The Muslims of British India*. Cambridge: Cambridge University Press, 1972.

Hirschmann, Edwin. *The White Mutiny: The Ilbert Bill Crisis and the Emergence of Indian Nationalism*. New Delhi: South Asia Books, 1980.

Hyam, Robert. *Britain's Declining Empire: The Road to Decolonization, 1918–1968*. Cambridge: Cambridge University Press, 2007.

Jalal, Ayesha. *The Sole Spokesman: Jinnah, the Muslim League, and the Demand for Pakistan*. Cambridge: Cambridge University Press, 1985.

Khan, Yasmin. *The Raj at War: A People's History of India's Second World War*. London: Bodley Head / Random House, 2015.

Long, Roger, and Ian Talbot, eds. *India in the First World War*. London: Routledge, 2017.

MacMillan, Margaret. *Women of the Raj: The Mothers, Wives, and Daughters of the British Empire in India*. New York: Random House, 2007.

Martin, Briton. *New India, 1885: British Official Policy and the Emergence of the Indian National Congress*. Berkeley: University of California Press, 1969.

Mehta, Uday Singh. *Liberalism and Empire: A Study in Nineteenth Century British Liberal Thought*. Chicago: University of Chicago Press, 1999.

Metcalf, Barbara D. *Islamic Revival in British India: Deoband, 1860–1900*. New Delhi: Oxford University Press, 2005.

Moore, Robin J. *Churchill, Cripps and India: 1939–1945*. Oxford: Clarendon Press, 1979.

Nehru, Jawaharlal. *The Discovery of India*. New Delhi: Penguin, 2010.

Nehru, Jawaharlal. *Toward Freedom: The Autobiography of Jawaharlal Nehru*. New York: John Day Company, 1942.

O'Malley, Kate. *Ireland, India, and Empire: Indo-Irish Radical Connections, 1919–64*. Manchester: Manchester University Press, 2008.

Omissi, David. *Indian Voices of the Great War: Soldier's Letters, 1914–18*. London: Palgrave Macmillan, 1999.

Ramnath, Maia. *Hajj to Utopia*. Berkeley: University of California Press, 2011.

Shaikh, Farzana. *Community and Consensus in Islam: Muslim Representation in Colonial India, 1860–1947*. Cambridge: Cambridge University Press, 1989.

Sinha, Mrinalini. *Colonial Masculinity: The "Manly Englishman" and the "Effeminate Bengali" in the Late Nineteenth Century*. Manchester: Manchester University Press, 1995.

Sinha, Mrinalini. *Specters of Mother India: The Global Restructuring of an Empire*. Durham: Duke University Press, 2006.

Wolpert, Stanley A. *Jinnah of Pakistan*. New York: Oxford University Press, 1984.

Wolpert, Stanley A. *Tilak and Ghokale: Revolution and Reform in the Making of Modern India*. Berkeley: University of California Press, 1962.

SOUTH ASIA AND THE WORLD, 1947 TO THE PRESENT

Aggarwala, Adish C. *Rajiv Gandhi: An Assessment*. New Delhi: Amish Publications, 1993.

Boo, Katherine. *Behind the Beautiful Forevers: Life, Death, and Hope in a Mumbai Undercity*. New York: Random House, 2011.

Cohen, Stephen Philip. *India: Emerging Power*. Washington, DC: Brookings Institution Press, 2002.

DeSilva, Kingsley. *India in Sri Lanka, 1983–1991*. Occasional Paper, No. 25. Washington, DC: Asia Program, Woodrow Wilson Center, 1992.

Frank, Katherine. *Indira: The Life of Indira Nehru Gandhi*. Boston: Houghton Mifflin, 2001.

Ganguli, Sumit. *Conflict Unending: Indo-Pakistan Tensions since 1947*. New York: Columbia University Press, 2001.

Guha, Ramachandra. *India after Gandhi: The History of the World's Largest Democracy*. New York: HarperCollins, 2007.

Guha, Sumit. *Environment and Ethnicity in India, 200–1991*. Cambridge: Cambridge University Press, 1999.

Jalal, Ayesha. *Democracy and Authoritarianism in South Asia*. Cambridge: Cambridge University Press, 1995.

Kalita, S. Mitra. *Suburban Sahibs: Three Immigrant Families and Their Passage from India to America*. New Brunswick, NJ: Rutgers University Press, 2003.

Kandar, Mira. *Planet India: The Turbulent Rise of the Largest Democracy and the Future of Our World*. New York: Scribner, 2008.

Lakshman, W. D., and C. A. Tisdell, eds. *Sri Lanka's Development since Independence: Socio-Economic Perspectives and Analysis*. Huntington, NY: Nova Science Publishers, 2000.

Mines, Diane, and Sarah Lamb, eds. *Everyday Life in South Asia*. 2nd ed. Bloomington: Indiana University Press, 2009.

Pierce, Fred. *When the Rivers Run Dry: The Defining Crisis of the Twentieth Century*. 2nd ed. Boston: Beacon, 2006.

Popham, Peter. *Lady and the Peacock: The Life of Aung San Suu Kyi*. New York: Experiment LLC, 2013.

Ray, Krishnendu, and Tulasi Srinivas. *Curried Cultures: Globalization, Food, and South Asia*. Berkeley: University of California Press, 2012.

Roy, Arundhati. *Power Politics*. Cambridge, MA: Harvard University Press, 2001.

Sen, Amartya. *The Argumentative Indian: Writings on Indian History, Culture and Identity*. New York: Farrar, Straus and Giroux, 2005.

Sharma, J. *Hindutva: Exploring the Idea of Hindu Nationalism*. 2nd ed. New Delhi: Penguin, 2011.

Shiva, Vandana. *India Divided: Diversity and Democracy under Attack*. New York: Seven Stories, 2005.

Singh, Prakash. *The Naxalite Movement in India*. New Delhi: Rupa, 1995.

Varshney, Ashutosh. *Ethnic Conflict and Civic Life: Hindus and Muslims in India*. New Haven, CT: Yale University Press, 2002.

Zamindar, Vazira-Yacoobali. *The Long Partition and the Making of Modern South Asia: Refugees, Boundaries, and Histories*. New York: Columbia University Press.

Websites

Digital South Asia
http://dsal.uchicago.edu/
Provides images and photographs arranged in databases organized by the original collections, books (including scholarly and pedagogical works), journals, newswpapers (including index/access guides to journals and newspapers, maps (catalogs of maps and maps themselves, ranging from historical to topographic), reference resources, a link to full-text dictionaries at Digital Dictionaries of South Asia (DDSA), electronic catalogs and finding aids for dispersed resources and collections, bibliographies, and many indexes, including periodical indexes and document delivery mechanisms. The site is also rich in statistical resources from the colonial period through the present (available in a variety of formats). Links to other Internet reources include a link to SARAI (South Asia Resource Access on the Internet).

Fatehpur Sikri
http://whc.unesco.org/en/list/255
UNESCO World Heritage site of the Mughal capital city featuring related documents, maps, and multilingual video.

Fatchpur Sikir
http://www.art-and-archaeology.com/india/fatehpur/fatmap1.html
Interactive map and tour of Fatehpur Sikri

Harappa.com
www.harappa.com
Perhaps the finest single Internet source on South Asia's first urban civilization, with a ninety-slide virtual tour and superb images of Harappan art and architecture. Also available at this site are digitized old photographs and early newsreel film of the Indian subcontinent, 1929–1947.

Indian Ocean in World History
www.indianoceanhistory.org/
This online educational resource shows the history of human trade, migration, and interaction in the Indian Ocean region through interactive maps.

Internet Indian Sourcebook
www.fordham.edu/halsall/india/indiasbook.asp
A large and varied collection of links and original source material on the history, religion, and culture of South Asia from the earliest times. Extremely useful site for obtaining free digital copies of foundational documents.

Manas: History and Culture of the British East India Company
www.sscnet.ucla.edu/southasia/History/British/EAco.html
Topical short essays supported by references to sources.

Modern South Asia Timeline: Social Movements, Political Events, and Intellectual Production
http://dart.columbia.edu/southasia/timeline/index.html
An interactive timeline, with hyperlinked documents, maps, short biographies, and other material, focusing on the modern history of the Indian subcontinent.

Perry-Castañeda Library Map Collection
http://www.lib.utexas.edu/maps/asia.html

The University of Texas offers an extensive online collection of digital maps of Asia including all South Asian nations and bordering states.

South Asia Outreach Center, University of Wisconsin, Madison
http://southasiaoutreach.wisc.edu/
Web resources; information on ancient civilization, religions, and countries of South Asia; a book-lending library for educators, film list, and K-12 lesson plans.

South Asia Resources South/Southeast Asia Library, University of California, Berkeley
http://www.lib.berkeley.edu/libraries/ssea-library
Provides overview sections to the Doe Library's many South Asia resources, databases, special collections, exhibits, and galleries, as well as subject guides. Interesting special collections on-line, such as "Court Fee and Revenue Stamps of the Princely States of India" and collections focused on South Asians in America (SANA), including historic Ghadar Party activities.

Taj Mahal
www.pbs.org/treasuresoftheworld/a_nav/taj_nav/main_tajfrm.html
This site, part of the Public Broadcasting System's Treasures of the World series, allows a visitor to navigate between stories and art involving the world's most recognizable building. Internal links located at the bottom of the homepage open short and enaging galleries that feature histories of the Mughal dynasty and its decline, offer insight into the life of Shah Jahan, and trace the architectural antecedents to the Taj as well as providing a virtual visit.

Virtual Art Exhibit: The Kushans
http://depts.washington.edu/silkroad/exhibit/kushans/kushans.html
Features virtual galleries offering insight into the first to third centuries CE, when political, economic, religious, and cultural contact between South Asia and Central Asia accelerated.

Virtual Art Exhibit: Mughal India's Timurid Heritage
https://depts.washington.edu/silkroad/exhibit/mughals/mughals.html

Virtual Art Exhibit: The Silk Road
https://depts.washington.edu/silkroad/exhibit/timeline.html
Opens with an interactive timetable tracing the Silk Road and its assoicated cultures that enables a viewer to open galleries on South Asia's connections to the Silk Road from 200 BCE to 1600 CE.

World History Connected
http://worldhistoryconnected.press.illinois.edu/
Open-sourced journal offering forums on world history topics, Internet guides, and interviews with world historians, with searchable archives increasingly rich in research and teaching on South Asia.

Acknowledgments

The task of placing any region into a world history perspective, let alone one as challenging as South Asia, could not even be attempted unless the author was, first of all, fortunate enough to have gurus (teachers) who sought to inculcate in their chelas (students) the highest ideals of the history profession and, second, able to benefit from the friendship, advice, and work of some of the finest practitioners of both South Asian and world history. This writer is indebted to many such gurus and fellow chelas, including Michael Adas, Aziz Ahmad, Michael Aung Thwin, Maitrii Victoriano Aung Thwin, Jerry Bentley, Dana Bernstein, Ned Burtz, Mary Parham Chin, Juan Cole, Ashin Das Gupta, Wendy Doniger, Ross Dunn, Richard Eaton, Andre Gunder Frank, John S. Galbraith, Kenneth R. Hall, Thomas D. Hall, Edward S. Haynes, Peter Hoffenberg, Michele Louro, Craig Lockard, Roger Long, Rila Mukherjee, Aloka Parasher, Kevin Reilly, Ronald "Robbie" Edward Robinson, Heather Salter, Damodar SarDesai, Mrinalini Singh, Peter N. Stearns, Robin Wiley, Stanley Wolpert who first introduced me to the wonders of India and the global reach of South Asian civilization.

I am greatly indebted to both and Anand Yang, a longtime colleague in World and South Asian History, and to Bonnie Smith, the co-editors of this series and to Nancy Toff of Oxford University Press for their collective patience and advice. I also wish to acknowledge the skills and talents of Alexandra Dauler, Elda Granata, Julia Turner, Johanna Baboukis, and Sonia Tycko as they guided this work into print.

NEW OXFORD WORLD HISTORY

 The
New
Oxford
World
History

GENERAL EDITORS

BONNIE G. SMITH,
Rutgers University
ANAND A. YANG,
University of Washington

EDITORIAL BOARD

DONNA GUY,
Ohio State University
KAREN ORDAHL KUPPERMAN,
New York University
MARGARET STROBEL,
University of Illinois, Chicago
JOHN O. VOLL,
Georgetown University

The New Oxford World History
provides a comprehensive, synthetic
treatment of the "new world
history" from chronological,
thematic, and geographical
perspectives, allowing readers to
access the world's complex history
from a variety of conceptual,
narrative, and analytical viewpoints
as it fits their interests.

Marc Jason Gilbert is the NEH-
supported Endowed Chair of
World History at Hawai'i Pacific
University. He is a founding
member and past president of the
World History Association and
editor of its affiliated e-journal,
World History Connected. He
has written extensively on South
Asian, Southeast Asian, and
world history. He is a coauthor
of *Cross-Cultural Encounters
in Modern World History* and
*World Civilizations: The Global
Experience*.

Index

Page numbers in *italics* refer to images.

Buddhism
  beginnings of, 22–27
  Chinese Buddhists, 43, 48
  in Classical Age, 46–47
  devotional, 39–40
  embraced by Ashoka, 33–35
  Mahayana Buddhism, 26–27, 39
  Theravada Buddhism, 26, 48–49
burial, 5–6, 9, 12
Burma, 48–49, 101, 111. *See also* Myanmar
business startups, 138

Calicut, 78
caliphate, 51–52
Cama, Bhikhaiji Rustom, 121
cane sugar, 43
car manufacturing, 137–38
cartridges, paper rifle, 102–3
caste system
  anti-discrimination laws and, 130
  Buddhism and, 20
  Gandhi and healing of divisions
    in, 123–24
  under Guptas, 43–44
  and introduction of modern law and
    science, 106–7
  origins of, 17–18
  Roy on, 96
  and "Sepoy Rebellion," 102
cemeteries, 5–6. *See also* burial
census, 106
Chaitanya Mahaprabhu, 66
chakravartin, 30, 34, 86
Chanakya, 30, 31–32
Chandogya Upanishad, 19–20
Chandra, Hemu (Samrat Vikramaditya),
    67–68, 69
Chandragupta Maurya, 30, 32
Charter Act of 1833, 100, 104, 112
Chelmsford, Lord, 116–17
Cheng Ho (Zheng He), 78
China, 37, 48, 131–32, 138
Chinese artists, 41–42
Chinese Buddhists, 43, 48
Chisti Sufis and Sufism, 66, 73–74
Christians, 75–76, 80
Churchill, Winston, 122–23, 125
"circle" theory of diplomacy, 31–32
civil disobedience, 119–20, 122, 123, 145
civilization, 2
Classical Age
  contact with Greece and Rome, 35–37
  Greco-Buddhist art, 39–40
  Greek conquests, 28–30
  Guptan Empire, 41–48
  Kushan Empire, 37–39
  Mauryan Empire, 30–35
Clement of Alexandria, 35–36
climate change, xiii, 142, 143

Clive, Robert, 93, 97–98
Coalgate, 138
Comprehensive Peace Accord (2006), 144
Congress Party, 132, 136
Constitution, 130
Cornwallis, Charles, 98
Cravath, Robert Drennan, 121
Cripps, Sir Stafford, 125
Cripps Mission, 125
cultural globalization, 147–48

Dadu, 66–67
da Gama, Vasco, 77–78
danda-niti, 32, 41
Dara Shikoh, 81, 82–83, 84
dar-ul-harb (Abode of War), 55
dar-ul-Islam (Abode of Peace), 55
Daulatabad, 60
Deccan, 2, 56, 60, 81
decolonization, 125–29, 147
deforestation, 10
Delhi Sultanate, 55–62, *63*
deregulation, 138
Derozio, Henry Louis Vivian, 96–97
dharma, 19, 20, 22, 23, 33, 43, 46, 47, 49
dhimmis, 52, 53, 60, 84, 85
Dholavira, 7
Din-i-Ilahi, 76
diplomacy, mandala theory of, 31–32
"Direct Action Day," 126
Disraeli, Benjamin, 108
drainage systems, 3
Dravidian language group, 11
Dupleix, Joseph-François, 93
Duroyodhana, 16

Edward VII, Prince of Wales, 108
Eightfold Path, 23
Einstein, Albert, xi
Elizabeth, Queen, 91–92
England. *See* Great Britain
English language, 100
European settlements, 89–90
Evangelism, 98–99

famine of 1877–1878, *110*
farming. *See* agriculture
"Fasting Buddha," 40
Fatehpur Sikri, 74, *75*
Faxian, 43
film, 148
fire sacrifice, 16–17, 19
First World War, 114–16
Fitch, Ralph, 74
Four Noble Truths, 23
French East India Company, 93

Gallipoli, 115–16
Gandhara, 39, 40